The Services Agenda

The Services Agenda

by

Rodney de C. Grey

The Institute for Research on Public Policy
L'Institut de recherches politiques

Printed in Canada

Legal Deposit First Quarter
Bibliothèque nationale du Québec

Canadian Cataloguing in Publication Data

Grey, Rodney de C.

The services agenda

(Essays in international economics,
ISSN 0826-4384)

Prefatory material in English and French.
Includes bibliographical references.
ISBN 0-88645-095-0

1. General Agreement on Tariffs and Trade (1947)
2. Service industries.   3. International trade.
I. Institute for Research on Public Policy.
II. Title.   III. Series.

HD9980.5.G74   1990   382'.45   C90-097554-7

Camera-ready copy and publication management by
PDS Research Publishing Services Limited
P.O. Box 3296
Halifax, Nova Scotia   B3J 3H7

Published by
The Institute for Research on Public Policy
L'Institut de recherches politiques
P.O. Box 3670 South
Halifax, Nova Scotia   B3J 3K6

Contents

Foreword

Trade in services emerged on the policy agenda in the 1980s as economic and technological developments expanded the scope for international commerce. These developments created new challenges for governments in formulating domestic economic policies and led to mounting international frictions. In part, these frictions arose because many of the barriers to trade in services stem from restrictions on investment or immigration which raise sensitive issues. In addition, there is no multilateral framework of rules governing trade in service, which could mediate international differences.

The economic developments creating the basis for expanding international services trade are rooted in the evolution of the industrial economies over the last several decades. It is becoming widely recognized that many consumer services previously generated within the household have migrated into the marketplace. Similarly many activities which might best be viewed as personal and social investment, and previously were undertaken within the family unit, now show up in our social accounts as health care, education, and social services provided through the public sector. And many services previously offered as internal activities within the hierarchy of organizations in primary or secondary industries now are marketed formally by service enterprises whose revenues therefore appear as part of the output of a formal service sector.

Thus the measured scale of the service sector grows, and many new activities come within the scope of public policies affecting market transactions.

Moreover, technological change increasingly makes possible a process of intermediation in service activities—a separation in space or time of the ultimate recipient of services from the original producer of those services. "Value-added" services along the way introduce new actors into the process of service provision, and the possibility of trade in such services across national boundaries brings within the scope of international negotiations and rules a vast range of activities previously missing from the trade policy arena.

Further, the nature of service activities moves trade away from a model of separated individual transactions and toward a structure of sustained relationships. The analysis of economic decisions, and of the possible impacts of public policy upon those decisions, becomes a very different and challenging exercise in these circumstances.

The growth of service activities based on such new technologies and more diverse, flexible organizational structures also introduces dramatically different approaches to competition and comparative advantage in international trade.

In place of strategies based on standardized products exploiting economies of scale in a settled organization of production, service-intensive, flexible production systems open up possibilities for global competition on the basis of custom services offered by flexible and adaptive organizations exploiting economies of scope in the utilization of a knowledge base and management skills.

Thus social investment in the creation and diffusion of knowledge, in education and training, is seen as a fruitful and productive investment—not just frivolous public consumption—and human capital is recognized as a durable asset on which longer term relationships in the organization of labour must be built. Comparative advantage in the international trading system is likely to reflect the extent of this knowledge base, the growth of human capital endowments, and the effectiveness of these organizational arrangements with the labour force.

Anticipating the need for greater analysis of these developments, Industry, Science and Technology Canada (formerly the Department of Regional Industrial Expansion) in 1984 initiated discussions with the Institute for Research on Public Policy. Following some preliminary work undertaken by the Institute, the Department launched in May 1986 the Service Industries Studies Program (SISP) aimed at investigating the structure and dynamics of the service sector and its component industries. The Institute contributed to that program by focusing its research on Canada's international trade in services, while the Fraser

Institute was asked to undertake a comprehensive examination of the growth of the service sector in the Canadian economy, and Statistics Canada was commissioned to review and develop the relevant underlying database. Industry, Science and Technology Canada will continue to work to develop a better understanding of the role of the service sector in the economy and to promote policies and programs in support of the international competitiveness of Canada's service industries.

The research program set up by IRPP was organized under four research modules, each dealing with a different aspect of the overall problem.

The first module, Trade in Services: A Theoretical Perspective, explored the various branches of economic theory to determine the positive and normative aspects of trade in services. Since the neo-classical trade and investment model was originally developed for analyzing goods trade, the research under this module was directed at identifying and exploring the various economic characteristics of services trade that must be incorporated into theoretical analysis of trade in services.

The second module, The Service Sector and Regional Balance, recognized that the extension of marketed services into broader inter-regional trade is a step—conceptually, if not chronologically—in the process leading to international trade, and therefore explored the role played by the service sector in the growth of regional economies.

The third module consisted of a series of case studies and dealt with the statistical and empirical issues encountered in analyzing trade in specific services. Transportation, financial services, computer and telecommunications, engineering services and real estate development and management were studied to explore the determinants of competitive position. These analyses were complemented by an exploration of the data already available on trade in services and foreign investment.

The fourth and last research module examined legal, institutional and negotiating issues particular to trade in services. These services issues emerged on the international agenda for trade negotiations in the 1980s, but the process was controversial. Developing countries expressed concern about sovereignty implications and many wondered whether the concepts of comparative advantage embodied in the GATT applied to trade in services. Yet the ongoing revolutions in global telecommunications, growing economic interdependence, and mounting international tensions over services issues compel governments to develop some formal framework for services. The scope and the implications of any such multilateral services agreement remain uncertain, however, reflecting both domestic pressures and international differences.

This study by Rodney Grey, a veteran Canadian trade negotiator, examines the proposals to negotiate GATT rules for trade in services. Grey traces the evolution of the international negotiating agenda throughout the 1980s, from the 1982 GATT Ministerial, where many countries resisted a vigorous U.S. proposal to bring services into the GATT framework, through the 1986 Punta del Este Ministerial Meeting, which carefully bridged differences over whether services trade issues should be on the GATT agenda, up to the Montreal Ministerial Meeting in December 1988, which proposed a negotiating framework for services in the Uruguay Round. The declaration of the Montreal Ministerial Meeting on services issues was adopted by the Trade Negotiating Committee for the Uruguay Round at its meeting in Geneva in April 1989 and will provide the basis for the final stage of the GATT negotiations.

The financial support of the Government of Canada for the initiation and conduct of this research program is gratefully acknowledged. Related publications from the program are listed at the back of this volume.

Rod Dobell
President
March 1990

Avant-propos

C'est au cours des années 80 que le commerce des services a fait son apparition à l'ordre du jour politique, lorsque les développements économiques et technologiques ont permis de donner de nouvelles dimensions au commerce international. Ces développements ont créé de nouveaux défis auxquels devaient faire face les gouvernements lors de la formulation de leurs politiques économiques locales et ont donné lieu à des frictions internationales de plus en plus fortes, qui ont vu le jour en partie du fait qu'un grand nombre des barrières au commerce des services provenaient des restrictions applicables aux investissements ou à l'immigration, ce qui a soulevé des questions pour le moins épineuses. De plus, il n'existe aucun ensemble de règlements multilatéraux pour gouverner le commerce des services, qui permettraient d'assurer la médiation lors des différends internationaux.

Les développements économiques qui sont à l'origine de l'expansion du commerce international des services proviennent de l'évolution qu'ont connue les économies industrielles au cours des dernières années. On se rend de plus en plus compte qu'un grand nombre de services aux consommateurs, qui autrefois étaient l'affaire des ménages, sont en train de devenir un des éléments de l'économie de marché. Similairement, beaucoup d'activités qu'on aurait pu qualifier d'investissement personnel et social, et qui comme tel relevaient de la responsabilité de la cellule familiale, apparaissent maintenant dans les dépenses publiques aux chapitres de la santé, de l'éducation et des autres services sociaux. Et beaucoup d'autres services, auparavant considérés comme partie intégrante des activités de fonctionnement des industries primaires et secondaires, sont actuellement l'objet du commerce d'entreprises de services dont les revenus apparaissent, par conséquent, comme inclus dans la production d'un secteur officiel des services.

Ainsi la dimension quantifiable du secteur des services est en pleine croissance, et de nombreuses activités nouvelles entrent dans le domaine de compétence de la législation relative aux transactions de l'économie de marché.

Les changements technologiques, qui plus est, facilitent de plus en plus le processus de médiation dans les activités de services et par conséquent la séparation dans l'espace et dans le temps entre celui qui fournit originellement le service et celui qui en est le bénéficiaire final. Les services avec "valeur ajoutée" introduisent tout au long de la chaîne de nouveaux participants dans le processus de prestation de services, et la possibilité du commerce de ces services entre les pays ouvre la voie aux négociations internationales et régit un vaste éventail d'activités inconnues jusqu'ici dans ce domaine.

La nature particulière des activités de services contribue à éloigner le commerce d'un modèle de transactions individuelles indépendantes pour le rapprocher d'une structure relationnelle consolidée. L'analyse des décisions économiques et des conséquences possibles d'une politique officielle sur ces décisions devient, dans ces circonstances, un exercice très différent et qui demande une nouvelle approche.

La croissance des activités de services dérivant de ces nouvelles technologies et de structures organisationnelles plus différenciées et plus souples entraîne un changement considérable dans les attitudes vis-à-vis de la concurrence et de l'avantage comparatif en commerce international.

En remplacement des stratégies de standardisation de produits mettant à profit des économies d'échelle au sein d'une organisation de production bien établie, les systèmes axés principalement sur les services et sur une production adaptée aux circonstances ouvrent de nouvelles possibilités sur le plan mondial. Les entreprises innovatrices et prêtes à s'adapter au marché peuvent offrir des services sur mesure, employant les économies d'échelle qui mettent à profit leur base de connaissances solide et les compétences administratives de leur personnel de direction.

Ainsi, les investissements sociaux en matière de création et de diffusion des connaissances, dans les domaines de l'enseignement et de la formation professionnelle, peuvent-ils être considérés comme des investissements productifs et non pas simplement comme des dépenses publiques sans signification. Le capital humain est reconnu comme un bien durable à partir duquel doit s'élaborer, dans l'organisation du travail, un système de relations à plus long terme. L'avantage relatif sur le plan du commerce international a toutes les chances d'être fonction de cette base de connaissances, de la croissance de ces ressources humaines et de l'efficacité des rapports d'organisation avec le monde du travail.

Dès 1984, prévoyant qu'il serait bientôt nécessaire de procéder à une analyse plus approfondie de ces nouvelles tendances, Industrie, Sciences et Technologie Canada (anciennement le ministère de l'Expansion industrielle régionale) prenait contact avec l'IRP pour discuter de cette question. À la suite de quelques travaux préliminaires entrepris par l'Institut, le ministère inaugurait en mai 1986 le Programme d'études sur les industries de services, dont le but était d'étudier la structure et la dynamique de ce secteur et des industries qui le composent. L'Institut a collaboré à ce programme en orientant plus particulièrement ses recherches sur le commerce international des services du Canada, alors que l'Institut Fraser entreprenait, de son côté, l'examen complet de la croissance du secteur des services dans l'économie canadienne et que Statistique Canada était chargé de revoir et d'améliorer la base de données fondamentale. Industrie, Sciences et Technologie Canada persévérera dans ses efforts pour améliorer la compréhension du rôle du secteur des services dans l'économie et pour promouvoir les politiques et les programmes afin d'appuyer la compétitivité internationale des industries de services canadiennes.

Le programme de recherches mis sur pied par l'IRP a été réparti en quatre modules portant chacun sur un aspect particulier du problème général.

Le premier, intitulé "Commerce des services : une perspective théorique", a été consacré à l'exploration des diverses branches de la théorie économique, afin de déterminer les aspects positifs et normatifs du commerce des services. Étant donné que le modèle néo-classique pour le commerce et les investissements était, à l'origine, destiné à l'étude du commerce des biens, les recherches dans le cadre de ce module ont visé à préciser et à identifier les diverses caractéristiques économiques du commerce des services qui pourraient être incorporées à l'analyse théorique de celui-ci.

Le second module, intitulé "Le secteur des services et l'équilibre régional", est parti de l'idée que la commercialisation des services à l'échelon interrégional était un premier pas, théoriquement sinon chronologiquement, vers l'internationalisation de ce commerce. Les recherches ont donc porté sur le rôle joué par le secteur des services dans la croissance des économies régionales.

Le troisième module a eu pour objectif l'étude d'une série de cas particuliers et des questions statistiques et empiriques qui se posaient au cours de l'analyse du commerce dans certains secteurs de services. Les transports, les services financiers, l'informatique et les télécommunications, l'ingénierie, l'expansion et la gestion de l'immobilier ont été examinés afin d'identifier quels facteurs déterminants permettaient l'accès à une situation concurrentielle. Ces analyses ont été complétées par une révision des données préalablement disponibles en matière de commerce des services et d'investissements étrangers.

Le quatrième et dernier module a été consacré à l'examen de questions particulières au commerce des services relativement à la législation, aux institutions et aux négociations. Ces questions sont apparues à l'ordre du jour international dans le cadre des négociations commerciales au cours des années 80, mais le procédé employé a soulevé la controverse. Les pays en voie de développement se sont inquiétés des implications de la question de souveraineté et un certain nombre d'entre eux se sont demandé si le concept d'avantage comparatif prévu par le GATT s'appliquait au commerce des services. Pourtant, les révolutions continuelles au niveau global dans le domaine des télécommunications, l'interdépendance économique grandissante et les tensions internationales de plus en plus fortes relatives au commerce des services ont forcé les gouvernements à mettre au point un cadre de travail officiel applicable aux services. La portée et les implications d'un tel accord multilatéral restent encore toutefois incertaines, ce qui reflète bien à la fois les pressions économiques et les différends internationaux.

Dans cette étude, Rodney Grey, négociateur commercial canadien chevronné, examine les différentes propositions pour que soient négociés les règlements du GATT applicables au commerce des services. Il récapitule l'évolution de l'ordre du jour des négociations internationales au cours des années 80, en commençant par la réunion des ministres du GATT de 1982, au cours de laquelle de nombreux pays ont résisté à une pressante proposition de la part des États-Unis d'inclure les questions relatives aux services dans le GATT, en passant par celle de 1986, à Punta del Este, au cours de laquelle a été réglée la question de savoir si les problèmes particuliers au commerce des services devaient être mis à l'ordre du jour du GATT, et en finissant par celle de décembre 1988, où un cadre de travail a été proposé pour les questions touchant le commerce des services, lors des discussions de l'Uruguay Round. La déclaration de la réunion des ministres de Montréal sur les questions de services a été adoptée par le Comité de négociation des questions commerciales de l'Uruguay Round, lors de sa réunion d'avril 1989 à Genève. Elle servira de base à l'étape finale des négociations du GATT.

Nous désirons, pour finir, exprimer notre reconnaissance au Gouvernement du Canada pour l'aide financière apportée dans la mise sur pied et la conduite de ce programme de recherches. La liste des autres publications issues de ce programme est publiée au dos de ce volume.

Rod Dobell
Président
Mars 1990

Acknowledgements

The author has received advice and helpful criticism from a number of trade policy specialists working on services issues, or working in individual services industries. He wishes to thank the following, who were of particular help: Peter Clark, John Curtis, Geza Feketekuty, Murray Gibbs, Harald Malmgren, Andrew Moroz, Daniel Roseman, Gary Sampson, Jeffrey Schott, Murray Smith. Of course, the errors, omissions and misjudgements are the author's own.

Ottawa—Codognan, 1990

The Author

Rodney de C. Grey joined the Department of Finance as Executive Assistant to the Minister (Hon. Douglas Abbot) in 1953. He served in Tariffs Section, attended Geneva tariff negotiations in 1956, Dillon Round 1960-62, Kennedy Round 1963-67 and Tokyo Round 1975-79. He was Assistant Deputy Minister of Finance, 1968-1975 and Ambassador for Canada to Tokyo Round. Since 1979, he has been Chairman of Grey, Clark, Shih and Associates, Ottawa, and associated with Malmgren, Golt, Kingston, of London. Author of several books and articles on trade policy, including *United States Trade Policy Legislation: A Canadian View*, published in the Essays in International Economics series.

Executive Summary

This study examines the proposal of the United States (supported by Canada and by the EC) that the trading nations should negotiate new international, multilateral rules to control restrictions on trade in services (including services provided by establishments, such as branches or subsidiaries of foreign controlled firms, as well as services sold across frontiers, such as computer services). Services are clearly a major element in national economies; services trade, broadly-defined, is of great importance in the operation of the world economy, particularly those services which are inputs to the production of other goods and services.

There are many restrictions on the free movement of services, on the ability of professionals (such as architects and lawyers) to sell their services in other jurisdictions, on the rights of services firms to establish affiliates in other countries, and on the rights of such affiliates to be treated on the same basis as domestically-controlled firms.

The post-World-War II period has seen the elaboration of a set of international rules governing trade in goods (the General Agreement on Tariffs and Trade—GATT); the "services proposal" of the United States, now being examined in the Uruguay Round of trade negotiations in Geneva, is that a similar set of international rules be developed to govern trade in services.

The U.S. proposal for a general or "framework" agreement to bring under international control restrictions on all traded services is examined in some detail. It is argued that, in realistic terms, little will be achieved by trying to formulate general rules about traded services; more may be achieved by negotiations in specific sectors. It has been possible to negotiate general rules about trade in goods because goods share one major characteristic: they are physical entities, the values and volumes of which can be recorded and brought within the scope of a taxing system when they cross a frontier. Services do not have this common feature. There are sharp differences between such services activities as air transport (for which there is already in place a sector-specific multilateral agreement, and a multitude of bilateral agreements), architecture (where recognition of professional qualifications is the central problem), or banking, a heavily-regulated industry in every jurisdiction.

The argument that there is a functioning set of rules about trade in goods (the GATT) and that therefore there should be and could be similar general rules for services is found to have little foundation. The GATT as a set of rules and as a system is in disarray; it might therefore be argued that for many smaller countries, including Canada and, of course, developing countries, more priority should be given in international negotiations to making the GATT effective with regard to trade in goods, before thinking of it as an analogue for rules on services trade. In particular, the problems of agricultural trade, of textile trade, the difficulties with the working of the dispute-settlement provisions of the GATT, the widespread abuse of the systems of contingent protection (anti-dumping and anti-subsidy provisions), the widespread recourse to bilateral trade-control measures outside the rules of the GATT "safeguard" system (Article XIX), and the collapse in practice of the GATT rule of non-discrimination all are evidence of the decay of the trade-agreement system centred on the GATT. In terms of trade policy, as it is practised, the services negotiations are only a side-show.

There are, of course, many multilateral and bilateral services arrangements; these are examined, as well as the various commercial treaties which cover services activities, such as the Canada/U.S. Free Trade Agreement and the Treaty of Rome (establishing the EC). The fact that some services industries, such as maritime transport and air transport, could not be covered by the "standstill" against new discrimination in the Canada/U.S. FTA is evidence of how intractable is protectionist sentiment in the various services sectors.

Now that the U.S. proposal to negotiate rules on services trade has been taken into the negotiations in Geneva, it is important—certainly for Canada—that this effort not be allowed to fail. But there are some dangers; one difficult issue, of critical importance to the smaller developed and developing countries, is dispute settlement. At present, there is no GATT basis for a GATT signatory withdrawing a concession on imports of goods, say, a bound tariff rate, because of some alleged failure of another country to open its services markets. If the result of the Geneva negotiations is to make this possible, the leverage of the larger entities (the U.S. EC, Japan) over smaller countries will be much enhanced.

Essentially, this study has been prepared as background to aid consideration of the proposals being discussed in Geneva in the Uruguay Round. The evolution of the services agenda from studies in the OECD in the early 1970s through the outcome of the Canada/U.S. FTA, in regard to services, and of the Montreal meeting of Uruguay Round ministers in December 1988 are examined in detail. But it has not been possible to include comments on more recent developments in Geneva, such as the tabling of comprehensive proposals by the EC, and the conversion by the U.S. of its set of concepts for a framework agreement on trade in services into the draft format of a formal agreement.

Chapter I

The Services Agenda

Most people who trade in goods between countries know that there is a structure of agreements between governments which set out limits or rules about how governments may intervene in such trade. These trade agreements specify what is the maximum rate of customs duty which may be levied for each different product; they specify that such tariffs are not to discriminate between goods from different countries, except where there is some economic grouping (in a 'free-trade area' or 'customs union'); they specify how goods are to be valued for duty (that is, how to fix the base for levying the import duty); they specify that, other than the levying of the import duty, foreign goods are to be treated under domestic tax system and other domestic legal provisions, on the same basis as domestically produced goods. These concepts of most-favoured-nation treatment (MFN) and national treatment (NT) have long been deployed in trade agreements. More recently, since 1947, they have been 'multilateralized'—that is, applied as between a group of signatories, using a standardized text based on well-established trade agreement concepts. This is the General Agreement on Tariffs and Trade. Its signatories, meeting as the Contracting Parties, and in its subordinate bodies, provide fora and rules for negotiating about trade barriers, problems in trade policy, and the conciliation and settlement of disputes between signatories.

But for international transaction in invisibles, as sometimes they are called, or *services*, there is no such comprehensive multilateral agreement or forum, although there are bilateral and multilateral agreements in some services industries, e.g., air transport.

Before, during and then immediately after the Multilateral Trade Negotiations of 1975-1979, (the Tokyo Round) U.S. officials and representatives of U.S. service industries began to organize meetings at which they promoted proposals to negotiate new and comprehensive rules for services trade, rather like the GATT rules for goods trade. They argued that the emerging problems posed by restrictions on services transactions (that is, sales of services from one country to another and the provision of services in a given market by an agency, branch or affiliate of a foreign-controlled company—that is, by an 'establishment' or 'facility') should be negotiable, and that there would be "gains from trade" by removing such restrictions. Since that time the trade policy community has had to consider to what extent the disciplines and modalities learned in regard to trade in goods could be transferred to the services sector in general—or to particular services sectors—or whether trade agreements could at least be analogues for services sector agreements or for a general agreement on services trade.

The United States put forward a formal proposal for consideration by its negotiating partners in October 1987. (This proposal is reproduced in Annex D.) Essentially, it proposed that restrictions on trade in services be addressed in two stages: first, a framework of general principles and second, agreements about specific services sectors. At present, the United States has elaborated only this proposal for a framework agreement.[1] Its main elements are as follows:

1. "Progressive liberalization"; this involves other countries agreeing that they will, over time, remove restrictions on services transactions.

2. It is accepted that countries have a right to regulate their services industries. It is restrictions on international transactions, broadly defined, that are to be addressed, not regulation as such.

3. A "standstill"; no new restrictions, as negotiated in the Canada-U.S. Free Trade Agreement (FTA)[2] with regard to a number, but not all, services sectors.

4. The agreement should apply to services that are traded across borders and to services delivered by facilities.

5. The application of the general code or framework would vary, sector by sector, within this general scheme. The specific concepts to be addressed, the United States has suggested, are:

- "transparency", a term that implies that government measures must be public and available to all interested parties, including other governments;

- "non-discrimination", that is, that all signatories of a services agreement should be treated alike; restrictions should be applied on the same basis to services imports or establishments regardless of source;

- "national treatment", that is, governments should treat foreign services sources on the same basis as domestic sources—as formulated in the United States' proposal, it is a demand for "free trade" in services, including those delivered by establishments, subject to stated exceptions;

- there should be detailed rules providing that state monopolies (or "state-sanctioned" monopolies) that provide services are not used as devices to discriminate against foreign competitors;

- there should be detailed rules limiting subsidies to services industries;

- there should be a right to offset "injurious" subsidies (but it is noted that the countervailing duty mechanism is not a practical approach to this issue); and

- there should be a dispute settlement system, perhaps modelled on the GATT provisions.

The organization of any study intended to clarify the emerging issues likely to arise in the Uruguay Round of multilateral trade negotiations, as well as the specific issues for Canada, is necessarily arbitrary, but it is clear that we should address a number of connected questions about the Geneva negotiations on services. The first is this: How important are negotiations on restrictions on trade and foreign direct investment to services enterprises themselves? Then we should ask: How important are such negotiations in the context of trying to manage the international economic system or systems—or at least trying to avoid a major crisis? Then it would be reasonable to ask: What is there to negotiate about? Here I wish to reiterate the view that was developed at quite an early stage among officials in Ottawa—that we should negotiate essentially sector by sector. The correctness of this view became more apparent as the major negotiating countries formulated their views in 1986 before sending ministers to Punta del Este. It became all the more apparent when Canada and the United States published their Free Trade Agreement, in regard to services. What was achieved, in general terms, was not very significant,[3] but what was achieved for certain specific services sectors (e.g., computer services and financial services) was of considerable importance. What has been proposed in Geneva in the way of *general, multisectoral, multilateral* rules is not, in fact, very substantial, except for the difficult and divisive question of dispute resolution (particularly, the scope for potential retaliation). A final question is: How should we negotiate? On that I prefer to be cautious, as is appropriate for one who is now an observer rather than a participant.

The Importance of Negotiations

On the first question, what is the relative importance of the services negotiations to services enterprises? There are, clearly, some annoying and petty restrictions on traded services, and there are restrictions on establishment and some discrimination against foreign-controlled services enterprises, once established, that are largely protectionist in aim and effect. Of course, the services enterprises that think they are affected adversely would like the bureaucrats responsible for foreign economic policy to do something about these restrictions and about individual cases of less than national treatment, particularly if this can be done in a negotiating forum where the necessary concessions can be found in other sectors of economic activity. However, some of these restrictions and some of the discrimination identified in earlier discussions in the OECD are either not very important or have been negotiated away in bilateral confrontations,[4] or could be negotiated away in quiet bilateral diplomacy, where it would be easier to indicate the potential of applied reciprocity than it will be in a more open multilateral forum in Geneva.

Among the long list of restrictions identified in the preparatory process, three groups seem important.

One is the complex of restrictions and discrimination in telecommunications—that is, in the communications services, including value-added or enhanced services, that transnational corporations in all sectors of activity rely upon. These restrictions on access to markets for telecommunications enterprises are, of course, not unrelated to discrimination in the markets for equipment. It is for consideration whether the issue of discrimination in equipment markets might be addressed in the same negotiating forum as the issue of restrictions and discrimination in services markets, that is, in a broad sector-specific negotiation.

Second is the complex of restrictions on establishment and the absence of national treatment in the financial services sector (or sectors, preferably). Here there are some difficult issues for Canada, but clearly the major issue at the international level is the reluctance of the Japanese authorities and, one supposes, the Japanese enterprises in the sector to accept that they must make a creditable show of reciprocity for the other major financial powers (the United States and Western Europe) in regard to the establishment in Japan of foreign-controlled financial services enterprises and in regard to the treatment accorded such enterprises once established. Japanese representatives, quite properly, express concern about discrimination against Japanese goods in foreign markets and about restrictions on Japanese-controlled enterprises. However, as a practical matter their policy in regard to exports of goods is highly discriminatory, based on bilateralism rather than multilateral rules, and they practise just as much protectionism and discrimination as the rest of the world will tolerate in regard to their domestic markets for goods and services (including, of course, those delivered by foreign-controlled companies in Japan).

The third group of restrictions on international services activities of economic importance is those in the labour market. Some services activities—such as consulting, engineering and architecture—frequently involve individuals bringing their specialized knowledge and skills to their potential clients in foreign markets. Restrictions on the ability of foreigners to enter national territory for the purpose of selling their services are restrictions on services trade. In practice, these restrictions take two main forms. One is to restrict the right to practise in a controlled or regulated profession (accountancy, architecture, medicine, law). In Canada and the United States, such regulation is often enforced at the provincial or state level and by professional bodies that do not necessarily welcome competition for their members. The other form of labour market restriction is that applied by immigration authorities, based on general rules regarding the rights of foreigners to enter and work in the domestic economy.

One tends to focus on these restrictions in the context of the services of so-called professions. However, there is also the issue of whether countries such as Canada, the United States or France would be prepared to accept the temporary entry of, say, construction workers employed, perhaps, by a foreign construction firm. It is not likely that Canada, for example, would be prepared to see a Korean firm build an airport or a pipeline in Canada with Korean construction workers. Yet it is in labour-intensive sectors such as these that developing countries may have services to export. If it seems necessary for the United States, for example, to demand fewer restrictions on the activities of U.S. computer services firms in Brazil, it would be reasonable for Brazil to ask in return that the United States allow Brazilian construction firms to compete on turnkey projects in the United States using Brazilian workers allowed to enter and work in the United States temporarily. It is doubtful, however, that there is much scope for negotiations along such lines, no matter how rational and economically coherent such propositions may be; it is of some interest that a leading representative of the U.S. financial services industry stated recently that the United States should address the issue of labour mobility in the Geneva services talks.[5]

It is not clear that these restrictions on services trade and investment are best negotiated by evolving general rules in a multilateral, multisectoral forum, as the United States proposes. The onus of establishing that such an approach will be productive is on the proponents of the proposition, primarily American services industry representatives and U.S. government represent-atives. They have not as yet made a convincing case, and, as already noted, the outcome of the recent Canada-U.S. FTA points clearly to specific sector negotiations as being the more productive route.

Those who are not advocates of the proposition are not required to prove the negative. But one can point to the inadequacies, indeed, the feebleness, of such efforts as the OECD Invisibles Code, the OECD Decision on National Treatment (of foreign-controlled enterprises), and the OECD Ministerial Declaration on Trans-border Data Flows (of April 1985) as evidence of how difficult it has been to agree on exchanges of meaningful rights and obligations in the services area formulated in general, across-the-board terms, even between the so-called market economies of the industrialized world.

The reality of restrictions in services is, of course, addressed in bilateral discussions invoking reciprocity—although there would be important negative consequences in applying reciprocity formulae retroactively. It would be unfortunate if the United Kingdom or the United States were to have to threaten to impose new restrictions on, or to disestablish, foreign-controlled services enterprises already established in these two jurisdictions. But the name of the game is and will be reciprocity—which is essentially a bilateral, not a multilateral, concept.

Of course, there are other petty restrictions that impose costs on the enterprises affected. But surely it is not necessary to hold a four-year jamboree in Geneva to deal with the discriminatory baggage-handling practices of some airport management enter-prises, or the tendency of South Korean insurance regulators to favor the friends of the South Korean regime rather than foreign-controlled enterprises. Moreover, now that the negotiations are finally beginning to move, questions are being asked about whether the interests of the United States, the *demandeur*, would really be served by a determined attack on barriers to services trade. The U.S. Office of Technology Assessment (OTA) has asserted that certain U.S. services industries could be as vulnerable to foreign competition as U.S. goods manufacturers have been.[6] The OTA report observes that there is "no compelling justification for the unusually high priority" the U.S. Administration has given to the Geneva services negotiations. Much the same point has been made by Robert Kuttner: ". . . services turn out to mean either banking, where the big advantage is passing to capital-rich Japan, or sectors such as construction, engineering or telecommunications, which are closely linked to leadership in manufacturing."[7] We need not necessarily agree with these negative views, but we should recognize that there is no consensus among American economic observers as to the utility of a negotiation about services trade.

In some services sectors other issues are relatively more important than trekking to Geneva. Given that many services sectors are regulated, the extent and legal format of such regulation as may be agreed, in different jurisdictions, to be necessary, are surely much more important issues. Of course, access by foreigners is an aspect of regulation; foreign competition may be an important factor for regulators (and U.S. members of Congress and Japanese bureaucrats) to take into account, but it remains that the definition and elaboration of an acceptable structure of regulation is the central question for many services sectors. We have seen how the debate about airline regulation, for example, has developed in the United States. (For Canada, the United Kingdom and France there is the related issue of getting the government out of the ownership of enterprises.) Clearly, some regulations in regard to airlines have restricted competition unduly, and there are some observers, such as Alfred Kahn, who argue that U.S. airline deregulation has, on balance, been good for the U.S. economy.[8] However, there are other observers, with unimpeachable free-market credentials, who have raised serious questions about the impact of deregulation. For example, Felix Rohatyn has said:

> We have deregulated the airlines and the resulting price wars did, indeed, lower fares. However, one airline after another is on its way to bankruptcy or to being acquired by another. The result will be a few huge airlines, with questionable financial structures, poor service with possibly higher prices, and worrisome safety factors.[9]

Most international travellers, particularly those who pay their own way, know that poor service and higher prices characterize how that industry performs now. As a *Business Week* writer said, "As any passenger knows, air travel has become a nightmare."[10] Surely this situation is a more important matter to address than are some of the governmental restrictions and discriminations against foreign enterprises in the aviation sector.

For the financial services sectors, important as the question of access to the German, Canadian and Japanese markets may be for the enterprises concerned, this is surely a second-order issue, as compared to other issues facing the managers of major financial services companies. To quote Felix Rohatyn again:

Deregulation of the financial markets has resulted in a explosion of private debt (and, I would add, of sovereign debt), unprecedented market speculation, and the sordid abuses in the financial industry that have been coming to light in recent months. Deregulation, as with most things in life, has to be done in moderation; it has been carried too far.[11]

Rohatyn is speaking essentially about U.S. financial markets and the conduct of the American financial services industries, but his views are equally applicable to other financial markets, e.g., the United Kingdom.

In considering what can be done in Geneva in a services negotiation, we should keep in mind that, whatever industry lobbyists may assert, the issue of access to foreign markets for some major services sectors is not really a first-order issue, even to them. But we should also look at the proposition from the public policy point of view. Governments have a responsibility for the management of the international economy that is not the same as the responsibility of the managers of corporations—which, it is said, is to direct their operations in the interests of shareholders.

The International Economic Context

In the context of managing the world economy, the issues raised by the enthusiasts for services negotiations in Geneva are surely not of great importance. It is not difficult to set out more important issues. One evident issue is how to achieve more effective economic policy co-ordination between the major economic powers. Another is whether and how to introduce some discipline over the vast pools of liquid assets sloshing about in financial markets, distorting exchange rates, negatively affecting private investment and macroeconomic policy decisions, and making the development of international trade relationships more difficult. Another is how to cope with the overhang of sovereign debt without producing a banking crisis. Yet another is how to bring into better balance government receipts and expenditures in certain major economies. Yet another is how to finance the renewal of infrastructure in the major industrial economies. These are some of the important economic issues that should be keeping ministers of finance, prime ministers, presidents, and even trade policy officials awake at night.

The Geneva trade negotiation is clearly a sideshow, but even in that sideshow the negotiations about services are surely not the major issue. In the context of the overall framework of the Uruguay Round, the negotiation about services restrictions is clearly not a major matter—and that this would be the case has been clear enough for long enough that one wonders why U.S. representatives applied so much leverage to get it agreed that services would be discussed in the next room to the GATT negotiations.

A much more important issue is how to open the markets of the advanced industrialized countries to the potential exports of manufactured products from developing countries other than Taiwan and South Korea, and how to keep them open. Only if this is achieved will the necessary flow of investment in new facilities in those countries occur. Another more important issue is how to reduce subsidization and provide some rules for trade in agricultural products. When one looks at the absolute failure of the trade policy system to provide a meaningful set of rights and obligations for agriculture trade, one must wonder why services industries are so eager to go to Geneva. Another and more interesting issue in the Uruguay Round is how to provide, in the trade policy system, for more effective protection of intellectual property, and the services industries have something at stake in this.

Furthermore, narrowing the focus to the trade policy system properly speaking, there are two interrelated issues that are, unfortunately, not likely to be addressed. The first issue is how to bring the contingency protection system—which, in practical terms, is a protectionist system—under control. The second is how to introduce, or rather, re-introduce, competition policy considerations into trade policy. All indications are that the thrust of the negotiations in Geneva, as regards these two issues, will be to refine, rather than to discipline, the protectionist impact of so-called trade remedy laws. If that is the case, the results of the Uruguay Round may well be protectionist.

Negotiating Issues

My third question concerned what there is to negotiate in regard to services. Insofar as general rules are concerned, there are really only two issues—everything else is sectoral, not general. One issue is how to make restrictions on trade and investment in services public and then potentially negotiable in subsequent rounds ('transparency' and 'negotiability'). The second issue is making the possible exchange of rights and obligations meaningful, in a contractual sense; that is, how are disputes to be addressed and what are to be the sanctions for breaches of the negotiated contract. This is, for developing countries (and perhaps even for Canada) the crucial issue in the services negotiations.

If the United States, for example, pays a developing country for the removal of some restriction, real or potential, on U.S. services export activities, by reducing a most-favoured-nation (MFN) tariff rate on some industrial good or binding a preferential rate of duty on such a good, then it follows that the United States could withdraw that concession on goods if the concession in the services sector were "nullified or impaired" (to use the language of GATT Article XXIII). At present, there is no GATT provision that allows a GATT tariff concession to be withdrawn as retaliation for the denial of a "benefit" in regard to services trade. It seems likely that an objective of the U.S. services industries and of the U.S. negotiators will be to get concessions on goods and concessions on services into one single agreement. The United States' ability to protect its services industries' exports (including the right of U.S.-controlled corporations in other countries to national treatment) will be buttressed by a right to withdraw concessions on goods under a procedure analogous to or incorporated in GATT Article XXIII.

There is no clear reason why developing countries should put their feet to the fire in this fashion, given that concessions on goods are, in any event, substantially conditioned by the deployment of the contingency protection system. There is no clear reason why Canada should support any U.S. proposals to this effect, even though it may be that Canada would be less at risk than developing countries in such an expanded system. Judging by what happened in the long period leading to Punta del Este, we should expect that the United States will apply great pressure, in the main bilaterally, to achieve an 'integrated' dispute settlement system. Our domestic sectoral interests, and our interests as a nation with important relationships with countries of the Pacific Rim, Latin America, and Europe, dictate that we should not support the United States (and also the European Communities and Japan) in any attempt to aggrandize its trade relations bargaining power in this fashion. The implications of this trade policy issue for our relations with the developing countries of our hemisphere, let alone with developing countries elsewhere, suggests a very cautious approach to dispute settlement as a services negotiations issue.

One other possible general issue will, one may hope, be deeply divisive if it is raised: that is the issue of remedies for 'unfair trade' practices. It has been suggested in the United States—but not, we should be clear, by the Administration—that the anti-dumping provisions, countervailing duty provisions, and other provisions regarding "unfair trade" (e.g., Section 337 of the Tariff Act) be extended, as is Section 301 of the Trade Act of 1974, to the services sector. The OECD Trade Committee is reported to have said that this would be desirable but impractical. This is a thoroughly perverse assessment. Given the skill and well-paid inventiveness of the growing group of specialized trade lawyers, it is clear that it would be practicable to apply the anti-dumping provisions to dumped services imports, or to apply the counter-vailing duty provisions to subsidized services imports—but, equally clearly, it would also be highly undesirable. We need to reform the contingency protection system, not extend it to other areas.[12]

There are, of course, unfair trade practices in the services area, but these might be better dealt with by more general Article XXIII-type procedures, under which the views of the international community would be sought before, rather than after, the application of a sanction or remedy.

How to Negotiate

We should turn to the fourth question: How are these issues to be negotiated? It should be evident from the general trend of this discussion, and particularly given the result of the Canada-U.S. FTA, that there may not be much that is useful, not much that creates trade, that increases welfare, flowing from the attempt to negotiate general, multisectoral, multilateral rules about traded services. Indeed, as experience with the Tokyo Round codes on anti-dumping and on subsidies/countervail might suggest, much that may be agreed may lead to negative, perverse, protectionist results. However, the reality and detail of restrictions can be addressed in sectoral negotiations; again, the outcome of the Canada-U.S. negotiation makes clear that this is the case. It is reported that the U.S. team is preparing a detailed draft agreement for the telecommunications services sector, certainly a key sector, if not the key sector. In a paper prepared for the Atwater Institute and published by the International Institute of Communications, I have set out how a GATT-like agreement might be devised for information trade or, as it could be called, traded computer services,[13] and much can be learned from the detailed provisions on this sector agreed to by Canada and the United States. The most difficult sectors to be dealt with in Geneva will be financial services, and here several sector agreements may be feasible. But in this area the main question, as far as the issue of market access is concerned, is achieving a reasonable measure of bilateral reciprocity in regard to establish-ment and national treatment—though mirror-image reciprocity for each country is virtually impossible.

There is one lesson we might well learn from the Tokyo Round in regard to these negotiations. If we take an OECD agreement—

which is unlikely to be drafted in precise language and which provides unsystematically for derogations but not for sanctions— and if we put such an agreement into a GATT-like framework, as was done with the OECD draft agreement on procurement, it may be possible to evolve a more workable agreement. One could, for example, consider taking the OECD Decision on National Treatment, with all its derogations, reservations and observations, to Geneva and turning them into scheduled, agreed lists of exceptions to national treatment in regard to services. The Canadian list would be long, but we would not be alone. This process would involve, necessarily, a form of standstill on restrictions in services trade. It would involve putting existing or potential restrictions, if not on the table, at least into an agreed schedule. That is the first step toward making restrictions negotiable.

Canada's Interests

As an epilogue, we may ask: What are Canada's interests and how can they be advanced, or at least secured?

As a trading nation we have an interest in allowing the negotiation process to operate as a stabilizing factor in trade relations, although we have perhaps paid too much on this account in the past. For some observers, particularly U.S. observers, that is virtually the whole case for going to Geneva. For Canada, it is the case that if our major trading partner, through its domestic political process, concludes that it wants negotiations in Geneva about services, it is difficult for us to stand aside or be naysayers. In any event, services are on the Uruguay Round agenda, even though Canadians and others may sense that the results may not be wholly positive. The U.S. Administration has argued that, by enlisting the services industries in favor of negotiations as a process, it is creating a new domestic coalition of interests in favor of multilateralism and non-discrimination. We may be sceptical about this political judgement, but it is very awkward for Canadian representatives to second-guess U.S. representatives about the U.S. domestic political process—although U.S. representatives have often been quite wrong on such matters.

We really have no choice but to accept the stated U.S. view, particularly now that we have hammered out the detail of a special bilateral agreement with the United States.

Having got this far, Canada has an overriding interest in not allowing a major multilateral trade negotiation to fail too obviously or to collapse. As this writer noted in 1979, the Tokyo Round was, for Canada, essentially a defensive negotiation, and the results were, in some major aspects, negative or illusory;[14] however, there has never been any shortage of commentators asserting that the Tokyo Round yielded a positive achievement of 'liberalization'. By the same token, we shall need to be able to say that the Uruguay Round is a success: that is our interest. On the substance aspect of the Geneva services negotiation, Canada's interest varies sector by sector, but the total gains to be made (or changes to be negotiated) will, in terms of their impact on Canadian services activities, be much less than the impact of the Free Trade Agreement.

Notes

1. The October 1987 'concepts' paper by the United States was circulated in the Multilateral Trade Negotiations (MTN) Group of Negotiations on Services (GNS) as MTN.GNS/W/24. The United States has more recently circulated a paper in the GNS on "Procedures for Reaching and Implementing a Multilateral Framework for Trade in Services" MTN.GNS/W/37 (16 May 1988). Other negotiating countries have put forward comments and proposals, for example: European Communities, MTN.GNS/ W/29 (10 December 1987); Canada, MTN.GNS/W/39 (16 May 1988); and Argentina, MTN.GNS/W/33 (March 1988).

2. *The Canada-U.S. Free Trade Agreement (FTA)* (Copy 10-12-87), Ottawa, Department of External Affairs: Part Four, pp. 194-256; see also *The Canada-U.S. Free Trade Agreement and Services/An Assessment* (Copy 01-09-88).

3. Jeffrey J. Schott, "Implications for the Uruguay Round", in Schott and Smith (eds.), *The Canada-United States Free Trade Agreement: The Global Impact* (Washington: Institute for International Economics, 1988); see p. 165, "The agreement is long on rules and short on liberalization."

4. Cho Yoon-Je, "How the United States Broke into Korea's Insurance Market", 10 *The World Economy* No. 4 (December 1987), pp. 483-496.

5. William Dullforce, "Trade-off in services urged", *Financial Times* [London], July 12, 1988, reporting the views of Mr. John Reed, President of Citicorp.

6. U.S. Congress, Office of Technology Assessment, *International Competition in Services/Banking, Building, Software, Know-How* (Washington, 1987).

7. Robert Kuttner, "The Prospect for the Summit: Political Gridlock", *Business Week*, June 8, 1987, p. 12.

8. See, for example, Professor Kahn's letter to the editor, *Financial Times* [London], September 8, 1987.

9. Felix Rohatyn, "The Economy on the Brink", *New York Review of Books*, June 11, 1987, pp. 3-6.

10. *Business Week*, May 25, 1987.

11. Rohatyn, p. 3.

12. There is a small but growing literature developing this argument. For an early comment noting the dangers of the trade regulatory system, see Rodney de C. Grey, "Some Commercial Policy Problems Ahead", Notes for a presentation, The Conference Board of Canada, Toronto, September 26, 1979: "It is certainly not clear that the new system, or better, the strengthened, re-designed, highly articulated, regulatory system will be less restrictive of imports into the United States than was the pre-Kennedy Round system . . . ".

   See also Rodney de C. Grey, "The GATT Codes on Non-Tariff Measures" in *Protectionism; Threat to International Order/ The Impact on Developing Countries* Commonwealth Economic Papers, No. 17 (London: Commonwealth Secretariat 1982); see particularly pp. 301-307.

13. Rodney de C. Grey, "Elements of a General Agreement on Information Trade", *Intermedia* (April 1987), pp. 18-23.

14. See first reference cited in Note 12 above.

Chapter II

The Services Proposal

The proposal provides our view of a set of rules to expand and liberalize the conduct of international trade in services. We must have a set of enforceable rules to cover services because this sector is the fastest growing in the United States and the world and because trade in goods and trade in services are inter-dependent.

> Opening comment by Ambassador Clayton K. Yeutter in tabling the U.S. proposal for a "Services Framework Agreement", November 4, 1987.

Background to the Proposal

The purpose of this chapter is to outline how the U.S. Services Proposal developed. In trying to trace the evolution of the proposal, it is important to recall that it was first in Paris at the OECD–not in Geneva, at GATT or UNCTAD—that the industrialized countries formulated their approach to what became the Tokyo Round of the GATT. The High Level Group on Trade and Related Problems set out the terms of possible trade negotiations in their Report of 1972 (the Rey Report)—a document that bears re-reading.[1] The Group prepared the necessary intellectual ground for the Tokyo Round and did address the issue of restrictions on traded services.

In Chapter IV of its report, the Group placed some emphasis on the removal of restrictions on insurance transactions and pointed to the imperfections in the OECD Code of Liberalization of Current Invisible Operations. The Group went on to comment that, for air transport, "there is little prospect of multilateral and genuine international competition as long as governments wish to protect their national airlines . . .". Despite deregulation, that 1972 verdict seems relevant in 1988. As for maritime transport, the Group noted that "transactions and transfers" (the subject matter of the OECD Invisibles Code) were free in principle, but that the United States had not been able to subscribe to the Note to the Code regarding discrimination in shipping; the Group went on to say that "other restrictive practices are maintained by governments and international shipping companies". The general conclusion of the Rey Group in regard to traded services was as follows:

> The Group considers that action should be taken by *the developed countries* to ensure liberalization and non-discrimination in the services sector. The Group's attention focused chiefly on insurance, when the time has come to hold discussions above the level of technical experts. However, the OECD should work out in more precise detail further steps to be taken also in the fields of tourism and transport, in particular shipping and, in consultation with the ICAO, air transport. As in the case of goods, consideration might be given to allowing developing countries a limited time to adapt themselves before undertaking the full commitments.[2]

Consideration of these proposals by this very senior and authoritative group of trade policy officials may help to make clear the nature of the discussion about the U.S. Services Proposal. First, the Group's proposals were not taken up, as no major negotiating country proposed, in any meaningful way, that liberalization of traded services be addressed in a comprehensive fashion in the Tokyo Round. Second, the approach was on an industry or sector basis; the Group apparently did not consider such horizontal or across-the-board concepts as most-favoured-nation treatment, right of establishment or national treatment, which obviously are relevant to 'liberalization' of some traded services, although a reference is made to "non-discrimination" in the passage just cited. Third, the Group failed to note the fact, and therefore to draw the necessary conclusions from it, that in regard to traded goods, it is accepted that countries may impose protective tariffs, but that there is no general technique for imposing a price barrier for protective purposes in regard to imported services. It is important to keep in mind that liberalization, in OECD terms, with regard to traded goods, had meant the removal of quantitative restrictions (that is, restrictions on transactions or the equivalent restrictions on payments, i.e., transfers), but not the removal of tariffs. However, when dealing with invisibles the OECD Secretariat and the Rey Group have used "liberalization" to mean a regime free of *any* barrier to imports, without addressing the issue of right of establishment. Such a usage may well suit the United States and the United Kingdom. Finally, the Group contemplated developing countries being given a limited time to adapt their services regimes to liberalization. The notion that for certain traded services (as for certain traded goods) developing countries—and indeed, many others —might wish to keep in place protective barriers for an indefinite period does not seem to have received consideration.

Since the U.S. Department of Commerce published its *Services Industries Study* in 1976, during the Tokyo Round, U.S. representatives have stated their proposals about restrictions on traded services separately, and with rather more emphasis than that given investment and establishment issues, in a variety of forums.

Following the conclusion of the Tokyo Round in July 1979, U.S. authorities urged the OECD Secretariat to address the issue of restrictions on trade in services more systematically. This work proceeded in several directions. First, the relevance and functional effectiveness of various OECD instruments were re-examined in regard to traded services; we note the more important of these in Chapter V. Second, a series of sectoral studies attempted to identify restrictions on trade by sector and possible courses of action in regard to particular services activities. Third, efforts were made to formulate or at least discuss trade agreement concepts relevant to trade in services, such as national treatment. In December 1985 these were pulled together in a discussion document by the Trade Committee; this document has not been formally published, but it has become generally available. It may be that it has the makings of some sort of normative code on services.[3]

Since the Tokyo Round concluded, the issue of whether restrictions on trade in services, broadly defined, should be the subject of multilateral negotiations to establish general rules regarding such restrictions has been raised in the GATT, in the OECD, bilaterally by the United States and in the annual Western Economic Summits—and no doubt on a number of other occasions. This proposal was in part accepted by the international community—reluctantly, by some countries—at the meeting of trade ministers at Punta del Este in September 1986. (The text of the relevant paragraphs of the Punta del Este declaration is in Annex C.)

In the GATT, the discussion was initially carried forward in the Consultative Group of 18 (CG18) which is a sort of executive committee for the 90-odd member countries. Prior to the ministerial meeting in November 1982, the U.S. proposal for a multilateral examination of traded services restrictions was reviewed in the preparatory group organizing the ministerial meeting. At that meeting there was considerable reluctance to accept a role for the GATT in regard to services; developing countries very much preferred that the discussion should go forward in UNCTAD. Finally, it was agreed that GATT signatories could, if they wished, undertake their own studies in regard to services trade and then make them available to others.[4] The 1982 compromise appeared to have virtually deprived the GATT—or at least the secretariat—of any real authority to address the Services Proposal, although developing countries had conceded that the GATT had scope, indeed some responsibility, for such services as were incidental to trade in goods (e.g., transport insurance). Nevertheless, a number of national studies were produced, several were circulated,[5] and there were some meetings, involving GATT secretariat attendance, of GATT representatives of countries interested in the Services Proposal or wishing to be informed about it.

Subsequent to the 1982 GATT ministerial meeting, two Western Economic Summits—1983 at Williamsburg and 1984 in London—recorded the agreement of the other major western industrialized nations with the U.S. proposal to initiate negotiations on services. In November 1984, the representatives of the Contracting Parties adopted a heavily negotiated text, which made one small step toward launching the negotiating process: namely, that the Chairman "will organize the exchange of information . . ." and the ". . . Secretariat will provide the support necessary . . .". In November 1985 yet another step toward launching the negotiation was taken: the Contracting Parties invited individual contracting parties "to prepare recommendations for consideration by the Contracting Parties at their next session". This work was carried forward by a committee chaired by Ambassador Felipe Jaramillo of Colombia, a committee separate from the committee examining other issues to be considered for the agenda of the negotiations. At long last—one might say finally, but it is really initially—ministers met in September 1986 in Punta del Este, to formally launch the new MTN. This meeting was analogous, in terms of the negotiating process, to the Tokyo meeting of 1973, which formally launched the Tokyo Round which, in turn, started moving only in 1975 and concluded in 1979.

At Punta del Este, Ministers agreed—reluctantly in some cases, as noted above—that negotiations on services should proceed in parallel with the negotiations on goods and be subject to GATT procedures and practices. The Punta del Este declaration set out the objective of services negotiations as the establishment of "a multilateral framework of principles and rules for trade in services, including elaboration of possible disciplines for individual sectors".[6] Only toward the end of the Uruguay Round will the question be addressed as to how the results of these negotiations on services may perhaps be fitted into the GATT framework of rules and obligations.

The U.S. Proposal

Of considerable usefulness in understanding the Services Proposal is an early statement by the United States Trade Representative, William Brock, published to coincide with the 1982 GATT ministerial session. Ambassador Brock's article anticipated the 1983 U.S. *National Study on Services* and offered this summary of the U.S. position:

> Objectives: The basic goal of any future negotiations should be to expand the opportunities for trade, making possible the economic gains that can be obtained from trade based on comparative advantage. A closely related objective should be to ensure that barriers to trade in services do not become a major obstacle to trade in goods. In order, then, to expand the opportunities for trade, such negotiations should focus on, first, the development of a stable institutional environment for trade in services, providing "predictability" in governmental actions and an orderly way for dealing with the problems that arise; and, second, the development of a negotiating process for reducing or eliminating barriers to trade in services, which to a large extent means addressing government regulations that discriminate between domestic and foreign suppliers of services.
>
> We should recognize the right of every government to establish its own social objectives for the regulation of services and the obligations of foreign suppliers of services to adhere to such regulations. At the same time, though, governments should assume an obligation to minimize the extent to which such regulations distort trade beyond the minimum necessary to achieve legitimate social objectives. Where such regulations are meant to protect domestic service industries, they should be clearly notified as trade restrictions.

Principles: Future negotiations might be guided by some of the following principles. Restrictions on trade in services should be made explicit and should be negotiable. All government regulations that are notified as barriers should be applied on a "national treatment" basis. Where national treatment is difficult to apply for technical or regulatory reasons, governments should commit themselves to minimize the distortion of trade inherent in such regulations. Government monopolies should operate on a commercial basis where they are in competition with foreign commercial enterprise and they should offer foreign and domestic customers the same reliability, quality and prices; that is, they should observe the principle of national treatment.

Procedures: Governments should be willing to consult with each other when problems arise with respect to their mutual trade in services and if they cannot resolve their differences on the basis of such consultation they should have access to a dispute-settlement procedure. New regulations that offset foreign suppliers should be notified in a timely way and foreign suppliers should be given an opportunity to discuss technical problems related to the application of such new regulations. Foreign suppliers of services should have the same access to government officials and to local courts as domestic suppliers of services.

Rights and obligations: Commitments entered into by governments as a result of negotiations should result in contractual rights and obligations. Governments should agree not to take other actions that would deny foreign countries the benefits of negotiating concessions, except under agreed circumstances. Where governments act in violation of their commitments, efforts should be made to reach a new understanding on the issues involved; otherwise, affected countries should have the right to take compensatory actions that would re-establish a balance of commitments.

Organisation of Future Negotiations: A considerable amount of staff work is needed before we can develop any concrete propositions for future negotiations. Within a common framework of principles, rules and procedures, negotiations could be organised either along sectoral lines or in terms of issue-oriented codes such as the GATT standards code negotiated in the Tokyo Round deliberations. We might be able to develop, for example, a regulatory code that could be patterned on the standards code.[7]

This is the elegant, compact statement of a negotiator. The essence of Ambassador Brock's proposal is that governments should negotiate a set of contractual rights and obligations with respect to services and trade and that governments should be able to take compensatory action for what they consider to be breaches of obligations by other governments. There is no suggestion that such compensatory action would be confined to the services sector at issue or to the services sector generally. For developing countries, and perhaps for all small countries, this may well be the crux of any negotiations regarding services in the Uruguay Round. It should be noted that the scope for retaliation in U.S. trade remedy legislation has gradually been expanded and goes beyond merely enforcing trade-agreement rights; the key provision, in this context, is Section 301 of the Trade Act of 1974, as amended by the Trade Agreements Act of 1979, the Trade and Tariff Act of 1984, and the Omnibus Trade and Competitiveness Act of 1988. From 1974, services have been included within the scope of this provision, including the scope for retaliation.[8]

As we examine the Services Proposal against the background of what has been said about the regime already in place, we should keep in mind that proponents of the proposal that GATT rules, or rules like the GATT, be extended to services may not be familiar with the extent to which the GATT system has been eroded, or may be unwilling to recognize the facts. They may see virtues in the GATT that are illusory, or they may see advantages from the point of view of their services entities, the interests of which they seek to serve, that may not be evident to others. We consider the GATT, as a system, in Chapter IV.

The most detailed, and still most useful, exposition of the U.S. proposal is in the *U.S. National Study* circulated to other countries negotiating in Geneva. The "working assumptions", as the text calls them, are as follows:

(1) trade in services, like trade in goods, is an engine of growth;

(2) liberalized trade in services, as in goods, benefits producers and consumers alike;

(3) protectionist measures that hamper trade in services retard every country's economic prospects;

(4) the regulation of some services to achieve national policy goals should be carefully weighed against the economic importance of liberalized competition.[9]

This last point, in our view, could be stated rather more simply: "There are gains from trade in services just as there are gains in trade from goods; however, there are other gains (from other policies). These various gains must be compared." The implication throughout the *U.S. National Study* is that gains from trade substantially outweigh gains from other policies. From the point of view of U.S. services corporations, that may be true, but this is an issue that each country taking part in the Uruguay Round may wish to examine in regard to each services sector.

Looking at the format for a set of rules, the *U.S. National Study* sets out a series of propositions, which we can evaluate in the light of our description of the existing regime. The Study addresses and comments on the possible approaches to negotiations. First, there are single-sector agreements open to all: "It would be difficult to maintain a consistent trade liberalizing bias among ... such independent agreements, and some could, in fact, become trade restrictive".[10] This has been the case with private sectoral agreements (e.g., shipping conferences and IATA), but the U.S. Study does not make it clear why, if governments really do agree on trade liberalization, they cannot impose their will in sectoral agreements at least as effectively as in a more general, multisectoral agreement.

Second, there could be bilateral single-sector agreements: "They run the additional danger of establishing restrictions against third countries if market sharing arrangements are included."[11] Again, one may ask why the mere form of agreement should impel governments to impose restrictions if they do not wish to. It is interesting that the Royal Bank of Canada initiative in favor of a Canada-U.S. free trade arrangement for data services stated explicitly that the objective is not restrictions against other countries and that it would not be in the interests of either Canada or the United States to seek a preferential arrangement.[12] It is important to recognize that neither U.S. nor Canadian representatives have presented the FTA as a preferential arrangement. However, the *U.S. National Study* goes on to say: "Given the structure of particular markets and overriding concerns of national security or economic development, *somewhat restrictive bilateral agreements may represent the greatest achievable degree of competition*."[13] (Emphasis added.) The Study cites agreements on civil aviation landing rights as a case in point.

A third approach is bilateral multisector agreements. This would make it possible to trade concessions in one services sector against concessions in another sector; clearly, this is a negotiating concept imported from conventional tariff negotiations. It is noted also that the principles of national treatment and transparency could be involved. (Surely transparency is a practice, a very valuable one, but not a principle or concept, in the sense that we can call national treatment a treaty principle.) The Study goes on to note that "the concept of most-favored-nation treatment, however, would be abandoned in favor of preferential systems based on reciprocal opportunities".[14]

Two comments are called for: first, if we followed the model of the pre-World War I "system of treaties", it is not necessarily the case that bilateral treaties covering a variety of areas of trade need abandon the principle of non-discrimination. The use of the unconditional most-favoured-nation (MFN) clause since the 1860s in trade relations is very powerful evidence to that effect. Countries adopt "preferential arrangements" because they choose to; alternatively, they adhere to a strict unconditional MFN clause because they see it as being in their interest. Their perception of their interest dictates the choice of treaty language, not vice versa.

Having virtually damned bilateral agreements, the *U.S. National Study* goes on to say: "Such bilateral accords might nevertheless operate as *models for developing the basic rights and obligations appropriate for a healthy multilateral services regime.*"[15] (Emphasis added.) Then the Study comes to the essential proposition: " . . . the trade of many services sectors face common problems whose reduction or elimination would facilitate a more efficient trading system. Ideally, all sectors should be moving in the same basic direction, albeit in different ways, depending on the sector. In order to accomplish such an objective, services could operate under a common framework applicable to all sectors with specific rules set out for individual sectors."[16] The Study then lists the elements in the common framework: "These principles include national treatment, minimization of distortion to trade, non-discrimination, the right to sell; procedures include transparency, due process, formal dispute settlement procedures, and provisions establishing the relationship of the framework agreement to other existing or future agreements, particularly those applicable to individual sectors."[17]

Defects in the U.S. Position

The Study comments on these principles and procedures and reviews the operation of the various multilateral and sectoral agreements that constitute the present regime and discusses, briefly, the nature of restrictions in the various sectors. While it is important to recognize that the Study is one of the most important documents to appear on services in international commerce, we should also be aware of some of its defects; they are the defects of the position the United States has been stating, in various documents, in Geneva and elsewhere, since the Study was published.

First, the Study makes a convincing case only that there should be some intensive multilateral study of the services sector or sectors, so that the international community can identify serious (i.e., costly) restrictions and decide whether and how they should be negotiated away. It does not make a case that there should be multilateral, multisectoral negotiations.

Second, the study asserts, but does not make a case, that *general* rules in the services sector would yield useful results; this may or may not be so, but essentially, this key proposition advanced by the United States is stated as a conviction. The exceptions that the United States itself will require, because of statutory limitations on the rights of non-nationals in certain U.S. service sectors, and the exceptions insisted upon by the United States to the "standstill" on new discrimination in the FTA (i.e., the various transportation industries) undermines this U.S. proposal.

Third, the Study seems to assume that the gains from services trade are large and distributed in such a fashion that all countries would gain, in economic terms, from more open regimes, and that these gains would, in political terms, more than equal the benefits of other policies, such as those—like Brazil's informatics policy—that emphasize the development of domestic capability. If this is so, then the U.S. proposal would have been strengthened by a demonstration of this rationale set out in factual terms.

Fourth, the *U.S. National Study* is not particularly concerned with the role of services in economic development. It is not responsive to the criticism that the GATT treats development more or less as an afterthought, as an issue to be dealt with by the formulation of "special and differential" treatment. This lack of concern for development considerations is no longer attractive to developing countries, and indeed this issue has been highlighted in the Argentine proposal to the negotiating group in Geneva and in the latest UNCTAD statement on services.[18]

Finally, the Study does not make the case that the international community should give priority to problems in regard to traded services—as against problems in traded goods, such as textiles and clothing, agriculture, steel, automobiles, semiconductors, electronic equipment, and the other goods sectors where the GATT discipline has long since virtually collapsed. It does not address the issue of whether the failure to realize gains from trade in these critical areas is greater than the failure to realize gains occasioned by restrictions on traded services. If we are to continue to give priority in the Uruguay Round to traded services, we need to inform ourselves as to whether the potential gains from removing restrictions are as large as the potential gains in other sectors of trade.

Recent Analysis of Services Issues

There is not a great deal of analytical writing about traded services, about the potential gains from trade in services, or about the scope for negotiations about traded services. It may be useful, therefore, to examine briefly some recent analytical statements by relatively independent commentators. Much of the recent literature is American, and, not surprisingly, much of it broadly supports the stated U.S. government position.

Two U.S. lawyers have advocated what could be called a 'services code'. Michael Cohen (then manager for public affairs of the American International Group, a group of insurance companies) and Thomas Morante (at one time an American Express Fellow at the Georgetown University Law Centre) argued that much difficulty arises from the lack of an agreed definition of services, from the related lack of an adequate catalogue of barriers to trade in services, and from the absence of adequate data.[19] (For example, many balance-of-payments statistics list 'invisibles' as a single category.) More important, they argued that the United States could improve its bargaining position in services: the anti-dumping and countervailing duty laws should be extended to services, and Section 301 of the Trade Act of 1974 ("other unfair trade practices" of governments) should be expanded. Section 301 has in fact been used with respect to service issues; for example in regard to border broadcasting (Canada) and insurance (Argentina).

The thrust of the Cohen/Morante proposal was this: "Such measures would indicate to the United States' trading and negotiating partners that the United States recognizes the importance of its services sector and is prepared to engage in protective practices, similar to those employed by other countries, to promote and direct its services sector. If the United States demonstrates to other countries its interest in promoting its services sector, ... negotiations will more likely be undertaken and successfully concluded." Further, "Because few developing countries can realistically make major advances as exporters of services to developed country markets, the developed countries may have to adopt a policy of making concessions that favor goods exported by developing nations in return for reductions of NTBs to services exports from developed nations." This is an argument for taking the services issue into a broad trade policy forum where there are rights and obligations regarding trade in goods, that is, for having traded services measures discussed in a framework in which conventional trade policy issues are also on the table.

Traditionally, the U.S. Council on Foreign Relations has been a source of 'liberal' pronouncements on trade policy. A paper on the services issue by William Diebold, Jr., a Senior Fellow of the Council (now retired), and Helena Stalson is a careful, much less committed approach than the paper by Cohen and Morante.[20] Diebold and Stalson state: "It should be an American objective to keep services practices, both in general and so far as possible in regard to particular services practices, from being treated as items on the North-South agenda." And later: "The United States should not let the pursuit of the liberalization of services . . . divert attention and energies from work on trade in goods." Earlier in their analysis, which is set out more in the form of questions than categorical policy proposals, Diebold and Stalson state: "The idea of a 'GATT for services' should also be rejected in favor of 'relating the existing GATT to services'". They address the issue of "unfair" practices in services and the question of reciprocity, stating that "There may be times when retaliation against foreign restrictive practices in services will be the best course, and when some degree of reciprocity will be a reasonable formula for arranging the mutual removal of restrictions."

Jeffrey J. Schott, then of the Carnegie Endowment for International Peace, now with the Institute for International Economics, and at one time a member of the U.S. negotiating team during the Tokyo Round, argues that the GATT, not the OECD, is the proper forum for services negotiations. He says: "[OECD agreements] consist of hortatory provisions of what countries should do rather than commitments by countries of what they will do. The OECD is a valuable *consultative* forum for developed countries. But it is not in effect a negotiating body . . . . By contrast, the GATT is a better forum for talks on trade in services, for it is the only international body that seriously negotiates binding agreements. It is the only place where developed and developing countries feel they can do business with each other."[21]

Trying to assess the attitudes of developing countries, Schott attributes their reluctance to become engaged in a round of services negotiations to three factors, as he thinks they are perceived by those countries: (1) other trade issues are more important—e.g., safeguards, textiles, agricultural products; (2) new rules regarding traded services may put many developing countries into a permanently inferior position; they will want to protect their infant service industries; and (3) restrictions by developing countries can be used to force the transfer of technology from developed countries. Schott believes that these worries are not really justified. However, in a more recent comment he has argued that the GATT negotiations should address immediate and important issues, such as trade in textiles promptly, and that services could be addressed by those concerned with the issue at possibly a later date. "Services," writes Schott, " clearly have a long fuse."[22]

The most detailed, and still the most useful, analysis of services from a non-governmental source is the study by Ronald K.

Shelp, then a vice-president of American International Group.[23] Shelp's book was a critical survey of the literature, of the state of play, and of the issues as of 1981. In terms of potential negotiations, he argued for what he calls a "shotgun approach": for doing what can be done in the OECD, in the GATT and in specific services sector bodies. As he sees it, we will then move gradually to detailed and comprehensive rules. However, like the authors of the *U.S. National Study,* Shelp does not address in any meaningful way the role of services industries in the development process, nor does he examine whether developing countries should realistically be expected to undertake meaningful obligations in regard to traded services or the establishment of foreign services firms. Shelp notes, however, that the barriers to trade in services imposed by developed countries and a few of the more advanced developing countries are the more significant: "The assumptions that barriers to services originate almost exclusively in developing countries is misguided . . .".

Shelp's book is now a basic text in the field, having supplanted, to an important degree, the earlier study by Griffiths, which is inevitably somewhat dated.[24] There is not surprisingly, a considerable amount of writing about specific sectors;[25] the few analyses we have noted above are those that deal with a general approach and that address the issue of general rules.

Another approach is urged by Peter Gray. He argues in favor of negotiations in selected services sectors and 'national treatment' negotiated on a basis of bilateral reciprocity; he proposes that negotiations should, in the first stage, take place among developed countries, and therefore not in the GATT but rather in the OECD. It is possibly too late to think of reverting to this approach, but it may yet be relevant in regard to specific sectors. Finally, we should note the major study by Geza Feketekuty, the senior U.S. official who for many years directed the formulation of U.S. official views on 'services' as a negotiating subject. His book appeared when this present study was in almost final form. It is a careful examination of the 'Services Proposal' consistent with the analysis in the U.S. National Study and the U.S. statements in Geneva. In a sense, this present paper can be taken as a commentary on these carefully articulated formulations.[26]

Earlier Proposals

All these issues and proposals have been considered in what we must assume are representative private sector bodies, such as the U.S. Chamber of Commerce[27] and the U.K. Committee on Invisible Exports.[28] At the international level, the private sector multisector body that has been the most active has been the International Chamber of Commerce. In 1981, the ICC Commission on Trade Policy and Trade-Related Matters issued its "Position Paper on Liberalization of Trade in Services".[29] This remains the most sweeping proposal yet formulated. In this lengthy and apparently carefully negotiated—perhaps over-negotiated—statement, the ICC proposed that:

(a) All services trade should be "conducted according to the principles of fair and open international competition".

(b) Traded services should be treated on an MFN basis.

(c) Restrictions on the purchase of foreign source services should be reduced "in as far-reaching and as reciprocal a manner as possible".

(d) Derogations should be subject to review and negotiations.

(e) New restrictions should be avoided "as far as possible"; if they cannot be avoided, new restrictions should "be temporary and subject to prior consultation and negotiation".

(f) The GATT should be extended to include trade in services; specifically, barriers to trade in services "should be tackled in a similar manner to the non-tariff barriers discussed during the Tokyo Round".

(g) "Industry-specific" negotiations should be aimed at "liberalization".

(h) Service contracts should be covered by the Tokyo Round Procurement Code, and the list of procurement entities should be made "as wide as possible".

(i) "National treatment" should be accorded to foreign service firms.

It would be difficult to think of a more all-encompassing request list. Of course, the U.S. mandatory prohibitions on foreign participation in certain service sectors (e.g., telecommunications), as detailed in the *U.S. National Study*, would make it impossible for even the United States to implement fully the ICC's proposal. It is not clear that the draftsmen in Paris were aware of this, or if they were aware, that they cared. While the ICC proposal does not seem to have gathered significant support, it does show what a group of private sector representatives—not just from the industrialized countries—or at least their advisers, believe is appropriate in the services sector. Few government officials would now go so far.

These various suggestions constitute the run-up to several attempts to set out in a systematic, detailed and organized fashion what might be the elements of a general agreement on services. So far, this has been expressed in terms of a series of concepts drafted in rather imprecise language; as one active enthusiast for a services negotiation observed, dealing in imprecise language is an attempt to avoid scaring off the less enthusiastic.

A number of broadly similar compilations of concepts have appeared in the past few years. One is the "Declaration on Trade in Services" appended to the U.S./Israel Free Trade Agreement of March 1985,[30] which was the first serious attempt to translate the Services Proposal into more precise language and undertakings, even if cast, at this stage, in terms of "best endeavours" only. Another is a statement submitted to the Contracting Parties to the GATT in July 1985 by the United States and reiterated in the two more recent submissions to the negotiating group by the United States.[31] The third is a document prepared by the Trade Committee of the OECD entitled *Elements of a Conceptual Framework for Trade in Services*.[32]

As regards the U.S./Israel Declaration, it is said by some U.S. observers that this declaration of intentions and principles, if cast in binding, contractual form, would make an appropriate general agreement on traded services. The key provisions are the paragraphs intended to prevent national regulation of a service sector from placing "undue, discriminatory restrictions on market access for services supplied from abroad"; the key concept (in paragraph 3) is "national treatment". An important point to note is that in this agreement the concept of a "commercial presence" as an alternative to "establishment" is introduced, and it is noted that, in the area of commercial banking, for example, a commercial presence "refers to the activities of representative offices, but not to agencies, branches or subsidiaries of commercial banks". Because the Declaration is cast in terms of "best endeavours", it was not technically necessary to exclude from the scope of the Declaration those services sectors where one party or the other has in place statutory restrictions on national treatment cast in mandatory form—such as banking, communications, maritime transport and air transport. The United States is not required by such a best endeavours undertaking to act in breach of mandatory provisions in its statutes.

If we were to compare this Declaration with the relevant provisions of the U.S./Israel Treaty of Friendship, Commerce and Navigation (FCN Treaty,)[33] we would see that there is considerable overlap with the detailed national treatment provisions of that treaty, but that the treaty, having statutory force in the United States, specifically excludes the above-named sectors from the scope of the national treatment obligation.[34] (It is fairly clear that much, although not all, of what is apparently being sought by the United States in the services sector is in fact covered, albeit in quite a different conceptual format, in the many FCN treaties the United States has negotiated.[35]

Yet another important consideration is revealed by the U.S. explanatory document: "The consultation procedure in the dispute settlement mechanism for the FTA will apply to goods and services".[36] A final point to note is the emphasis on transparency, which U.S. spokesmen have elevated from the status of a desirable practice (as in Article X of the GATT) to a "principle"—as in paragraph 7 of the list of principles in the Declaration. Indeed, in all U.S. formulations of what the United States seeks in services, the publication of all laws and regulations and the obligation to act publicly, not privately, in regard to the regulation of services enterprises, figures importantly.

The Current U.S. Proposals

Turning now to the more comprehensive Statement submitted to the GATT by the United States, and reflected in the more recent U.S. proposals, a number of points emerge.

1. What the United States seeks is a "contractual under-standing". As a practical matter, this implies that the agreement be cast in terms of precise, first-order obligations, supported by a system for dispute settlement and a system of enforcing sanctions.

2. The United States has made it clear that it excludes from the discussion of services certain categories under the "services" heading in the balance of payments accounts—namely "financial flows such as capital and labor remittances". The U.S. Statement notes, succinctly, that these "represent the disposition of earnings of the factors of production of both goods and services".

3. The U.S. Statement asserted that "Foreign [service] enterprises will not be able to take advantage . . . of commercial opportunities so long as the problems of investment are not addressed *in a framework similar to what we have suggested to cover trade in services.*" In the current proposal the notion of traded services and services delivered by facilities have been merged.

The United States now envisages that a legal framework to embody the general principles might include provisions along the following lines:

1. Transparency: We have noted the importance of this practice.

2. National treatment: All regulations affecting services industries would be governed by an obligation to treat foreign suppliers on the same basis as domestic suppliers. However, "where regulations limit the total number of enterprises [in a

sector] national treatment by itself might not assure reasonable market access . . . additional commitment might therefore be necessary."

3. Open regulatory procedures: Here the United States urges that other countries adopt the U.S. practice of publishing regulations in draft form, or as proposed regulations or rules, and providing an opportunity for interested parties to comment.

4. Public monopolies: Because in some countries some services are treated as public monopolies, it is important that there be provisions ensuring that such monopolies do not use their power to disadvantage foreign services suppliers.

5. Dispute settlement: Here the U.S. text is carefully drafted; it is silent on the key issue of whether a dispute settlement provision should allow compensation in the goods sector for alleged restrictions in a services sector. This will necessarily follow if, in the trade negotiations, countries secure concessions from the United States in the goods sector by offering concessions in their services sectors. The U.S. proposal reads: ". . . provision should be made for the establishment of independent panels to assist in resolving the dispute, including provision for compensation by a party whose trade opportunities have been impaired because of a foreign practice inconsistent with the framework." On the face of it, this does not go quite as far as Article XXIII of the GATT, which deals with *any* action that nullifies or impairs a benefit under the Agreement, whether or not such action is inconsistent with the Agreement.

6. Market access: This concept is intended to include "an appropriate degree of initial market access" and then "procedures for reducing barriers to trade in services". As regards "initial market access" the agreement "should cover" *existing* protective measures and restrictive licensing systems that limit access by foreigners to the domestic services market and should deal with any new restrictive measures. The procedures for the reduction of barriers to trade should be "along sector and functional lines". And as the Statement makes clear, the United States envisages that commitments would be stated in detailed and precise terms.

7. Sectoral negotiations: The United States envisages a number of sector-specific understandings that would deal with the problems unique to each sector, but in a manner consistent with the framework outlined above. The United States has not made clear whether a sector such as civil aviation—where the scope for national treatment is, under present practice, rather

restricted, and where there is a functional international, inter-governmental sectoral agreement—would be covered. The Statement merely notes that "priority" should be given to an understanding on international information flows.[37]   Presumably in these sector negotiations the United States should seek cover for those restrictions on foreigners that are mandated in U.S. legislation (e.g., in the communications sector).

8. Functional negotiations: By this term the United States means adapting and adopting some of the "basic concepts and principles of the GATT codes dealing with non-tariff barriers to trade, such as standards and procurement".   The Statement went on to note that it will be necessary to consider how the concepts of an understanding on intellectual property issues might apply to traded services.   The Statement was silent on whether the "basic concepts and principles" of the GATT Anti-Dumping and Subsidies/ Countervail Codes should be adapted to traded services.   Clearly the issue of "unfair trade" can be considered a "functional" issue; the United States has not, in fact, advocated that the GATT arrangements on unfair trade (that is, GATT Article VI) be extended to trade in services, but it flagged "unfair trade practices" as an issue for the negotiations.[38]

9. Finally, the U.S. Statement refers to the issue of a parallel arrangement on investment.

It is not a criticism—far from it—to say that this U.S. Statement and the November 1987 Statement are negotiating documents.

The OECD Approach

Another document that sets out a comprehensive approach to negotiating on services is the OECD Trade Committee's report.[39] The report is in four sections: "Definition(s)", "Principles", "Balanced commitments by national governments", and "Issues related to liberalization approaches and to negotiations".

Under "Definitions(s)", the Committee notes that a framework agreement would cover "the flow of services from one country to another", but notes that there are "other related aspects"— movement of persons and investment—and that the term "trade in services" should cover the financial transactions and transfers related to such trade.   This reflects the longstanding OECD formulation in the Invisibles Code: "transactions and transfers". The U.S. proposal, however, addresses the question of "commercial presence" without explicitly addressing the investment issue, as well as the questions surrounding movement of professionals.

Under "principles", the OECD covered much the same ground as the U.S. Statement, albeit using a more convoluted, cautious drafting style. However, it is fair to say that the formulation by the OECD Trade Committee of a set of principles in terms not radically dissimilar to those advanced by the United States reflects (1) the considerable effort at consensus building by the United States in the OECD and in other forums of the industrialized countries; (2) the acceptance, to a degree, by the European Communities, or rather by certain member states and by the Commission, that they do have a positive interest in negotiations on services; and (3) the adoption by the United States of a somewhat less aggressive style, combined with a policy of silence in regard to potentially critical issues, such as "unfair trade" and retaliation.

In the third part of the OECD Trade Committee report, the issue of "balance" is raised. This is the issue raised by the fact that in some countries some services sectors are regulated by sub-national levels of government (e.g., insurance in the United States) while in other countries the same sectors may be regulated by the central government. Thus there may be an issue of securing balance between the commitments of various national governments. Here is an issue that will obviously concern Canada, both as an importer of services and as an exporter of services.

Finally, under the general heading of "Issues related to liberalization approaches and to negotiations", the OECD report notes that it will be necessary to spell out countries' obligations with respect to procedural issues such as notification, consultation, invoking safeguard provisions, dispute settlement and so forth.

All these issues have been dealt with in some detail in earlier OECD documents. This particular document indicates that a certain consensus has been developed among OECD countries—at least a limited consensus as to what the issues are, though certainly not what the solutions are.

Recent Developments

If we turn to more recent developments, which have taken place against the background of the discussions and proposals outlined above, we should look, first, at an important statement prepared by Professor John Jackson, an American expert on the GATT and on trade law generally, and then at what the Canada-U.S. FTA provisions on services suggests in regard to the Geneva negotiations.

John Jackson's recent article[40] (which has, fortunately, been circulating in draft for some months) is addressed to the structure

of a possible set of agreements on services and the related institutions. Like the present writer, he envisages that most substantive
detail will be addressed only in sector-specific agreements; he is
more optimistic than the present writer in arguing for setting up a
services forum or institution to direct future negotiations and deal
with disputes. But he is pessimistic, perhaps unduly so, about the
scope for achieving more than agreement on an institutional
arrangement in the Uruguay Round: "It will not be possible to
build, within the period of the Uruguay Round negotiations, a
complete set of such rules. It seems best to recognize this and to
focus instead on the institution and structure which would be put
in place. Such a structure should allow the satisfactory solution of
substantive rules over a period of some decades . . ."

The outcome of the Canada-U.S. FTA negotiations is of great
importance, because here is an example of two rather like-minded
negotiating governments, with not dissimilar legal philosophies,
who found how little could be achieved in regard to services, *in
general terms*. The FTA provides for a 'standstill' on discrimination—that is, for national treatment in future measures regarding
services activities. However, existing measures are not affected.
Moreover, a major group of services activities—trucking, shipping,
air transport and railway transport—are not covered by the
standstill obligation. Moreover, right of establishment (if we
define that to include takeovers of domestic firms by foreign firms)
is subordinated to the investment provisions of the FTA, although,
in practical terms, this may not mean a great deal. The problem of
the temporary entry at immigration of professionals was addressed, but not in the sense of creating any right for a qualified
person in a regulated profession in one country to reside
permanently and practise his profession in the other country. The
one exception is in regard to architecture—for which the FTA
notes the arrangements being worked out for reciprocal recognition of professional accreditation. The FTA does define, very
carefully, what we could call a 'right of commercial presence'—and
the drafting may be useful in Geneva—but this right is created
only with regard to new and additional measures, not existing
measures, and not for all services industries.

But for two services sectors the FTA does develop detailed
agreements on access: "enhanced telecommunications and computer services" and financial services (which is defined to exclude
insurance). At this point we need not examine these particular
bilateral sector arrangements—in the main they relate almost
exclusively to the Canada-United States situation. But the point
is made that the real progress—the real liberalization of access
achieved in the FTA—is at the sector-specific level. Discussion
henceforth of the Services Proposal surely has to take proper

account of what was achieved, and what was not achieved, in the Canada-United States negotiation.[41]

Notes

1. OECD, *Report by the High-Level Group on Trade and Related Problems* (The Rey Report) (Paris: 23 August 1972). C(72) 175.

2. Rey Report, p. 64.

3. OECD, *Elements of a Conceptual Framework for Trade in Services* (Paris: OECD Secretariat, Trade Committee), TC/WP[85]9, 1985.

4. The text of the Ministerial Declaration of 29 November 1982; the text of the "conclusions adopted by the Contracting Parties" on 20 December 1984; and the decision of the Contracting Parties on 28 November 1985 and Part II of the Punta del Este Declaration are attached as Annex C.

5. The U.S., U.K., EC, Canada, Australia, Japan, and Netherlands studies have been circulated.

6. GATT, "Ministerial Declaration on the Uruguay Round", Press Release No. 1396, 25 September 1986.

7. Ambassador William Brock, "A Simple Plan for Negotiating on Trade in Services", 5 *The World Economy*, No. 3 (November 1982).

8. The most useful explanation of the retaliatory provisions of Section 301 of the Trade Act of 1974, as amended, is in *Report of the Committee on Finance*, Senate No. 96-249, July 17, 1979, pp. 234-244. (This is the Senate Committee's report on the legislation implementing the Tokyo Round agreements.)

9. *U.S. National Study on Trade in Services/a Submission by the United States Government to the General Agreement on Tariffs and Trade* (Washington: Office of the Trade Representative, December 1983).

10. *U.S. National Study*, p. 10.

11. *U.S. National Study*, p. 8.

12. See Rowland C. Frazee, *It's Canada's Turn* . . . (Montreal: Royal Bank of Canada, 1983), and Rodney de C. Grey, *Traded Computer Services/An Analysis of a Proposal for Canada/ USA Agreement* (Montreal: Royal Bank of Canada), esp. at

p. 2: "An Open-ended Arrangement". See also Rodney de C. Grey: "Elements of a General Agreement on Information Trade", 15 *Inter Media* (March 1987), 18-23.

13. *U.S. National Study*, p. 8.

14. *U.S. National Study*, p. 8.

15. *U.S. National Study*, p. 8.

16. *U.S. National Study*, p. 8.

17. *U.S. National Study*, p. 8.

18. "Communication from Argentina" MTN.GNS/W33, 22 March 1988; UNCTAD, *Trade and Development Report 1988*, Report of the Secretariat (New York: United Nations, E.88.11.D.8); see Part Two: "Services in the World Economy", especially Chapter VI, "Service Strategies for Development".

19. M. Cohen and T. Morante, "Elimination of Non-Tariff Barriers to Trade in Services: Recommendations for Future Negotiation" 13 *Law and Policy in International Business* (1981), pp. 495-519.

20. William Diebold, Jr. and Helena Stalson, "Negotiating Issues in International Services Transactions" in William R. Cline (ed.), *Trade Policy in the 1980s* (Washington: Institute for International Economics, 1983), pp. 581-609.

21. Jeffrey J. Schott, "Protectionist Threat to Trade and Investment in Services", 6 *The World Economy* No. 2 (June 1983).

22. Gary Clyde Hufbauer and Jeffrey J. Schott, *Trading for Growth: The Next Round of Trade Negotiations* (Washington: Institute for International Economics, September 1985), pp. 89-90.

23. Ronald K. Shelp, *Beyond Industrialization/Ascendancy of the Global Service Economy* (New York: Praeger, 1981).

24. Brian Griffiths, *Invisible Barriers to Invisible Trade* (London: Macmillan, for the Trade Policy Research Centre, 1975).

25. See, for example, Ronald K. Shelp, "The Proliferation of Foreign Insurance Laws: Reform or Regression?" 8 *Law and Policy in International Business* 1976).

26. H. Peter Gray, "A Negotiating Strategy in Trade in Services", 17 *Journal of World Trade Law* No. 5 (September/October 1983). Geza Feketekuty, *International Trade in Services/An*

Overview and Blueprint for Negotiations (AEI/Ballinger, 1988).

27. See *Report 1978-1980*, International Service Industry Committee of the Chamber of Commerce of the United States (Washington, 1980).

28. British Invisible Exports Council; *Liberalization of Trade in Services* (London: April 1984); (An assessment paper prepared by the LOTIS Committee. (London, April 1984.)

29. International Chamber of Commerce, Paris, Document No. 103/34, Rev. C1, 1981-C9-30.

30. *Declaration on Trade in Services/From the U.S.-Israel Free Trade Agreement* (March 1985) OECD, Paris, Working Party of the Trade Committee, TC/WP/85/24.

31. L/5838, 9 July 1985, and U.S. documents cited in Note 1 to Chapter I.

32. Cited in Note 3 above.

33. U.S. Department of State, *Treaties and Other International Acts Series* (TIAS) 2948, 1951-54, Publication 5490.

34. Article VII (2).

35. The U.S. has 43 FCN-type treaties. The more recent ones tend to exclude professionals providing services from the scope of the standard national treatment provisions. See Geza Feketekuty, "Barriers to International Trade in Professional Services" Chicago *Legal Forum*, No. 1 (1986). The standard articles on national treatment in a U.S. FCN treaty read as follows (this particular version is from the U.S./Israel FCN treaty):

    1. Nationals and companies of either Party shall be accorded national treatment with respect to engaging in all types of commercial, industrial, financial and other activity for profit (business activities) within the territories of the other Party, whether directly or by agent or through the medium of any form of lawful juridical entity. Accordingly, such nationals and companies shall be permitted within such territories: (a) to establish and maintain branches, agencies, offices, factories and other establishments appropriate to the conduct of their business; (b) to organize companies under the general company laws of such other Party, and to acquire majority interests in companies of such other Party; and (c) to control and manage enterprises which they have established

or acquired. Moreover, enterprises which they control, whether in the form of individual proprietorships, companies or otherwise, shall, in all that relates to the conduct of the activities thereof, be accorded treatment no less favourable than that accorded like enterprises controlled by nationals and companies of such other Party.

2.   Each Party reserves the right to limit the extent to which aliens may establish, acquire interests in, or carry on enterprises engaged within its territories in communications, air or water transport, banking, or the exploitation of land or other natural resources. However, neither Party shall deny to transportation, communications and banking companies of the other Party the right to maintain branches and agencies to perform functions necessary for essentially international operations in which they are permitted to engage.

3.   The provisions of paragraph 1 shall not prevent either party from prescribing special formalities in connection with the establishment of alien-controlled enterprises within its territories; but such formalities may not impair the substance of the rights set forth in said paragraph.

4.   Nationals and companies of either Party, as well as enterprises controlled by such nationals and companies, shall in any event by accorded most-favoured-nation treatment with reference to the matters treated in the present Article.

Article VIII

1.   Nationals and companies of either Party shall be permitted to engage, within the territories of the other Party, accountants and other technical experts, executive personnel, attorneys, agents and other specialists of their choice. Moreover, such nationals and companies shall be permitted to engage accountants and other technical experts regardless of the extent to which they may have qualified for the practice of a profession within the territories of such other Party, for the particular purpose of making examinations, audits and technical investigations for, and rendering reports to, such nationals and companies in connection with the planning and operation of their enterprises, and enterprises in which they have a financial interest, within such territories.

2.   Nationals of either Party shall not be barred from practicing the professions within the territories of the other Party merely by reason of their alienage; but they shall be

permitted to engage in professional activities therein upon compliance with the requirements regarding qualifications, residence and competence that are applicable to nationals of such other Party.

3. Nationals and companies of either Party shall be accorded national treatment and most-favoured-nation treatment with respect to engaging in scientific, educational, religious and philanthropic activities within the territories of the other Party, and shall be accorded the right to form associations for that purpose under the laws of such other Party. Nothing in the present Treaty shall be deemed to grant or imply any right to engage in political activities.

36. See *U.S. Proposal on Trade in Services Provisions on the U.S.-Israel Free Trade Area*, photocopy, 1984.

37. A position also supported by Grey in the two works cited in note 12 above and in "The Service Industries: A Note of Caution About the Proposal to Negotiate General Rules About Traded Services", in *Canada and the Multinational Trading System*, Vol. 10 of the studies for the Macdonald Commission. p. 36.

38. The U.S. brought forward "unfair trade practices" in regard to services in the discussions immediately before the Punta del Este meeting; in June 1986 the U.S. proposed a paragraph for possible inclusion in the Ministerial Declaration (which was not accepted) which read as follows

Proposed Text for Ministerial Declaration

In recognition of the growing importance of trade in services to the effective operation of the global economy, it is agreed that liberalization of trade in services through negotiations is desirable. Such negotiations should aim at ensuring that international trade in services is as open as possible through the development of a multilateral services agreement setting forth principles and procedures for the conduct of international trade activities in services. Such agreement should establish disciplines governing services trade, taking account of the legitimate objectives of national laws and regulations applying to services, and should also address specific trade barriers and unfair trade practices encountered by particular services sectors, as identified during the course of the negotiations.

Prep. Com (86) W/34, 11 June 1986. It is also explicitly addressed in the November 1987 Statement (Annex D).

39. Cited in note 3 above.

40. John H. Jackson, "Constructing a Constitution for Trade in Services" 11 *The World Economy* [London] No. 2 (June 1988), pp. 187-202.

41. See FTA, Chapter Fourteen, "Services", Annex 1404, "A. Architecture B. Tourism C. Computer Services, etc."; Chapter Fifteen, "Temporary Entry for Business Persons"; Chapter Sixteen, "Investment"; and Chapter Seventeen, "Financial Services".

Chapter III

Trade Policy Aspects of the World Services Economy

A number of features of the international services economy are relevant to the proposal to negotiate new rules about restrictions on international transactions in services. They are examined in this chapter. We do not attempt to set out a general description of the services economy in any one country or countries, or to describe in statistical terms the growth of international services activities. The reasons for not doing so are twofold. First, it is fairly obvious that there is a growing commerce in services, that a number of service companies (e.g., banks) have an interest in establishing themselves in other countries and selling their services there, and that a wide range of services (e.g., repairs to equipment, insurance, transportation) are integral to trade in goods. Second, there are already a number of adequate descriptions of services in the world economy. For example, the *U.S. National Study,* contains a useful general description. The Canadian government's submission to GATT on services also contains some useful general descriptive material on Canada's part of the international services economy. There is also a substantial volume of literature describing how the structure of domestic economies and of the international economy is changing because of the enlarged role of services activities and developments in particular services sectors, particularly changes in relative productivity.[1]

This chapter sets out a series of observations and points for consideration that appear to be important in assessing the likely developments in the Geneva negotiations.

Distinguishing Between Trade in Goods and Trade in Services

The first issue to consider is the difference, in trade agreement terms, between trade in goods and trade in services. It is customary to think of goods trade as taking place in different 'sectors' with important differentiating economic characteristics: the economics of the garment trade or the trade in numerically-controlled machine tools are manifestly different from the economics of commodity trade—say, tin or wheat. But from the point of view of trade agreement drafting, goods have one important characteristic: being material, they can be entered at customs, inbound or out-bound; the movement across the frontier, whether by truck or pipeline, or from ship to customs warehouse, provides a physical and temporal point at which a charge or fee or quantitative control can be imposed.

In relatively underdeveloped economies without elaborate or competent bureaucracies, the movement of goods (as well as persons and means of transport) across frontiers is often the occasion on which the state imposes such a fee. The structure and format, indeed, the language of trade agreements has developed around this common characteristic of traded goods. But services lack such a single common characteristic; attempts to classify services have proved less than useful from the point of view of drafting agreements about international commerce. It is not surprising that, in the goods sector, agreements about particular products are essentially, at best, arrangements to control quantities traded and/or prices (e.g., the Tin Agreement); at worst, they are mere producers' cartels. By contrast, in the services sectors of international commerce there are a number of highly developed regulatory agreements (including, most importantly, conciliation and dispute settlement provisions), such as the International Telecommunication Convention, administered by the ITU, and the Convention on International Civil Aviation (the Chicago Convention), administered by ICAO.

For the purposes of our discussion of the prospects for negotiations, we can classify all goods trade in one sector, then consider whether each category of services trade should be treated as a separate sector, or whether traded services have sufficient characteristics in common that they can be treated, for any significant negotiating purpose, as a single category. The Canadian *Back-*

ground Report noted that services might be classified into four broad categories, considered in terms of their relationship to goods:

Category One: Services *embodied* in goods (e.g., motion picture films, sound recordings, books and computer tapes).

Category Two: Services *complementary* to trade in goods (e.g., shipping, including port services, handling and storage; other transportation (air, rail, road, inland waterways) including handling, warehousing and storage at loading and delivery stations; insurance and reinsurance of cargo for fire, theft and similar risks; banking related to trade in goods such as the financing of imports and exports; brokerage, such as transport and insurance brokers; and advertising for products trade internationally).

Category Three: Services that *substitute* for trade in goods (e.g., franchising, chartering, leasing, and repairs and maintenance).

Category Four: Services that are traded *without a relationship* with goods (e.g., banking, other than that related to trade in goods, life and other types of insurance not related to trade in goods; professional services such as accounting, architectural, engineering, legal and medical; real estate; telecommunications, data processing and information services; and travel).

This classification suggests that it would not be unreasonable to consider the GATT as having some responsibility for at least Category Two, in that restrictions on such services (or discriminatory charges, e.g., for port services) can adversely affect goods trade and can be, in effect, disguised tariffs or restrictions on goods. The GATT Contracting Parties asserted such a competence in 1953, when they began to consider the issue of discrimination in transport insurance; however, this early effort of the Contracting Parties in the services area had very little result.[3]

However, when we consider this classification more closely, we see that there are some difficulties. For example, one can argue that many goods are little more than "embodied" services, e.g., private automobiles embody transportation. Moreover, many types of services can be embodied in goods—the value of which may not reflect the value of the services, e.g., architectural and engineering plans. It appears that Category One may involve quite a number of different types of service activities. Conversely, a number of services that normally require the physical presence of the service provider can now be delivered without such a physical presence, but through the employment of some electronic device—e.g., banking by electronic teller. This phenomenon of the embodiment of services in goods, and 'disembodiment', is not only of interest to professional economists; it also has trade policy implications.[4]

From the point of view of analyzing the Services Proposal in the context of current international trade policy there are two issues here: (1) how are certain goods that embody services to be valued at customs, e.g., computer tapes; and (2) what sort of regime should apply to services that can be delivered internationally over telecommunications systems. For example, what are the implications, in terms of the regulation of architectural practice and in terms of the regulation of transborder data flows, of an American architectural firm forwarding copies of its detailed working drawings over the telephone wires to a Canadian or European client's computer for use in that jurisdiction?

When we examine Category Three, we see that a number of unlike activities have been lumped together. Franchising, for example, is an activity much like licensing the use of a patent or trademark; it is a "substitute for trade in goods" in somewhat the same sense as producing goods in a branch plant in another country to serve the market in that other country—rather than exporting to that other country—can be called a "substitute for trade". In this light, it is not clear that franchising is really a service activity; if it is, it may belong in a category by itself. "Chartering and leasing" are not substitutes for trade in goods, but alternative ways of disposing of the title to goods; the choice between buying or leasing, say, construction machinery or railway cars is a financial and fiscal matter, but the article being bought or leased performs the same functions (or services) regardless of who retains title or how the 'service' embodied in the article is purchased.

'Repairs' as a category raises other conceptual issues. Why is it, for example, that the installation of an automobile exhaust system, including the value of the parts involved and the labour required, is counted as the production of a 'good' the first time it is done for a particular vehicle, but if it is required to be done a second time (i.e., the exhaust system is repaired) the whole operation is considered a 'service'? If we count the production of exhaust system spare parts as the production of goods, what is the utility of treating the subsequent installation labour as a 'service'? Repairs are, of course, an important item in international trade in regard to such activities as air transport and shipping; the value of repairs performed abroad has traditionally been considered an import of goods when the repaired article is entered at customs. There is an analogous problem regarding construction. Engineering advice and project supervision certainly have a service character, but construction activities as such are properly excluded. For any particular project, there will be difficulties in deciding what proportion of the total cost of a project is made up of services.

Other attempts to classify services have been based on economic criteria. For example, we could divide services into four categories: producer or intermediate services (that is, services, such as data processing, that are necessary to the production of goods or other services); *distributive* services, such as wholesaling and retailing; *social* services, such as the services of governments; and *personal* services such as entertainment, personal care, medical services and life insurance.[5] Such a categorization is important for economic analysis, for example, for the study of changes in labour markets, changes in industrial structure, and divergent trends in productivity. It is also important, when we consider the particular problems of developing economies in relation to services trade, to recognize the critical role of high-technology services in the production of many types of goods and services—for example, computer-assisted design and computerized control of manufacturing in the manufacture of automobiles, or computerized reservation systems for airline operation.

But these attempts to categorize services are not helpful when we try to organize trade agreement rules about services. As a tentative working approach one may conclude that each service belongs in its own category; attempts to categorize or group services will not be very productive or, in the formulation of rules regarding international trade, will lead to only a few statements of such generality as to create no meaningful rights or obligations. It is perhaps not surprising that it is in relation to *particular* services, such as air transport or telecommunications, that it has been possible to develop detailed international agreements. That is not to say that these arrangements are adequate or that it is necessarily in existing sector institutions that new negotiating efforts should be made.

The Classification Problem

Our working hypothesis is, therefore, that traded *goods* are one category and traded services comprise a series of dissimilar categories. This obviously has significant implications for the negotiation of general, multisector rules. There is one major caveat on the assertion that one service activity is unlike another service activity: increasingly, a number of internationally traded services rely on the flow of information, or are themselves the flow of information, from and to computerized installations over tele-communication systems. One can call this information flow 'informatics'. The international services economy (that is, the sum of transactions between services entities (corporations, systems or individuals providing services) and purchasers in all countries, including affiliates of those entities in other countries, and the transactions affected by foreign establishments) is information-driven and informatics-based. Thus, in a practical sense, if informatics as a sector were to be addressed it might be that a number of the problems (i.e., restrictions) facing other services sectors would also be addressed. (Of course, some key barriers would remain, e.g., restrictions related to the operations of foreign-controlled banks in Canada, professional accreditation, commercial presence.) That is not to say that, for example, investment banking as a sector could easily be addressed in any detail under the same heads of agreement as, say, reinsurance as a service activity—but rather that both are now important users of a producer or intermediate service: informatics. As Harald Malmgren has pointed out, it is important, in considering just how the services negotiations may develop, to try to envisage what sort of rules we will need for the informatics-based services economy of the 1990s and 2000s, not for the less internationalized, less wired services of the early 1980s.[6]

There is another problem of classification. The established practice of statistical agencies, in counting international transactions, is to consider transactions in 'visibles' (merchandise trade) and 'invisibles'. 'Current invisibles', however, cover not only pure 'service' transactions, such as the sale of engineering services, but also dividends and interest on debt. Thus some earlier discussions of the 'services proposal' were confused because the magnitudes at issue were drawn from statistics on 'invisibles' taken as a single broad category. For example, in the study published in 1982 by the British private sector group, Liberalization of Trade in Services Committee (LOTIS), much attention is given to the contribution of U.K. investment to U.K. earnings on 'invisibles'; this was clearly a misconception.[7] Similarly, the Canadian *Background Report* of 1982 referred to the fact that the "overall service deficit" of Canada had grown from 2.5 per cent of GNP in 1971 to 4.5 per cent in 1981: "This deterioration in the net position of the service account can be traced almost entirely to Canada's growing deficit in terms of interest, dividend and miscellaneous investment income payments."[8]

This too was evidence of confusion. Underwriting fees and brokerage fees earned in Montreal or Toronto, or London or New York, are fees for services and can properly be included in a discussion of issues in the services sector. But interest and dividend income, that is, transactions that represent the rent of capital or the return for risk taking are outside the concept of services, and they do not figure on the emerging agenda. Since 1984, Statistics Canada has separated investment income from services transactions in the category of invisibles, in presenting the System of National Accounts (see Table 1).[9] However, it is difficult to factor out fees for services from interest, because interest payments often include services other than money borrowed (e.g., banks provide market information). However, this 'bundling' of services is becoming a thing of the past among bankers as non-bank competition grows and banks try to turn each activity into a profit centre.

There is another statistical difficulty with respect to the magnitude of trade in services. In general, the data are inadequate; moreover, data on profits from service transactions carried out by establishments (that is, controlled in one country but established in another) are difficult to assemble. Statistics Canada notes that, with regard to banking, for example: "... data on banking services are not available separately from other banking transactions and are implicitly included in investment income transactions. Canadian banks, as multinationals, can carry on their international service activities from their subsidiaries abroad. The revenues from these sources would flow into Canada through profits, as opposed to services."[10] Given that the services agenda clearly includes questions about the restrictions that may apply to the establishment of foreign-controlled services companies and about the differences, if any, that may be appropriate in the treatment accorded such companies, once established, it is unfortunate that we know so little about the magnitudes involved.

More recently, the U.S. Congressional Office of Technology Assessment (OTA) reviewed U.S. statistical reporting on services, including revenues of establishments, in the sense discussed above and concluded that services trade, broadly defined, and the U.S. surplus in such trade, have been much larger than previously calculated (by the Department of Commerce Bureau of Economic Analysis). The accompanying table (drawn from the OTA report), which excludes banking, shows nonetheless the importance of revenues of establishments in this reassessment of the scale of international services activities (see Table 2).[11]

The Magnitude of Services Sectors

There are also difficulties in judging the overall magnitude of the services sector in a given economy. It is evident that many so-called advanced industrial countries are in fact service economies, that is, calculated in terms of employment. Changes in the structure of production and in labour markets are of great significance.[12] Just as in an earlier period employment in agriculture declined with the increasing mechanization of agriculture and the development of extensive cultivation techniques, so more recently

Table 1
Current Account,
Canadian Balance of International Payments, 1984

Previous Presentation			New Presentation
	RECEIPTS		
	($ millions)		
Merchandise Transactions	112,218	112,218	Merchandise Transactions
Non-Merchandise Transactions	23,730	23,730	Non-Merchandise Transactions
• Service Transactions: (including invest- ment income)	20,365	14,189	• Service Transactions
		6,176	• Investment Income
• Transfers	3,365	3,365	• Transfers
Total Receipts	135,948	135,948	Total Receipts
	PAYMENTS		
	($ millions)		
Merchandise Transactions	91,493	91,493	Merchandise Transactions
Non-Merchandise Transactions	41,094	41,094	Non-Merchandise Transactions
• Service Transactions: (including invest- ment income)	38,542	18,572	• Service Transactions
		19,970	• Investment Income
• Transfers	2,551	2,551	• Transfers
Total Receipts	132,586	132,586	Total Receipts
Balance	**3,362**	**3,362**	**Balance**

Table 2
Comparisons of U.S. Balance of Payments and Foreign Revenues Figures for Services
(in billions of current U.S. dollars)

	Exports	Imports	Balance	Overseas revenues of affiliates of U.S. companies	U.S. revenues of affiliates of foreign companies
Commerce Department figures:					
1983	41.80	35.40	6.4		
1984	43.80	41.50	2.3	Not compiled	
OTA estimates:					
1983	67.84	52.66	17.0*	87.97	69.75
1984	69.91	57.74	14.0*	Not available	

* based on mid-range of OTA estimates for exports and imports.

employment in manufacturing has declined because of the application of capital-intensive techniques, even in such traditionally labour-intensive sectors as primary textiles.[13] Many service activities, it would appear, have been less easy to mechanize, and therefore gains in productivity may be relatively lower. Hence, as the mature economies expand, relatively more labour is drawn into services activities. U.S. services employment is estimated to have represented 64 percent of the labour force in 1965, 71 per cent in 1975, 75 per cent in 1985.[14] U.S. figures suggest that there has been a relatively steady expansion since the 1950s in services employment, including during periods of recession; goods-producing industries, however, showed substantial declines in employment in each recession. The figures shown in Table 3 were compiled by the U.S. Department of Labour.[15]

These changes in the level of services employment lump together a large number of structural shifts in economic activity. In the personal services sector, where there is no great amount of trade (if we define trade narrowly, and in the sense it is used in the goods sector, to mean the provision of a service in one country to a customer in another), there may well have been an increase in such services as laundromats, dry cleaning centres, physical fitness centres—but not all these represent an increase in economic activity. Some service facilities have replaced domestic labour by household members; there is probably some associated increase in leisure.

Table 3
U.S. Employment Changes by Sectors

Recession	Goods-producing industries (non-agricultural)	Services (including government)
1957-58	-10.0%	+ 0.07
1960-61	- 6.4%	+ 0.90
1969-70	- 7.3%	+ 3.10
1973-75	-11.9%	+ 3.30
1981-82	-11.2%	+ 0.60

Clearly there are major differences in the types of services activities available and customarily purchased in different economies. In North America and Western Europe, there has been a decline in employment in households for domestic servants. Many will recall that in the 1930s many North American families of only modest means, both farm and non-farm, had occasional, if not regular, domestic help. In Africa and South and South-East Asia, even a modest income makes possible relatively lavish domestic assistance, on a scale only the most wealthy can contemplate in Western Europe or North America. In Japan, patterns of services employment are again different. The high levels of employment and service found in retail outlets, restaurants and hotels in Japan reflect a traditional pattern or structure of services activity; these are either "inefficient" or "service-oriented", depending on one's point of view.[16]

One major type of service activity, office work, is common to many service sectors, such as banking or insurance, as well as to goods production. New methods of information storage and communication are changing the nature of this type of service employment. There is much talk of the office of the future, but we are clearly at an early stage of its development. It may be that there will be significant gains in productivity in this area, and therefore less rapid growth of employment, but it is not clear that there has been great improvement in the quality of the product (i.e., the level of service) in all the areas concerned. Much of this change is, of course, based on the use of informatics techniques.[17]

Legal Treatment in Services Sectors

The intriguing questions of just how employment and production structures are changing, and the resulting impact on productivity levels, do not directly concern those obliged to focus on the question of what restrictions exist on *international* transactions in the services sectors, and whether and how rules might be agreed to bring such access restrictions under some effective scrutiny and surveillance. We should note, of course, that a number of services enter only marginally into international trade (narrowly defined), but that, conceptually, virtually all services (with the exception, perhaps, of some governmental services) can be produced by foreign-controlled entities. Thus the issue of the legal treatment to be accorded foreign-controlled entities in services sectors is of broad relevance.

In the case put forward, for example, by Brock or Malmgren, in favor of a system of rules regarding services, both those traded and those delivered by establishments or facilities, much has been made of what are taken to be two characteristics of services: that service industries are often regulated, and that service industries are often public or publicly-regulated monopolies. Both these statements are true, but neither of these characteristics sharply distinguishes services sectors from the goods sector. Many types of goods are subject to detailed technical regulation—foods, pharmaceuticals, electrical goods, automobiles. In the main, in regard to goods, it is the product itself that is subject to regulation. In services sectors, products are also subject to regulation, e.g., insurance contracts, air transport contracts, but regulations may also apply to establishments, e.g., insurance companies, airlines. A first and substantial attempt to devise rules and procedures to limit the trade-restricting effects of regulations applying to goods is the GATT Standards Code;[18] not surprisingly it has frequently been suggested that the principles and concepts of this code could be used in regard to services sectors.

It is true that certain services have been taken to be natural monopolies and have frequently been taken into the public sector on the basis that the public interest is best protected by the provision of such services by state monopolies. The perceived alternative has been regulation of private monopolies by independent boards or by other governmental agents. Examples of sectors where monopolies exist differ from country to country. For example, in France the postal system and the telephone system are publicly operated monopolies. In the United States the telephone system is not a monopoly but it is regulated, though less so, it appears, than heretofore. In the United Kingdom the railway system is a public monopoly, although for a long period there were privately owned railways operating under regulation.

In the goods sector, the fact that public monopolies are the main purchasers of particular categories of goods in some countries, but not in others (for example, telecommunications equipment and electricity generating equipment) has meant that access to markets has been restricted not only by tariffs but also, and often more significantly, by procurement policies. Attempts to negotiate rules on procurement (in the Tokyo Round and now in the Uruguay Round) have not been very productive. It is obviously difficult, for example, to agree on rules regarding the procurement of electricity generating equipment, when in one country, France, electricity generation is the function of a national public monopoly, in another, Canada, it is largely a function of provincial public monopolies or provincially regulated companies, and in a third country, the United States, its mainly a private sector activity. Banking, air transport and insurance are service sectors where some countries have either publicly operated monopolies or nationalized operating entities. This asymmetry—the existence in certain goods subsectors of public monopolies in some countries but not in others—has made it difficult to strike bargains to reduce barriers to trade. This same problem of asymmetry is likely to be significant in various services sectors, particularly in regard to developing countries. It is possible that deregulation and privatization may increase the scope for negotiating effective sector-specific trade rules.[19]

The Gains to be Made

Finally, in this series of comments on the services economy from the point of view of whether trade in services can be brought under effective international or trade agreement rules, there is the question of whether there will be gains from liberalizing trade in services. It is to the judgement that there are 'gains from trade' that democratic governments, subject to the pushes and pulls of interest groups, must react. This question can be, and has been asked in terms of the theory of international trade,[20] but it is not necessarily an interesting question for trade negotiators. They are faced with the fact that producers of certain services in a number of countries, e.g., the United States and the United Kingdom, believe that their interests would be advanced (i.e., that there would be gains for them) by removing restrictions that bear on their trade. U.S. officials hold to the view that there would be gains for all countries from freer trade in services—that is, not only for the services exporters of the North, but also for the developing economies of the South. This is being asserted more as an article of faith than as substantiated economic analysis; it leaves the United States open to the criticism that if it is so concerned about the gains from trade in the services sector for developing countries, should not equal effort and equal priority be given to realizing the gains from trade and letting new comparative advantages work in the regard to those goods sectors, such as leather goods, textiles, garments, and even steel, where developing countries have export capacity.

Without disputing that there may indeed be gains from liberalizing trade in services, we should note that:

1. Gains from trade are likely to be large in industries that use one or another factor of production intensively, where there are sharp differences between factor endowments between countries, and where there are large-scale industrie; with decreasing costs. Countries with large volumes of relatively skilled low-priced labour will gain substantially from trade in such labour-intensive areas as garments, electronics assembly and construction. Countries with large pools of capital stand to gain from trade in capital-intensive, decreasing cost industries, but capital mobility may make large amounts of capital available at many competing locations. It has not been demonstrated, in this context, that in services sectors the gains from trade are necessarily large.

2. It is difficult to measure or estimate potential gains from trade, but easy to identify what may seem to be short-term or immediate losses from the removal of given restrictions. This is a recurrent problem for negotiators of trade agreements designed to remove restrictions on trade.

3. It is difficult to assess the value of potential gains from trade against other practices of economic and political value such as the maintenance of sovereignty, or the building up of domestic capability in particular services sector. These other objectives are not necessarily issues of importance only to developing countries. The United States has taken exception to Brazil's policy of developing domestic capacity in the computer equipment and services sectors—but how is this different, in economic terms, from the Canadian policy, in force for many years, that the banking sector should be reserved for Canadian-controlled enterprises, or from U.S. policy in regard to the production of sugar? It will clearly be a mistake to assume that concern for sovereignty or for building up domestic capacity (the 'infant industry' argument) is somehow immoral and should be the subject of retaliation. To suggest that unless the interests of the potential services exporters of

the North prevail, restrictions will be placed on exports of goods from developing countries is not, on reflection, a very convincing demonstration of the virtues of free trade, whatever the political logic may be in terms of forging a freer trade coalition in the United States.

In the next chapter we examine the existing trade relations system as it applies to goods. Then in the following chapter we move on to look at existing regimes in regard to services. In examining the trade relations system, and indeed, in examining services regimes, it will be important to keep in mind our working hypothesis that services activities are sharply differentiated, although increasingly some of them are dependent on informatics as an intermediate service.

Notes

1. See *U.S. National Study*, Section 1, p. 13. "Services in the World Economy", Section 2, p. 20. "Services in the United States Economy"; Canada, Task Force on Trade in Services, *Background Report* (Ottawa, October 1982): "The Services Economy", p. 6; Ronald Kent Shelp, *Beyond Industrialization/Ascendancy of the Global Service Economy*, Jonathan Gershuny and Ian Miles, *The New Service Economy/The Transformation of Employment in Industrial Society* (London, Pinter, 1983), Chapter 3; Jacques Nusbaumer, *Les Services/Nouvelle Donné de L'Économie* (Paris: Economica, 1984). Geza Feketekuty, *International Trade in Services* (Cambridge, Mass.: AEI/Ballinger, 1988). United Nations Conference on Trade and Development/Report by the UNCTAD Secretariat, *Production and Trade in Services: policies and their underlying factors bearing upon international service transactions*, TD/941/Rev. 1. New York, U.N., 1985; *Services and the Development Process* TD/B/1008/Rev. 1, New York, U.N., 1985; *Trade and Development Report 1988*, New York, U.N., E.88.D.8, Part Two.

2. Canada, *Background Report*, p. 7.

3. See Raymond J. Krommenacker, "Trade Related Services in the GATT", 13 *Journal of World Trade Law* No. 6 (1979) pp. 510-522.

4. For a comment, see Jagdish Bhagwati, "Splintering and Disembodiment of Services and Developing Nations", 7 *The World Economy* No. 2 (1984), pp. 133-143.

5. See H.L. Browning and J. Singleman, "The Transformation of the U.S. Labour Force: the Interaction of Industry and Occupation", 8 *Politics and Society* (1978), pp. 481-509.

6. Harald B. Malmgren, "Negotiating International Rules for Trade in Services", 8 *The World Economy* No. 1 (March 1985), pp. 11-26. For comment on informatics as a sector, see Rodney de C. Grey, *Traded Computer Services/An Analysis of a Proposal for Canada/U.S.A. Agreement* (Montreal: The Royal Bank of Canada, 1983). The proposal examined in this paper is turned into a detailed agreement in the Canada-U.S. FTA, in Part C of Annex 1404.

7. Liberalization of Trade in Services Committee (of the Committee on Invisible Exports); *Liberalization of Trade in Services* (London: November 1982), especially Appendix A.

8. Canada, *Background Report*, p. 15.

9. Statistics Canada, *System of National Accounts/Canada's International Trade in Services, 1969 to 1984* (Ottawa: June 1986), p. 12.

10. *System of National Accounts*, p. 49.

11. Office of Technology Assessment, *Trade in Services: Exports and Foreign Revenues* (Washington: 1986), p. 4; the explanation of why banking has been excluded is set out at p. 40. See also *The Economist*, September 20, 1986: "Without any statistical reforms, American policy makers will not know what they are talking about if trade in services comes under the GATT umbrella."

12. An authoritative study of the U.S. services sector, which reached a wide audience, is Eli Ginzberg and George J. Vojta, "The Service Sector of the U.S. Economy", 244 *Scientific American* No. 3 (March 1981); the basic study of the Canadian services sector is U.K. Ranga Chand, "The Growth of the Service Sector in the Canadian Economy", 13 *Social Indicators Research* (1983), pp. 339-379. (This article contains a short bibliography of material of particular relevance to Canada.)

13. See Eli Ginzberg, "The Mechanization of Work", 247 *Scientific American* No. 3 (September 1982).

14. From *Wall Street Journal (Europe)*, September 22, 1986: "U.S. Growth in Services May Moderate Cycles".

15. *Wall Street Journal* (as cited in note 14). For a detailed comment on changes in the structure of the market for services the United States, see Emma Rothschild, "The Real Reagan Economy", *New York Review of Books*, June 30, 1988; "The Reagan Economic Legacy", *New York Review of Books*, July 21, 1988.

16. Victor R. Fuchs, *The Service Economy* (New York: NBER, 1968).

17. Vincent E. Guiliano, "The Mechanization of Office Work", 247 *Scientific American*, No. 3 (September 1982); Martin L. Ernst, "The Mechanization of Commerce", 247 *Scientific American*, No. 3 (September 1982); Gershuny and Miles (see note 1 above).

18. For the GATT Standards Code; 26S *BISD*, 8-32. For a discussion of this code from a Canadian point of view, see D. Cohen, "The Intersection of Consumer Protection Law and International Trade: Implications for Canadian Regulators", in *Canada and International Trade, Conference Papers*, Vol. 1, Institute for Research on Public Policy, 1985), pp. 235-310; the references in this paper provide a useful bibliography of relevant studies and cases, which it will be necessary to examine if it were seriously proposed to use the Standards Code as a model or analogue for services negotiations.

19. We do not enter into the debate on deregulation and privatization, but see, as examples of studies on these issues in regard to the structure of services sectors, Almarin Phillips and Mitchell Berlin, "Technology and Financial Services: Regulatory Problems in a De-regulated Environment", Discussion Paper No. 8, June 1985, Fishman-Davidson Centre for the Study of the Service Sector, Wharton School, University of Pennsylvania; Gerald R. Faulhaser: "Deregulation and Innovation in Telecommunications", Discussion Paper No. 14, January 1986, Fishman-Davidson Centre.

20. See Alan V. Deardorff (comment by Ronald W. Jones), "Comparative Advantage and International Trade and Investment in Services", Discussion Paper No. 15, Fishman-Davidson Center.

Chapter IV

The Trade Relations System

The Services Proposal, if implemented, would require that the trade relations system, which deals primarily with trade in goods, be extended in some form to services, whether traded across borders or delivered by establishments, or that the system for goods be taken as an analogue for a system regulating restrictions on trade in services. The purpose of this chapter is to consider the complex of treaties, bilateral agreements, codes, declarations, and protocols that constitute the trade relations system. This is a somewhat different approach than to consider, as an economist might, the benefits of lower tariffs and non-discrimination. What we need to recognize is that the trade relations system is extremely complex, extremely detailed and shot through with reservations and derogations and—most important—that major trading countries or entities often act in breach of the formally agreed rules. "Organized non-compliance with the rules", to borrow a phrase often used by the late Jan Tumlir, is a feature of the system as it exists and, some would say, increasingly so.

GATT: The Main Concept

The trade relations system consists of all the bilateral and multilateral trade agreements, the institutions that administer such agreements, and the practices and precedents under these arrangements. The General Agreement on Tariffs and Trade

(GATT) is, for industrialized countries other than the USSR, the main component of the system and central to its operation.[1] There are, however, numerous other instruments of public and private international law that constitute key elements of the trade relations system.

The GATT is an inter-governmental, multilateral instrument of public international law, a trade agreement on the classic model, based on a most-favoured-nation (MFN) clause drafted in the unconditional form. It replaced a number of pre-war bilateral treaties linked by unconditional MFN clauses. The GATT, however, is more than merely a standardized agreement; because it is a multilateral agreement, it has been possible to cast many obligations in a form embodying an obligation on the part of each signatory (a contracting party) vis-à-vis all other contracting parties. This is important, for example, with regard to obligations on tariff rates. A contracting party, when it assumes an obligation to apply no more than the rate of X per cent to a specified imported good, has assumed an obligation toward all other contracting parties. If the rate is to be raised, it is not a question of negotiating only with the single other country with which the original agreement to lower the rate was negotiated (as in the 'system of treaties'), but with all the countries specified in Article XXVIII— that is, the original negotiating country and the principal supplier (which may be a new supplier, or the European Communities, which has aggregated the trade interest of its member states), subject to consultations with all others that can show a supplying interest.

The GATT also institutionalizes and multilateralizes the process of consultation and dispute settlement and provides a forum for the negotiation of trade problems. When the GATT was concluded in 1947, it was rightly considered a radical advance on the sort of arbitrary and unilateral trade policy pattern that reigned prior to World War II, and it represented a major element in the construction of a broad system of international order.

Looking at the GATT from a distance, it seems reasonable to argue that this noble structure should be enlarged to shelter services, or perhaps that we should construct another structure, another comprehensive multilateral agreement, to cover services in a fashion analogous to the GATT. However, to accept such a proposition as valid, one has to overlook at least two facts: first, in practice many powerful governments prefer to settle trade issues by methods that derogate from their GATT obligations; second, many important areas of trade—e.g., most of agriculture, textiles and garments, steel, automobiles, certain electronics—are regulated by applying rules other than those of the GATT or by ignoring GATT obligations.

The problem is not with the GATT text, but with governments, which do not have the will (i.e., the political coalition of interests) to live by the rules they have put in place.[2] Moreover, there is the problem created by the fact that some GATT provisions are inadequate or open to abuse, notably Article VI (and the Tokyo Round codes) governing the use of anti-dumping and countervailing duties. Many observers would argue that Article XIX, governing emergency action in regard to imports of particular products, is deficient; I share the view, often expressed to GATT delegates by the late Sir Eric Wyndham Whyte, that the issue is not deficiency in drafting but the unwillingness of governments to follow the rules. Be that as it may, imperfect as the GATT is, and unwilling as governments often are to adhere to their GATT obligations, the GATT is the centrepiece of the trade relations system for the western industrialized nations.

Regarded as an institution, the GATT is merely a committee of representatives of contracting parties to the agreement, and its secretariat merely the secretariat of the Interim Committee of the International Trade Organization. The GATT has no corporate existence; there is no GATT entity with decision-making powers distinct from the powers of the signatories meeting together. It has no executive board, as the International Monetary Fund and the World Bank do; its collective authority, such as may emerge on any particular issue, is merely the aggregated commitment of the contracting parties. Commercial policy is so sensitive politically, so particularized in a regional or constituency sense, so subject to the play of special interests, that it has not been possible to consign sovereignty to a supra-national body.[3] Two efforts have been made to turn the GATT into a corporate, supra-national body. Both—the International Trade Organization and the Organization for Trade Cooperation—failed to be born.[4]

Another portion of the trade relations system is the set of arrangements ancillary to or amplifying the GATT—the arrangements that have made the GATT what two observers usefully labelled a "multi-tier system"[5] in the sense that there are tiers of rights and obligations. There are, for example, the protocols of accession or association with the GATT entered into by a number of countries that cannot apply all the GATT articles (in the main, the non-market countries) or that do not choose to apply all the GATT articles (e.g., Switzerland). There is a Multi-Fibre Arrangement (MFA), which provides a special set of rules for two sectors of trade (textiles and textile products) that many GATT signatories assert should be dealt with outside the GATT proper. There are various elaborate interpretative notes to the GATT articles (e.g., the Anti-dumping Code and the Subsidies/Countervail Code) to which not all GATT countries are signatories. There are the agreements that extend elements of the GATT system itself as between the signatories of such agreements, i.e., the Tokyo Round agreements on procurement and on standards, and there are the sector agreements worked out in regard to agriculture (bovine meat, dairy products).

Bilateral Arrangements

Another important part of the trade relations system is the set of bilateral trade agreements. There are several categories here. First, there are a number of longstanding bilateral trade agreements between GATT signatories; the agreements may, in some cases, still be in effect or may have a different legal basis than the GATT. The text of a provision referring to a given trade agreement concept, such as MFN treatment, may not be the same as the GATT article. An interesting case is the pre-World War II trade agreement between the United States and Canada. In Canada the provisions were given statutory effect and remained part of Canadian law; by an exchange of notes in 1947 it was agreed that the agreement would "be inoperative for such time as Canada and the United States of America are both contracting parties to the General Agreement on Tariffs and Trade . . .".[6] The United States suggested many years ago that this treaty be terminated, but the Canadian reaction was to retain it against the risk of some unforeseen development in U.S. policy, particularly given that Canada and the United States had no comprehensive treaty of Friendship, Commerce and Navigation (FCN Treaty), to use the American term. The FTA, of course, makes this earlier arrangement of only historical interest.

The second category is composed of bilateral arrangements for the conduct of trade between GATT signatories and non-signatories, such as the United States/USSR[7] and United States/China agreements.[8] The list of such trade agreements must be lengthy, given that many developing countries have entered into special bilateral arrangements with China and with the USSR.

Third, and of considerable importance, are the various bilateral agreements that go beyond the GATT and that in one way or another supplement, perhaps even in a contradictory fashion, GATT obligations. An example is the Canada-U.S. agreement on the automotive products sector, which the United States implemented on a formally and overtly discriminatory (i.e., preferential) basis, therefore requiring a waiver (under the provisions of GATT Article XXV) from the MFN obligation under GATT Article I.

Another example is the set of bilateral agreements regulating trade in such products as steel, textiles, garments and automobiles. If we take as a measure the amount of trade covered and the change in the terms of trade effected by these bilateral agreements, they must be considered of great importance. Indeed, most countries, including the United States, the European Communities and Canada, devote considerable trade policy resources to negotiating and administering such agreements. It is perhaps convenient to ignore these trade-restricting arrangements when citing the merits of the GATT as a system, but this is surely misleading. The MFA, for example, is part of the GATT system, even though it is a derogation from the provisions of Article I.

A sub-category of bilateral arrangements should also be mentioned because of its economic importance. One example is the understandings, renewed annually, between the Japanese automobile industry and the U.K. automobile industry, according to which the Japanese limit their automobile exports to the U.K. What may, in the United States or Canada, require discussion between governments, because of the implications for the private sector of anti-trust and competition law—for example, arrangements such as those to limit Japanese exports of automobiles— may in other jurisdictions be achieved by arrangements negotiated in the private sector. Such private sector arrangements fulfil the same function for the United Kingdom as is performed for Canada by the somewhat more formalized arrangements at the inter- governmental level. Such bilateral arrangements vary, of course, all the way from formal treaties to the loosest sort of under- standing—but the latter may have, in practical terms, substantial effects.[9]

Going beyond bilateral trade agreements, there is the set of broader bilateral agreements known in the United States, as we have noted above, as Friendship, Commerce and Navigation (FCN) treaties, which deal with such issues as the legal status of traders and companies, transportation issues, and access to courts. These are comprehensive agreements, covering a range of commercial matters other than the terms of access for imports, which are usually the main subject of a trade agreement. Many countries have had recourse to this device, and consequently FCN treaties are an important part of the overall system. The United States, for example, is party to some 43 FCN treaties. According to the *U.S. National Study* (which points out, of course, that these are important in regard to traded services and services estab- lishments), about half of these pre-date World War II. The post- war FCN treaties tend to deal less with shipping and transport issues and more with the protection of direct investments.[10] It is of interest that before the United States and Canada sponsored Japanese participation in the GATT (in 1955)[11] the United States negotiated a comprehensive FCN Treaty,[12] which, like other FCN treaties, provided a treaty basis for arrangements going beyond the GATT and, to some extent, duplicating the GATT (which does not have treaty status in the United States—being only an "executive agreement"). The United Kingdom also negotiated a treaty with Japan; it came into effect in 1962 and was of the same comprehensive character as the United States agreement, going beyond the narrow range of subjects covered by a trade agreement.[13]

Canada has not embarked on the negotiation of comprehensive FCN treaties, for reasons that are now somewhat unclear. It may be in part because such issues were sometimes covered in treaties negotiated by the U.K., some of which extended to Canada, and in part because, in the 1920s and 1930s, Canadians were developing their own structure of commercial treaties. They focused on tariffs because that was the most important issue, in practical and political terms. In the post-war period, Canadian trade policy officials, less numerous than their counterparts in London, Paris, or Washington, were obliged to concentrate on tariff issues and on tariff negotiations; this was the agenda set by U.S. priorities. The Canada-U.S. FTA has to be interpreted in light of the fact that there is no Canada/U.S. FCN treaty, but that the United States does have FCN treaties covering some of the same issues (e.g., entry of business persons) with other countries.

Possibly the time has come for an independent assessment of whether Canada's international economic activities would be served by the negotiation of comprehensive FCN-type arrangements—say, with the EC, Japan, Sweden, Switzerland.

Another part of the trade relations system, particularly when we take into account the critical role of direct investment as a vehicle for trade in both goods and services, are bilateral investment treaties. Such treaties deal with the treatment to be accorded foreign investors—e.g., the extent and definition of national treatment, compensation in the event of expropriation, the transfer of profits, and the settlement of disputes. A number of Western European governments, notably that of the Federal Republic of Germany, and the United States, have negotiated a series of such bilateral treaties designed to protect, and thus encourage, direct investment.[14] The *U.S. National Study* notes that OECD countries other than the United States have signed 150 such investment protection treaties; it also asserts that U.S. treaties negotiated to date (with Panama, Egypt, Senegal) are considerably more detailed than those negotiated by other countries.[15]

Commodity Agreements

Yet another portion of the trade relations system is made up of the commodity agreements (e.g., tin, cocoa, coffee, OPEC). The Havana Charter—which, it is important to recall, covered a range of issues wider than commercial policy—devoted 16 articles to such agreements.[16] They were conceived as an integral part of the post-war international economic order struggling to be born. Commodity agreements are not operated under the aegis of or under the terms of the GATT (although there is a reference in the "general exceptions" provisions of Article XX.)[17] But they are part of the system. For countries dependent on the export of a particular commodity that is the subject of an international agreement, the success or failure of such an agreement may be of greater importance to that country than all the GATT provisions; e.g., as the International Tin Agreement was at one time for Malaysia.

Customs Unions and Free Trade Areas

Another, and major, part of the trade relations system is the set of arrangements establishing discrimination in the application of tariffs and other trade-regulating devices as between various countries. The GATT made provision for customs unions and for free trade areas, on the assumption that such arrangements increase income and trade—if they are genuine customs unions or free trade areas. Other than that, there would have to be waivers (of GATT Article I obligations) for preferential arrangements that do not meet the GATT criteria and that therefore breach the MFN clause and the "no new preference" rule of Article I, paragraph 2. In the category of discriminatory or preferential arrangements we can lump together such different arrangements as the tariff preferences flowing from application of the Treaty of Rome and the various subsequent accession treaties (the arrangements for the accession to the EC of Spain, Portugal and Greece, for example, will be, for a considerable period of time, tariff preferential arrangements, although not only so); the European Free Trade Area (EFTA) arrangements; the agreements between EFTA countries and the EC (providing for tariff preferences in the industrial sector); the Generalized System of Preferences (under the aegis of the United Nations); the arrangements between the EC and the large group of developing countries (the African-Caribbean Pacific group of developing countries (ACP)); the preferential arrangements between various groups of developing countries, such as the ASEAN preferences and the preferences under the Treaty of Cartagena, establishing the Andean Pact; the Canada-U.S. Automotive Products Agreement and, more recently, the Canada-U.S. FTA. The list is so long and covers so much trade that it might be appropriate to say that this category of trade policy arrangement is more important than the GATT itself—as indeed it is for the member states of the European Communities and for Canada.

Private International Trade Laws

Trade policy officials devote most of their time and energy to negotiating and administering arrangements *between governments* (e.g., the GATT, bilateral trade agreements, voluntary export restraints under the MFA, etc.) and to devising or manipulating such agreements and arrangements to satisfy, to the extent judged necessary or inevitable, the demands of domestic interests. This focusing of trade policy officials on relations between governments, on detailed measures that have come to require a degree of consent from the governments of other countries, has led many of them to overlook the fact that, for private sector entities engaged in trade, a significant part of the trade relations system does not involve active administration by governments.

Formal inter-governmental arrangements are, indeed, only a part of the overall trade relations system. There is a substantial body of international trade law that rarely involves governments, in the sense of administering the system, although, of course, government representatives may be involved in international attempts to redraft, modernize or codify such law.[18]

If we glance at recent work in this area, we note such matters are addressed as the law applicable to the international sale of goods; counter-trade practices; contract forms (for transactions in particular commodities, e.g., pepper, tropical timber); 'cost-plus fee' contracts; 'standard' contracts; publishing contracts; general conditions of delivery of goods and of particular commodities; international trade terms; *force majeur* and hardship clauses; limited liability clauses, penalty clauses, terms of avoidance in contracts, and so forth. The list of issues falling within the ambit of private international trade law is very long. A very substantial number of international organizations, both intergovernmental and non-governmental, are actively involved. The point of importance is that, for a particular trader engaged in a particular international trade transaction, these detailed provisions in private international trade law are part of the trade relations system and may be, for the particular case, more important than, say, the GATT-bound rate of tariff or whether there is a tariff preference bearing on the goods.

From this brief catalogue of the various components of the trade policy system, a catalogue that is at best only illustrative, we can see first that the system involves far more than the GATT articles and, second, that the system must look quite different to one country than to another. A country dependent on one commodity will consider the relevant commodity agreement of the greatest importance; a developing country may focus primarily on the preferential arrangements available for its exports; an exporter of agricultural products may be aware that there is, as a practical matter, no functionally effective system of rights and obligations.

GATT Principles in Practice

Having looked briefly at the trade policy system in a formal sense, we should look in more detail at the GATT, to examine further the basis for the proposal that the GATT should be extended to services or, more modestly, that the GATT should be an analogue for a comprehensive agreement on services.

The GATT is based, as we have noted, on the commercial policy chapter of the Havana Charter. As a treaty text, it involves a number of principles:

(a) *Non-discrimination* as between sources of imports or destinations of exports, as provided for in Article I, a most-favoured-nation clause drafted in the unconditional form.[19] The Article requires that concessions (including procedural arrangements) formally agreed with one GATT signatory have to be extended unconditionally—that is, without other specific payment—to all other GATT signatories and that all rules regarding trade be applied on the same basis to all GATT countries. This requirement has been followed in regard to tariff reductions formally agreed to in the various tariff negotiating rounds but has not been followed by the United States for the Tokyo Round agreements on subsidies/ countervail and procurement. Moreover, and more important, there are the specifically discriminatory quota regimes regarding textiles, garments, steel, automobiles and electronics. Managed trade is rarely non-discriminatory.

(b) As a corollary of (a), the provision (in Article I, paragraph 2) that *no new margins of tariff preference* are permitted. Despite considerable reluctance on the part of the United States,[20] it was agreed that existing tariff preferences need not be abolished; they could be maintained but were to be subject to reduction by negotiations. However, no new margins of preference were to be created, except those consequent on the creation of a free trade area or a customs union, under Article XXIV.

Clearly, these obligations have been very widely ignored. Leaving aside the question of whether some of the arrangements may (or may not) be justified under Article XXIV, there are, as we have noted above, the tariff preferences accorded by the European Communities to goods from other European countries and from countries around the Mediterranean, as well as countries in Africa, the Caribbean and the Pacific

(ACP) affiliated by means of the Lomé Convention. In addition, there are the many tariff-preferential and quota-preferential arrangements entered into by developing countries, which stop short of contemplating free trade in the sense of Article XXIV. There is the tariff preference given Canadian automotive products by the United States and the covert preferences accorded to U.S. products by Canada under that arrangement. To cite these examples is not to express a judgement; it is only a statement that the no new preference rule has been of little force and effect. Since the 1950s trade policy has focused on creating new preferential arrangements and, in parallel, coping with emerging issues, such as discriminatory steel quotas.

(c) The concept that *trade should be regulated primarily by the tariff*, that is, by a price mechanism, not by quantitative measures (except in limited and defined circumstances). Some progress was made in removing quotas, initially on a discriminatory basis, in Europe (i.e., by discriminating against imports from the dollar area). However, in parallel with that liberalization, and in parallel with the substantial reductions of tariffs negotiated in a series of multilateral negotiations under the GATT, extensive systems of quantitative restrictions have been developed: textiles, garments, agriculture, steel, autos, electronic entertainment equipment. Significant sectors of the international trade in goods are, in fact, administered or managed by governments or by quasi-governmental agencies, or with the tacit consent of governments, on a quantitative basis. Here again, a central concept or principle of the GATT system has been systematically ignored.

(d) The concept of *national treatment*. Given that the tariff was to be the permitted technique of intervention to regulate competition between imported goods and domestic goods, Article III provided that once the tariff was paid, imported goods were to be treated within the domestic market exactly as domestic goods—for example, in regard to the levying of commodity taxes.

One important exception to this Article III provision is procurement by governments of goods for their own use. The Article is silent, of course, on the procurement of services. This procurement exception has not been rigorously interpreted; the exception does not appear to cover, for example, the purchase by government agencies of capital equipment to make products for resale, such as the purchase of electricity generating equipment. However, trade in such goods is quite frequently controlled by restrictive procurement rules providing for a preference for domestic producers. The Tokyo Round procurement code was an important first step in narrowing the scope of the procurement exception, but it did not deal with the procurement of many categories of goods in which countries such as Canada could be efficient producers, e.g., electricity generating equipment. In sum, the wide interpretation given by individual signatories to the procurement exception in the national treatment provision has, for many producers, made the concept of national treatment of little effect.

(e) The concept that trade is to be conducted by entrepreneurs, reacting to prices as determined in open markets, independent of government direction. More briefly, *the GATT assumes the existence of market economies.* It was thus logical to take the tariff—a price mechanism—as the only permitted technique of intervention. However, state-controlled entities engaged in buying and selling do not always act as though they were independent economic agents, guided only by commercial considerations (despite Article XVII). Moreover, how are trade relations between so-called market economies and non-market economies to be regulated? The market economy countries have had to adopt concepts of bilateral reciprocity, usually in terms of quantitative balancing, in dealing with the non-market economies, or they have adopted such GATT devices as anti-dumping duties in ad hoc and rather convoluted forms.[21]

(f) The concept that *governments retain a right to protect* their domestic producers, in defined circumstances, against what they judge to be unacceptable or intolerable import competition. This concept is the basis of Article VI, which permits action against dumped or subsidized exports—if such imports cause or threaten *material* injury to domestic producers—and of Article XIX, which permits action to limit imports held to cause or threaten *serious* injury to domestic producers (sometimes called safeguard action). Action under Article VI is the subject of very detailed procedural provisions in the two Article VI codes relating to anti-dumping and subsidies/countervail (the former developed initially in the Kennedy Round and then elaborated in the Tokyo Round). As we shall note below, Article VI action is the centrepiece of the contingency protection system. As for Article XIX, it has been reasonable to assume that an important part of the value of the GATT to small countries, such as Canada, was that they secured, by virtue of Article XIX, a measure of protection against arbitrary and discriminatory import restrictions by the larger countries. The willingness of major trading countries to resort to techniques of managed trade when

Article XIX situations develop casts doubt on the validity or utility of this GATT provision; it also reveals the unwilling-ness of major trading countries to live by the rules they have put in place. The problem of Article XIX action, and surrogates for it, is part of the rationale for the Canada-U.S. FTA; it is the subject of Chapter Eleven of that Agreement: "Emergency Action".

(g) The concept that *trade barriers should be reduced.* As the preamble to the GATT makes clear, the GATT is not about free trade, or even about tariff-free trade, to be more precise. The GATT was about freer trade—about reducing the high tariffs of the 1930s—about doing so on a basis of non-discrimination (that is, getting rid of tariff preference schemes, such as those aimed at the United States, particularly the so-called Ottawa Agreements of 1932), and about getting rid of quantitative controls on trade. Certainly tariffs are now lower, at least on industrial products. But, taking account of quota arrange-ments in agriculture, autos, steel, textiles and garments, together with the increase in the use of Article VI measures, we could ask: are trade barriers really, overall, significantly lower now?

To measure the impact of decisions about the quantities that may be imported in sectors where trade is managed, to measure the impact of various contingency measures, particularly given the importance of precedent in their application, to measure the trade impact of U.S. and EC agricultural policies, for example, particularly of the EC variable levies and the various export restitutions, would be extremely difficult. One is tempted to argue that the enormous expansion in world trade since 1945 demonstrates that, on balance, barriers to trade have been reduced. But, then, increases in managed trade are managed increases, as experience in agricultural trade and in the negotiation of textile and garments restraints makes clear. It may be that increasing specialization of production and increased trade has occurred because of technological changes, because of the growth of transnational corporations (which are able to internalize trade policy), because of the decisions regarding industrial policy in such new centres of production as Korea, Taiwan, Hong Kong, and of course, Japan, and not primarily because of such net reduction of barriers as may be have been effected.

(h) Finally, there is the concept that *trade relations issues are to be addressed* not by unilateral and arbitrary measures but *by consultation and negotiation.* However, the concept of negotiating reductions in barriers to trade, negotiating detailed understandings, and consulting about, then negotiating toward, the resolution of disputes and difficulties, and doing all this in a multilateral forum and in the framework of multilateral rules and accepted practices, works better when the disparities of power between the entities involved are not too great. Now that we have two superpowers, many, if not most, trade policy issues are negotiated between them and the resulting decisions imposed upon the rest of the participants. Of course, there may be some room for securing some accommodation of the interests of smaller countries by ingenious and informed representation. As for the GATT dispute settlement practices, it is not clear, judging by a number of recent cases, that either the procedures or the standards of panel adjudication are always satisfactory, even for the larger partners.[22]

The Erosion of the GATT System

We have set out a brief summary of the principles of the GATT, with some comments to indicate to what extent these principles are being followed or not followed. It might be concluded from those comments that the GATT, as a set of rules and procedural agreements, is no longer functionally effective, if it ever was. It no longer serves adequately the interests of smaller countries (such as Australia and Canada); in fact, it no longer serves sufficiently well the interests of the larger entities—which themselves need rules and agreed procedures, if only to protect themselves against themselves, that is, against the unremitting pressure of special sectoral and regional interests. Hence the increasing resort to bilateral negotiation and bilaterally agreed limits on trade.

Several factors have been at work in this erosion of the GATT system. In the post-Tokyo Round period an important shift in emphasis in the trade policy system has become more evident; the shift is away from reliance on *fixed* measures or techniques of intervention (tariffs) to regulate the competition between imports and domestic production, and toward much greater reliance on *flexible and contingent* methods of protecting domestic producers (e.g., textile voluntary restraint agreements, anti-dumping proceedings).[23] This switch in emphasis occurred gradually. In what we might call the period of multilateralization, from the Havana meeting to the launching of the Tokyo Round in 1973, the thrust of trade policy appeared to have been to organize negotiations around the conventional technique of intervention—the import tariffs of the negotiating countries. However, it is now evident that, as tariffs were reduced and bound against increase, pressure for protection against import competition, much of it arising from new sources, occasioned greater recourse to the various contingency measures. In the period immediately before and during the Kennedy Round of 1963-67, the U.S. Administration was driven to use its anti-dumping provisions more and more frequently. Moreover, there was increasing concern about the ease with which large transnational corporations could indulge in injurious hidden dumping; the French, for example, tried to legislate against such practices. On the other hand, there was increasing concern about the scope that anti-dumping systems allow for harassment of legitimate trade. This led to the attempt in the Kennedy Round to codify administrative procedures for the use of anti-dumping measures.

We might note, as an aside, that this codification of anti-dumping rules and procedures had the perverse, but not necessarily unforeseen, result that all signatories to the negotiated code acquired rights to use all the varied procedural devices or administrative techniques that had been drafted into the code at the request of one or another negotiator. Thus each signatory could, and some did, enact anti-dumping provisions that could be applied, in some particular respects, in more restrictive ways than the systems in effect before the negotiation. Indeed, one result of negotiations designed to regulate the use of contingency measures, in contrast with negotiations to reduce tariffs, is likely to be an increase in the overall capacity of governments to restrict trade. This sort of perverse result of negotiations—which, in terms of the stated agenda, are exercises in trade liberalization—was evident in the outcome of the negotiations on subsidies and countervailing duties and in the revision of the anti-dumping code in the Tokyo Round. (This might suggest to realists that there will be some risks in negotiating codes regarding the reasonable regulation of service industries.)

The United States having made clear it believes that a services negotiation should address the problem of unfair trade practices, the central role of the contingency protection mechanism in the trade policy system becomes most relevant. It is important to recognize that the domestic implementation of the contingency protection system involves a mass of detailed and subordinate legislation. The nature of state intervention in the market and price structure requires a large bureaucratic establishment, the staff of which must necessarily be assumed to be capable of having a detailed knowledge of a large number of transactions occurring at any given time. Even for the most highly developed state, it is difficult to work this apparatus responsibly. Substantial deployment of the contingency system, such as was involved for steel in the United States and the European Communities, lumber in the United States, and corn in Canada, requires that the bureaucracy scrutinize evidence about a large number of transactions taking place in a given period of time and make decisions—as to the consistency or inconsistency with detailed rules—about contracts made outside the national jurisdiction. This means, in effect, that only a large industrial state can rely on a contingency system of trade regulation. In this important sense, the contingency system is biased in favor of the large entities. This factor will be at work if contingency measures are adopted in regard to services.

As a practical matter, the anti-dumping and countervailing duty systems, as sanctioned by Article VI of the GATT, protect producers in large economies more effectively than such measures protect producers in small economies. Moreover, measures taken by the governments of major countries are likely to have a much larger impact on producers in small, export-oriented economies than do the measures applied by the governments of those smaller countries to exports from larger countries. (One might compare the impact of the U.S. action against Canadian lumber with the impact of Canadian action against U.S. corn.) Nor does the contingency system deal with injurious import replacement measures. A modest attempt to deal with this issue was made in the Tokyo Round arrangements on subsidies. It was made clear that the injurious effects of import replacement subsidies (as a practical matter, available mainly in the larger economies) on firms in smaller countries could be proceeded against under provisions derived from Article XXIII of the GATT.[24] However, as a form of intervention, such a proceeding in Geneva is considerably less effective than a countervail action under domestic law.

There is a similar bias in the operation of the GATT safeguards system of Article XIX and in the various devices for avoiding the discipline of that article and for avoiding the issues of structural adjustment, i.e., the orderly marketing arrangements, voluntary export restraints, and industry-to-industry understandings, which, taken together, make up managed trade. The discipline of GATT Article XIX is based on the threat of retaliation or having to pay compensation. The threat of requiring payment for taking safeguard action is credible enough when invoked in disputes between trading entities of roughly the same order of power, and it is certainly credible when invoked by a large trading entity against a smaller entity, particularly if that smaller country receives economic assistance from the larger entity or is otherwise indebted to it. In this context, the increasing resort to managed trade techniques, which can be invoked by a major entity with relative ease, is perhaps the most obvious evidence of the decay of the GATT system.

It is important to recognize that the central concept in the system of contingency protection—taking the phrase to include Article VI measures and Article XIX measures (and surrogates thereof)—is the concept of injury: injury to producers, injury to an industry, injury or prejudice to the importing country.[25] However, the GATT tradition (based on the Hatters' Fur case)[26] takes injury essentially as a matter for the government of the importing country to decide upon. The exporting country has the onus, if it does not agree with an injury determination, of making a case that injury has not been caused or threatened. This is manifestly difficult to achieve. Moreover, despite the setting up of committees of signatories to the Tokyo Round Codes, and despite prolonged discussion about the modalities of Article XIX, there is as yet no adequate apparatus of international surveillance. This defect in the international system has been reinforced by the fact that in importing countries, most importantly in the United States but also in Canada, injury as a concept has been taken into domestic trade relations law primarily as a legal concept devoid of economic content. This has buttressed the restrictive and protective effect of the system of contingency measures.

To state the issue in as moderate terms as possible, it is not at all clear that the system of contingent protection—coupled with the specialized regimes of sectorally managed trade, operating in the context of the lower but still relevant tariffs as negotiated in the Tokyo Round and the extensive regimes of tariff preference enacted since the 1950s—is less restrictive, less interventionist, less trade distorting, less trade diverting, less costly for consumers and less anti-competitive, than the older system which relied in the main, it was thought, on published schedules of import fees applied on an unconditional most-favoured-nation basis. I expressed this view in a speech in September 1979 at a meeting organized by the Conference Board of Canada; it was received with much scepticism by trade policy experts who had not taken part in the Tokyo Round or who had decided to present the outcome of the negotiations as 'liberalization'.

This situation poses some major problems for trade relations policy, particularly for a small industrialized country. The key question, given the Services Proposal and other proposals to extend the aegis of the GATT, is whether we should be devoting our efforts and our negotiating skills to trying to extend this system, or to create an analogue of this system, to services and to high-technology products. Alternatively, would it not be more prudent and more helpful in creating (or re-creating) some international order to try to bring managed trade under a degree of international scrutiny and to try to control the excesses of contingent protectionism.

From the point of view of developing countries, it would be more useful to talk less about the possible gains from trade that will accrue to the services firms and high-technology enterprises of the industrialized North and more about the imperative of open markets in the North for the agricultural and industrial products of the South—that is, applying the GATT rules in regard to goods.

In this way, developing countries might earn the funds to meet at least the interest payments on their international debts, and the new investment that industries in those countries require would be encouraged.

Notes

1. For the current text of the GATT, see the Contracting Parties to the General Agreement on Tariffs and Trade, *Basic Instruments and Selected Documents, (BISD)*, Vol. IV, Text of the General Agreement, 1969.

2. There is a growing literature on the disarray, the decay, of the GATT. See, for example, Harald B. Malmgren, "Threats to the Multilateral System", in William R. Cline (ed.), *Trade Policy in 1980s* (Washington: Institute for International Economics, 1983); Rodney de C. Grey, "The General Agreement After the Tokyo Round", in John Quinn and Phillip Slayton (ed.), *Non-Tariff Barriers After the Tokyo Round* (Montreal: Institute for Research on Public Policy, 1982); Rodney de C. Grey, "Contingency Protection, Managed Trade, and the Decay of the Trade Relations System", in R.H. Snape (ed.), *Issues in World Trade Policy* (London: Macmillan, 1986); Gerard Curzon and Victoria Curzon, "The Multi-Tier GATT System", in *The New Economic Nationalism*, A Battelle Conference, edited by Otto Hieronymi (London: Macmillan, 1980); and "The Undermining of the World Trade Order" *Jahrebach fur die Ordnung von Weitschaft und Geselleschaft*, Band 30; Jan Tumlir, "The Protectionist Threat to International Order", 34 *International Journal* (1978-79); "Need for an Open, Multilateral Trading System", 6 *The World Economy*, No. 4 (December 1983); and "International Economic Order: Can the Trend be Reversed?", 5 *The World Economy* No. 1 (March 1982).

3. The Havana Charter involved the concept of an International Trade Organization, which would have had substantial power as an institution and would have involved reference to the International Court of Justice for the resolution of certain disputes. Neither the ITO nor its successor, the Organization for Trade Cooperation, negotiated during the GATT Review Session in 1955, received the necessary national legislative endorsement. For the text of the Havana Charter, see United Nations Conference on Trade and Employment, held at Havana, Cuba, *Final Act and Related Documents* (Lake Success, New York: 1948), Interim Commission for the International Trade Organization. The GATT is based,

largely, on Chapter IV, "Commercial Policy". For the differences between the Havana Charter provisions and the GATT provisions, see GATT Contracting Parties, *Analytical Index*, as revised in 1986, available in photocopy.

4. For an authoritative discussion of U.S. policy in negotiating the GATT and tariff reductions, as well as an authoritative discussion of the structure of trade agreements, see Harry C. Hawkins, *Commercial Treaties and Agreements/Principles and Practice* (New York: Rinehart, 1951). Hawkins was a senior official in the U.S. State Department charged with the negotiation of the reciprocal trade agreements; he frequently negotiated with representatives of Canada, such as Norman Robertson and Hector B. McKinnon. For a useful description of the pre-war bilateral trade and tariff negotiations in which Canada was involved, see J.L. Granatstein, *A Man of Influence/Norman A. Robertson and Canadian Statecraft 1929-1968* (Ottawa: Deneau, 1981), Chapter III, "Trade Negotiator".

5. Gerard Curzon and Victoria Curzon, "The Multi-Tier GATT System".

6. "Agreement Between Canada and the United States of America Supplementary to the General Agreement on Tariffs and Trade of October 30, 1947", in Canada/Treaty Series, 1947, No. 27, at p. 92.

7. "Agreement Between the United States and the Union of Soviet Socialist Republics Regarding Trade (1972)". U.S. Department of State *Bulletin*, Vol. LXVII, No. 1743, November 20, 1972, at 595; cited in Jackson (ed.), *Documents Supplement to Legal Problems*, pp. 413-422.

8. "Agreement on Trade Relations Between the United States of America and the People's Republic of China", Presidential Proclamation 4697 of October 23, 1979; *Federal Register* Doc. 79-33030.

9. For an account of how arrangements were put in place to limit Japanese exports of automobiles to Germany, to take one example, see the extract from *Handelsblatt*, May 5, 1986, translated in 9 *The World Economy* No. 3 (September 1986), pp. 273-274.

10. *U.S. National Study*, p. 75.

11. For "Protocol of Terms of Accession of Japan to the General Agreement on Tariffs and Trade", see 45 *BISD* 7-10 (Geneva, 7 June 1955).

12. For U.S./Japan FCN Treaty, TIAS 2863, *U.S. Treaties and Other International Agreements*, 2063-2133, April 2, 1953.

13. U.K./Japan treaty: Japan, No. 2, 1962: Treaty of Commerce, Establishment and Navigation between the United Kingdom of Great Britain and Northern Ireland, (London and Japan; HMSO, November 14, 1962).

14. International Chamber of Commerce, *Bilateral Treaties for International Investment* (Paris: International Chamber of Commerce, 1980).

15. *U.S. National Study*, p. 76-77.

16. *Havana Charter*, Chapter VI, Inter-governmental Commodity Agreements, Articles 55-70.

17. Article XX, sub para (h), provides that the GATT does not preclude the adoption of measures "undertaken in pursuance of obligations under any intergovernmental commodity agreement which conforms to criteria submitted to the Contracting Parties and not disapproved by them or which is itself so submitted and not so disapproved", *BISD*, Vol. IV, p. 38.

18. See the reports of the United Nations Commission on International Trade Law (UNCITRAL). A comprehensive survey of work going forward in the modernization of private international trade law will be found in the *Report of the Secretary-General* of (UNCITRAL) to the Fourteenth Session, Vienna, 1981, A/CN.9/202. The examples of issues being addressed is based on this document.

19. The two forms of the most-favoured-nation clause are examined in detail as series of reports of the International Law Commission, beginning in 1969. See the *Yearbook of the International Law Commission* for 1969 and subsequent years.

20. For a discussion of U.S. attitudes in regard to preferences, see Harry G. Hawkins, *Commercial Treaties and Agreements/ Principles and Practice*, Chapter XI, pp. 108-118.

21. The relevant Anti-dumping Code provision is Article 2, paragraph 7.

22. There is extensive literature on the GATT dispute settlement practices; to cite only some of the most important:

> Robert E. Hudec. *The GATT Legal System and World Trade Diplomacy*, New York, Praeger, 1975.

> _____. *Adjudication of International Disputes*, London, Trade Policy Research Centre, 1978.

> _____. "GATT Dispute Settlement after the Tokyo Round: An Unfinished Business", 31 *Cornell International Law Journal*, pp. 391-432.

> Ivo Van Bael. "The GATT Dispute Settlement Procedure" 22 *Journal of World Trade*, No. 4, 1988, pp. 67-77.

The text of the "understanding" negotiated in the Tokyo Round is in 26S *BISD*, pp. 210-218; this includes an "Agreed Description of the Customary Practice of the GATT".

23. A number of other observers have perceived that the balance of the trade relations system is changing. See, for example, J.M. Finger, H. Keith Hall and Douglas R. Nelson, "The Political Economy of Administered Protection" (a paper prepared in the U.S. Treasury Department, Office of Trade Research); in this paper the authors use the phrase "administered protection" to include the two categories of "managed" trade, such as the MFA measures, and "contingency" measures, such as anti-dumping and countervail; Robert E. Baldwin: "The Changing Nature of U.S. Trade Policy Since World War II" NBER Conference on the Structures and Evolution of Recent U.S. Trade Policy, 1982, and "Trade Policies Under the Reagan Administration" NBER Conference on Recent Issues and Initiatives in U.S. Trade Policy, 1983.

24. 26S *BISD*, Articles 12 and 13 of the Subsidies/Countervail Code, p. 71-72.

25. On the concept of "injury" see Rodney de C. Grey, *Injury, Damage and Disruption*, UNCTAD Secretariat, Geneva, 1981. (UNCTAD/MTN/217).

26. Jackson, *World Trade and the Law of GATT*, p. 560.

Chapter V

Existing International Regimes for Services

In earlier chapters, we examined the Services Proposal and noted briefly the characteristics of the services economy. We noted that services appear to be becoming relatively more important in advanced industrialized economies and that, in any event, the services sector or sectors dominate—at least in employment terms—the modern industrialized economies. We also noted that the present international trade relations system, centred in the GATT, deals primarily with goods, although bilateral FCN treaties cover a considerable range of service activities. The purpose of this chapter is to look at existing international regimes in regard to services.

To examine the Services Proposal in an orderly way one must consider the international legal and institutional regime or regimes that exist for traded services and examine what is being done within intra-governmental bodies (GATT, OECD, ICAO, ITU) to address the issue of constructing rules for services trade. We shall see that all the substantive attempts at rule making (national treatment, most-favoured-nation treatment, reciprocity, etc.) can be and are being applied in various services sectors and can be applied differently in one sector than in another. For example, in air transport, reciprocity in regard to the allocation of international routes is well established, whereas in banking, in the United States at least, national treatment is the practice.

The fact that different rules have developed for different sectors is most relevant when we consider trade in data services. Data processing services are a key intermediate service for other services sectors (banking, insurance, air transport) and for many goods-producing sectors, such as automobile manufacturing. The transborder movement and processing of data is a major traded service. Many of the problems that proponents of the Service Proposal think they are addressing might well be swept up in a more limited but more intensive examination of the issues surrounding traded data services and foreign direct investment in data services capacity.[1]   There is thus an emerging case for addressing, if not the services sector in general, then perhaps this major service activity on a rather narrower basis.

Services Under GATT

It is appropriate to start a review of the present international regime for traded services with an examination of the GATT, because so much recent discussion about services has focused on the GATT as a possible future locus and analogue for a general agreement on traded services. In its original 35 articles, the GATT addresses only one services issue directly: cinema film quotas (Article IV)   It addresses this service trade restriction because European (and particularly U.K.) quotas on imported (i.e., U.S.) films were a contentious issue in the 1930s. U.S. film companies were forced to produce 'quota' films in Britain, in order to safeguard access to the U.K. for their Hollywood films. Thus the U.S. authorities were under pressure to deal with this issue in the early post-war period; it duly appeared in the Havana Charter for an International Trade Organization.[2] As the text of the Article makes clear, what was essentially a restriction on a traded service was described in terms of a restriction on traded goods: "internal quantitative regulations relating to exposed cinematograph films".

The GATT makes a passing reference to insurance (in Article X). There is a requirement to publish promptly rulings, administrative decisions, and regulations "pertaining to the classification or the valuation ... of products ... affecting ... transportation, insurance ...". It is not surprising, therefore, that the one substantial effort in the GATT to address a services issue explicitly has been in regard to transport insurance. In the 1950s there was an attempt to develop a set of rules regarding such insurance, but this attempt came to very little, primarily, it is understood, because of opposition from developing countries. They could not support the recommendation that enjoined non-discrimination—that is, no legislated preference for domestic suppliers of insurance. (Such an obligation is more properly labelled 'national treatment'.) The developing countries concerned took the view that they must be allowed to protect their domestic insurance industries by a legislated preference for such domestic suppliers, just as they are allowed to protect domestic producers of visible goods by the imposition of an agreed price barrier at the frontier against foreign goods (i.e., a customs tariff).[3]

Questions about restrictions on trade in services were not addressed directly or in any organized way in the Tokyo Round, although at the time the United States manifested considerable interest in the services sector and in the existence of restrictions on the export of U.S. services.[4] There were some restrictions on services that related to trade in goods, and these were identified on Tokyo Round request lists. The European Economic Community, for example, raised the issue of the insistence by a number of non-market economy countries that goods be transported by their domestic carriers; the surcharge on ocean freight imposed by Argentina and a 'maritime tax' imposed by Brazil; and 'flag' discrimination by these two countries. The EEC also raised the restriction on the use of foreign-built vessels under U.S. cabotage legislation (the Jones Act). The United States listed requests concerning insurance restrictions in Poland, Nigeria, Argentina, Colombia and Venezuela.

The most important reference to services in the agreements resulting from the Tokyo Round is the explicit provision regarding services in the Agreement on Government Procurement.[5] Article I(a) defines the scope of the Agreement as "any law, regulation, procedure and practice regarding the procurement of products by the entities subject to the Agreement. This includes services incidental to the supply of products if the value of these incidental services does not exceed that of the products themselves, but not service contracts *per se*".

The signatories to the Agreement accepted to negotiate, no later than the end of the third year of the Agreement, the coverage of the Agreement; Article IX(b) requires that the Committee of Signatories explore the possibility of adding service contracts to the scope of the undertakings set out in the Agreement. In February 1983 the Committee of Signatories agreed to initiate the necessary preparatory work. Recognizing that governments are major purchasers of such services as consulting engineering and data services, the Committee identified service contracts as one of the elements for inclusion in its work program. Countries have exchanged their preliminary request lists (of the purchasing entities to be covered), and discussion is now proceeding in the Uruguay Round on the basis of national suggestions for improvements in the text of the Agreement. If the Procurement Code, limited as it is to certain "entities", could be extended to services contracts, that would be a real and not unsubstantial measure of liberalizing trade in services.

The Tokyo Round Agreement (or Code) on Customs Valuation also addresses what are, in effect, services issues.[6] For example, the Code makes clear that the agreed valuation base may <u>not</u> include a number of services incidental to the supply of certain goods—and thus that such services cannot be subject to the customs tariff: "charges for construction, erection, assembly, maintenance or technical assistance, undertaken after importation of imported goods" are excluded if they are not included in the price of the goods at issue. A number of transactions of a services character also arise in connection with the calculation of the value of 'assists'—that is, services provided by an importer to the producer abroad. Moreover, payments for licences and royalties are added to the value for duty. These particular services are thus, in effect, made subject to the tariff. More importantly, the Code makes clear that signatories are free to include in the valuation base (that is, to levy a tariff on) all or part of all costs, insurance, and transport related to the shipment of the goods from the point of sale to the point of importation. This Code provision was not a new feature in valuation law, it was merely clarified. For countries that have valued imports for customs duty on essentially an ex-factory basis and may now, under the Code, elect to value them on the basis of including costs, insurance and freight to point of importation, the Tokyo Round valuation code sanctioned a new tariff on services. It is of interest that what are, in effect, tariffs on these services were advocated, or at least agreed to, by the United States, the country that is now the main advocate of removing restrictions on services.[7]

Services also figure in the Subsidies/Countervail Agreement.[8] The Illustrative List of prohibited export subsidies, which are actionable under the Agreement, includes "internal transport and freight charges on export shipments, provided or mandated by Government, on terms more favorable than for domestic shipments . . . ", "the delivery by governments . . . of products or services for use in the production of exported goods, on terms and conditions more favorable than for delivery of like directly competitive products or services for use in the production of goods for domestic consumption", and "the exemption, remission or deferral of prior stage cumulative indirect taxes on goods and services used in the production of like products when sold for domestic consumption". These provisions are aimed at restricting the scope for subsidizing exports; this subsidization of goods by subsidizing intermediate services is actionable under the GATT countervailing duty provisions. Obviously, it would be only a short step to making subsidized services *per se* subject to countervailing duties.

OECD Provisions Regarding Services

The Organization for Economic Co-operation and Development (OECD) has also formulated and put in place obligations in regard to international services transactions. We should first consider the relevant OECD Codes on the Liberalization of Capital Movements and the Liberalization of Current Invisible Operations, the Declaration on Investment and Multinationals, and the Decision on National Treatment.[9]

As regards the Code on Capital Movements, member countries have agreed, by adhering to this Code, to abolish restrictions on long-term capital flows (as distinct from short-term speculative transactions). The Code would seem, therefore, to apply to investments in service industry establishments (*inter alia*) such as hotels; however, it does not provide a *right of establishment*. There have been discussions at the OECD as to how a right of establishment might be added to the Code. Clearly there are difficulties, in that many countries not only have policy objections to conceding a right for foreigners to establish affiliates in particular sectors, some also have legislative prohibitions, notably the United States.

Discussion in the OECD resulted in a Decision of the Council of the OECD (April 4, 1984) that added what would appear to be a significant obligation to the Code: "The authorities of Members shall not maintain or introduce regulations or practices applying to the granting of licenses, concessions, or similar authorizations, including conditions or requirements attaching to such authorizations and affecting the operations of enterprises, that raise special barriers or limitations with respect to non-resident (as compared to resident) investors, and that have the intent or the effect of preventing or significantly impeding inward direct investment by non-residents.[10] This decision is intended to make clear that the freedom of non-residents to invest is not to be frustrated by sectoral regulations that in effect inhibit or preclude foreigners from conducting business.[11] To this extent the Code creates a sort of partial right of establishment. The scope of the amendment can be understood only in the light of a close reading of the Code, but it would appear that this amendment will make necessary a reworking of the existing reservations, observations or derogations that various member countries have appended to the Code, and perhaps the filing of new reservations.

An important example of how the Code works is the interpretation of the Code given by the OECD Committee on International Investment and Multinational Enterprises (CIIME) to the effect that laws conferring a public or private monopoly on particular enterprises in all of the activities in particular sectors do not breach the obligations to "liberalize" capital movements. This is clearly important in such sectors as transport and telecommunications. This clarification of what the Code means may well have some impact on investment in service industries, because, as has often been noted, in some service industries it is possible to serve a market only by means of a physical presence in the market, that is, by the establishment of facilities requiring investment.

The OECD Code on Invisibles has very substantial bearing on services trade (as distinct from foreign direct investment in services establishments). One would assume, from a more than cursory reading of the Code, that services trade between member countries of the OECD would be required to be unrestricted, except for explicit reservations to the Code. The Members have agreed to "eliminate between one another . . . restrictions on current invisible transactions and transfers". (Transaction has the usual meaning—the incurring of an obligation; transfer means the actual movement of funds and relates to the fact that many OECD countries have had exchange controls that limit transfers of funds required to fulfil obligations that are otherwise legal, e.g., for the purchase of foreign insurance contracts.) The reservations and derogations to the Code are extensive; moreover, in terms of its specific sectoral coverage the Code now seems incomplete, and there has been rather more progress in regard to the details of obligations for some sectors than for others. For example, insurance has been treated in much more detail than other sectors.

The scope of the Code was carefully weighed in the *U.S. National Study* and summed up as follows:

> As a vehicle for further liberalizing trade in services, the Invisibles Code appears to have drawbacks and advantages. Drawbacks would include (1) the current limitations on membership to OECD Members; (2) the apparent ease with which obligations can be reserved and derogated from; (3) the absence of strong enforcement mechanisms, binding arbitration, dispute settlement mechanisms, concepts of compensation or penalties; and (4) the general, though not complete, absence of rights of establishment and to conduct business and of national treatment from listed liberalization measures.

> The advantages . . . are probably, first, that it is already in force and second, that, with the requisite political will of the Members its annexes could be extended to broaden its scope and strengthen its disciplines as is presently being done with respect to insurance. Explicit extension to additional industries not currently covered, along with broadening the scope of application of national treatment and the rights of establishment and to conduct business appear possible. However, the extent to which the Code could be made more binding or implemented with greater

discipline with respect to reservations and derogations is uncertain.[12]

The third OECD instrument with relevance to services is the set of declarations and decisions regarding multinational enterprises. The 1967 Declaration covers a set of "Guidelines for Multinational Enterprises" and includes the Decision on National Treatment.[13] Canada has filed a number of what amount to reservations in regard to this decision and has listed those aspects and details of national and provincial legislation under which foreign-controlled corporations are treated less favorably than domestically-controlled corporations.[14]

The OECD set of codes and decisions makes a relatively coherent system. Foreign investment is addressed, to an extent, under the Code on Capital Movements. Once that investment is made, the foreign-controlled enterprise is to be given national treatment, subject, of course, to the many reservations so created and observations filed by member countries adhering to the Decision on National Treatment. This Decision obviously is of great importance to those service sectors where a presence in the market is required to serve that market. The Invisibles Code then covers transactions and financial transfers in regard to traded services. But four important difficulties remain: (1) an extensive area of non-compliance, represented by the large number of reservations, observations, and derogations; (2) the absence of dispute settlement procedures controlled by effective sanctions; (3) there is no effective discipline over sub-national governments that are not subject, in regard to some particular matter, to the control of the national authorities[15] and (4) the fact that non-OECD countries are not involved.

As a result of member governments agreeing that the Organization should look more intensively at services, the OECD Secretariat prepared a number of detailed sector studies and some analysis of the relevant trade agreement concepts. The most important visible result of this work, with regard to individual sectors, is the Declaration on Transborder Data Flows, which was adopted by OECD Ministers in April 1985. This Declaration, which sheds some light on the inherent difficulties of attempting to negotiate meaningful rights and obligations in the services area, is reproduced as Annex B to this study. It will be noted that all that could be clearly and unequivocally agreed was that "further work should be undertaken" and "to cooperate and consult".

The latter obligation assumed by governments by virtue of this Declaration is already established by the agreement establishing the OECD itself; it is therefore not a new obligation. For the rest, Ministers took refuge in language that is at best normative and at worst mere exhortation: to "seek transparency", to "develop common approaches", to "consider possible implications". It is not being critical of the officials and ministers involved to say that this is a meagre result, considering all the effort that went into negotiating the Declaration. That it is such a meagre result suggests that there may be little scope at present for a substantial and meaningful exchange of contractual rights and obligations in this key service sector.

The UNCTAD Guidelines

A third important multilateral institution that addresses horizontal issues and sector-specific issues is the United Nations Conference on Trade and Development (UNCTAD). Under the umbrella of this body, a code of conduct has been drawn up on an important horizontal issue of relevance to service activities, namely, the guidelines on restrictive business practices.[16] The guidelines address the same issue as the OECD does in its Council recommendation on co-operation regarding restrictive business practices.[17] The OECD, being an organization of limited membership, often addresses—with its particular style of drafting— obligations and issues that are addressed in other bodies and in institutions of broader membership, such as UNCTAD.

There are also certain sector-specific arrangements devised within UNCTAD, notably in regard to liner conferences and insurance.[18] The work of UNCTAD in insurance has been directed (by the Committee on Shipping) to developing standard marine insurance practices and (by the Committee on Invisibles and Financing Related to Trade—CIFT) to the strengthening of the national insurance markets in developing countries and to improving the terms and conditions of reinsurance. More recently, developing countries have expressed an interest in having UNCTAD address the range of general issues raised by the Services Proposal, and the Secretariat has therefore produced a number of important studies for the Trade and Development Board.[19]

Other International Services Regimes

In a more comprehensive review of the existing international regimes for trade in services, it would be necessary to look at the activities of EFTA, the Andean Pact, the ASEAN grouping, the Council of Europe and the United Nations regional Economic Commissions. These have ranged over such issues as restrictive business practices, foreign direct investment, and privacy in regard to data services. What we have done here is to draw attention to those important instruments developed in institutions where further significant work on the modalities of rules on traded services and foreign direct investment in service facilities is likely to take place and to be of concern to Canada.

There are also important international rules or understandings regarding traded services developed in various specialized sector-specific bodies: ICAO, ITU, the International Maritime Consultative Organization (IMCO), and the World Intellectual Property Organization (WIPO), all of which are intergovernmental bodies, and the International Air Transport-Association, (IATA), which is a private sector-specific institution. What is important is that international arrangements in the sector-specific institutions often take the form of agreements on standards or norms of behaviour that all signatories undertake to follow. This format is necessary to ensure the functioning of the international component of a service industry—e.g., air transport or telecommunications. Arrangements of this sort may create what amount to multilateral treaty rights, which are called into existence essentially for functional or operational purposes. ICAO and the ITU are examples of services sector arrangements the objectives of which are to set norms of conduct in the sector and promulgate standards for adoption by national governments in regard to their chosen service entities. Much of the work of the ITU, for example, is of this character. The ITU originates such standards as those governing the interface of computers with other computers linked by telecommunications systems; these interface standards are then given the force of law by appropriate national legislation.[20]

In the air transport area, there is a functional division among four authorities. The ICAO has instituted a number of standards of conduct necessary to ensure that there will be a working international air transport system. Like the ITU provisions, these do not normally involve explicit MFN or national treatment formulations; rather they are cast in the form of rules that signatories adopt to govern their own conduct and that confer in practice a measure of non-discrimination.

At the level of the carriers, standards or norms (e.g., what may be charged for cabin services) are agreed in the private sector association, IATA. These are primarily private rules to regulate competition; for that reason they have been increasingly criticized from the point of view of the consumer. There is also a third component: the bilateral air route and air services allocation agreements, negotiated between governments, under which international routes are allocated and the number of national carriers agreed to for each route. These agreements are re-negotiated frequently, given changes in the pattern of demand for air transport, and are usually conceived of as reciprocal or balanced packages of air route and service rights of comparable value.

Given the growth of air transport, these particular service sector arrangements occasion major and continuing negotiations.

The fourth component is regulation by the national government. Such regulation covers a variety of international aspects: the licensing of foreign-produced aircraft and the approval of foreign airline fares for services to the country concerned. More recently, deregulation—or rather, the narrowing of the authority of the domestic regulatory agency with regard to fares and services standards—on the part of the United States has, in the perspective of certain other countries, created a number of problems for their more closely regulated systems. For example, where their airline companies are in direct competition with U.S. carriers there have been disputes about fares, frequency of services, and levels of cabin service. The same conflict of perception or difference in emphasis as between users' and producers' interests is evident in the continuing debate between the U.K. authorities, which favor greater competition between carriers, and the authorities of other EC member countries with regard to intra-European air fares.

If it were decided in the process of international discussion that more detailed international agreements covering the services sectors are in fact desirable, one technique would be to develop other sector-specific agreements of the norm-setting character of the Chicago Convention or the International Telecommunications Agreement. It would be necessary to determine which of the other service sectors would lend themselves, at least in a technical sense, to this sort of approach. Banking might well be considered in such a fashion, as the recent efforts to agree on risk/asset ratios suggests; so too might transborder data services, as the detailed sector agreement in the Canada-United States FTA suggests. As we have already noted, we may need to consider whether in regard to trans-Atlantic and trans-Pacific trade in data services—given its role as an intermediate service—some of the emerging issues could be dealt with sooner and more effectively on the ICAO-ITU model, rather than by addressing issues or various types of access barriers horizontally, across the whole range of the services industries.

Another approach, obviously, is to deal with issues between governments in a bilateral fashion, by means of a bilateral exchange of concessions and obligations. The United States has recently been addressing some of the investment and establishment issues in the services sector in this manner, with respect to various developing countries (e.g., Panama, Egypt), and focused on services in the free trade arrangement with Israel and, in more detail, in the FTA with Canada.

Commercial Policy Agreements

In our survey of the present international regime for services, we should not overlook the existence of a number of broad commercial policy agreements, agreements on the avoidance of double taxation, and investment protection agreements.[21] The pre-war commercial policy treaties (the more comprehensive ones being the FCN treaties) frequently dealt with such matters as the right of persons of the one country to non-discriminatory treatment before the courts of the other country, and non-discrimination in the levying of charges in relation to shipping (e.g., harbour taxes). Sometimes these were cast in terms of national treatment, sometimes in terms of most-favoured-nation treatment.

Many of these issues have been ignored in more modern trade agreements; they are addressed in such multilateral instruments as we have noted, under specialized bilateral pacts, such as agreements on the avoidance of double taxation, or in instruments negotiated in whole or in part between governments, but administered as part of private international law. We have already noted that many of such issues as, for example, terms of sale, have been addressed by the United Nations Commission on International Trade Law (UNCITRAL).[22] Disputes about these various matters are often dealt with under agreed international arbitration procedures, although more difficult issues may be taken to particular national courts that are prepared to accept jurisdiction.

The bilateral investment protection treaties are obviously of considerable importance with regard to those service industries that require a corporate presence or establishment to deliver a product. Most of these treaties are concluded between developed market economy countries and developing countries; they began to become important in the early 1960s. The Federal Republic of Germany had concluded more than 50 such agreements by the end of 1983. Switzerland has also negotiated a number of such treaties; other OECD countries and even developing countries (vis-à-vis other developing countries) have signed such arrangements. Typically, 'foreign investments' and 'investor' are defined fairly broadly, and the protection given by such treaties is apparently important. The specific clauses deal with such matters as fair and equitable treatment, national treatment, most-favoured-nation treatment, security (of investment), compensation in the event of nationalization, repatriation of funds and dispute settlement. Many of these treaties are in fact similar because they are modelled on the 1967 OECD draft convention on the protection of foreign property.

The network of treaties on the avoidance of double taxation is also of importance to service entities. There are approximately 400 such treaties, over half concluded between members of the OECD. Many of these treaties have been renegotiated in recent years, and the new texts draw on the 1977 OECD model convention or the 1979 United Nations model.[23] It is of interest that these treaties often contain specific reference to taxes on profits from shipping and air transport; for example, the Canada-U.K. agreement of 1978 provides that "Profits derived by an enterprise of a contracting state from the operation of ships or aircraft in international traffic shall be taxable only in that state".[24]

The extent to which many aspects of services transactions and investment in services can be covered in a bilateral treaty formulated in general terms is illustrated by the U.K.-Japan treaty of 1962.[25] This treaty received considerable attention in trade policy circles because of its discriminatory safeguard arrangements, which were in fact the principal subject dealt within the U.K. government statement on the treaty. However, the treaty covers many other matters in great detail, including even such matters as freedom of worship and burial or cremation of the dead. The latter, which is a service industry, is to be subject only "to any non-discriminatory, sanitary or medical requirements laid down by the authority of that territory".

The thrust of the treaty is to ensure MFN treatment—when that is the appropriate technique for creating rights and/or taking account of the national treatment rights previously accorded by Japan to the United States, and, in regard to persons and companies ("all legal persons except physical persons"), national treatment, to the extent feasible. Cabotage is explicitly excluded from the scope of national treatment, by Article 20 (5). Establishment issues, broadly defined, are dealt with on an MFN basis; Article 6(1) states that "the companies of one Contracting Party shall in any territory of the other be accorded treatment not less favorable than that accorded to the companies of any other foreign country in all matters relative to the carrying out of *all kinds of business*, including *finance*, commerce, industry, *banking, insurance, shipping*, and *transport*, as well as in all matters relative to the *establishment* and *maintenance* for such purposes of branches, agencies, offices, factories and other establishments appropriate to the conduct of this business". (Emphasis added.) It is significant, from the point of view of this paper, that two such important services markets and services exporters as Japan and the United Kingdom have accorded each other these MFN rights in regard to specified services industries. Given that the U.K. is the host country of many foreign services companies' affiliates, the rights given Japan would appear to be substantial.

In the period ahead it may well be that the bilateral treaties, making use of the established concepts of national treatment and most favored nation treatment, will be perceived as useful and perhaps the preferred routes for creating international rights and obligations that can be multilateralized by an MFN clause, either unconditional or conditional, in the same fashion as in the pre-World War I system of treaties. Whether the Canada-U.S. FTA (with respect to services) will be, in regard to some issues, a model or an excuse for preferences in services trade, remains to be seen.

The Treaty of Rome

Finally, in our survey of the international services regime, we should consider the situation within the European Communities. The Treaty of Rome establishing the European Economic Community envisaged the freeing of trade in services as well as trade in goods. It provided for the free movement of persons of one member country into employment in another country; significantly, it included sectors that are regulated—often self-regulated, such as the legal and medical professions—and the abolition of limitations on establishment for entities controlled in other member states. There remain, of course, some state-imposed barriers to the free movement of goods within the EC, but it is fair to say that such barriers have been significantly reduced as a result of the operation of the Treaty.

However, extensive barriers to trade in services are still in place, despite the provisions of Article 59 of the Treaty, which states that "restrictions on freedom to provide services within the Community shall be progressively abolished during the transitional period". For the original six member states, that period ended in 1970. It is an interesting comment on the Services Proposal that in one of the most advanced services sectors (i.e., non-life insurance), and one for which there is supposed to be a completely free market within the EC—"guaranteed in theory by the Treaty of Rome", reinforced by the EC Council's co-insurance directive of 1978, and in regard to which the annexes to the OECD Code on Invisibles would be thought to prescribe the removal of all barriers among the advanced industrialized nations—there is no common market within the EC. This issue has been addressed by the European Court of Justice. The advocate-general's opinion, in a case brought by the Commission and supported by Britain and the Netherlands, was that certain restrictions applied by Denmark, France, Germany and Ireland were in breach of Article 59 of the Treaty of Rome; in December 1986 the Court accepted this opinion.[26]

A proposal on insurance has been approved by EC finance ministers. This proposal contemplates that the EC should move to a free market in non-life insurance, provided that mass risks are excluded from the scope of liberalization. (Mass risks are risks such as personal injury and motor vehicle insurance.)[27] As noted above, the services issue has also been addressed in regard to intra-European air fares; the United Kingdom has undertaken a measure of deregulation and is prepared to approve substantially lower fares between the U.K. and other European points. Only the Netherlands has agreed, and the U.K. proposal has been sharply rejected in other European capitals.

There is an analogous issue with regard to cabotage. The United Kingdom has opened its coastal shipping trade to the vessels of other EC countries, but other EC countries exclude foreign vessels, including the vessels of their EC partners. It is understood that U.K. ministers are strongly of the view that their country has not received the benefits it expected from joining the Communities, in the sense that the United Kingdom has lowered barriers to imports of goods from its EC partners, but those countries have not removed their restrictions on U.K. services exports.[28]

It will be useful to keep in mind the remarkable lack of progress in freeing trade in services over the 32 years since the Treaty of Rome established the European Economic Community as we consider the prospects for implementing the Services Proposal.

Conclusions

From this short survey of major international instruments regarding traded services and foreign direct investment in services entities three conclusions emerge:

1. We should not exaggerate the contrast between the international regime for goods and that for services. The main difference is that in respect of goods there is a multilateral agreement and a multilateral forum where a number of (although not all) issues concerning traded goods may be discussed and negotiated. The rights and obligations affecting goods are, in the main, those that were formerly (pre-war) the subject of bilateral treaties multilateralized through the MFN clause. With regard to investment, taxation, establishment and national treatment, goods and services are treated in much the same manner, frequently under the same instrument. Moreover, in the services sector there are a number of specialized sectoral agreements of a norm-setting character; these have been deemed necessary to provide functionally effective international services.

2. Nonetheless, the international regime for services is somewhat fragmented, may be incomplete, and is not in any sense a coherent system. Given the other issues facing governments with regard to the operation of the world economy, this fragmentation and lack of coherence may not be very important. Nevertheless, one is tempted to conclude that some

set of additional rules of a general character could not but help improve discipline over restrictive and protectionist unilateral actions—and it is quite clear that there is much protectionist sentiment in service industries.

3. Implicit in this conclusion, which underlies the Services Proposal and much of the recent literature supporting proposals to negotiate general rules on traded services and to strengthen the rules regarding foreign direct investment in services entities, is the assumption that the trade policy system in the GATT—that is, the general set of rules regarding goods—is working satisfactorily. As we have seen, this assumption has little basis in reality. A second assumption is that the GATT rules can be adapted to traded services, or at least that the GATT can be an analogue for a set of general rules for traded services. The basis for this assumption is not evident. That is not to say that the GATT may make a useful model for a forum or institution to address services trade issues.[29]

Notes

1. See, for example, the key article by Joan E. Spero, "Information: The Policy Void"; 48 *Foreign Policy* (Fall 1982), and the proposal by Rodney de C. Grey, *Traded Computer Services*.

2. Article 19 in Chapter IV, Commercial Policy, of the *Havana Charter*.

3. For a more extensive discussion, see Raymond J. Krommenacher, "Trade Related Services and the GATT", 13 *Journal of World Trade Law* (November-December 1979), pp. 510-522.

4. See U.S. Department of Commerce, *U.S. Service Industries in World Markets: Current Problems and Future Policy Development* (Washington: December 1976).

5. GATT, 26S *BISD*, pp. 33-55.

6. GATT, 26S *BISD*, pp. 116-153.

7. For a general discussion of the Valuation Code see Saul L. Sherman and Hinrich Glashoff: *A Businessman's Guide to the GATT Customs Valuation Code* (Paris: International Chamber of Commerce, 1980).

8. GATT, 26S *BISD*, pp. 56-83.

9. OECD, *Code of Liberalization of Capital Movements* (January 1976); *Code of Liberalization of Current Invisible Operations* (June 1988); *Decision on National Treatment* (21 June 1976); *Declaration on International Investment and Multinational Enterprises* (21 June 1976).

10. OECD, Council, Decision of the Council/Amending Annex A to the Code of Liberalization of Capital Movements, C(83) 106 (Final).

11. An example of such sectoral regulation affecting the freedom of foreigners to invest is the restrictions in the Canadian Mining Regulations. See Annex A for the text of the Canadian 'reservations' to national treatment.

12. *U.S. National Study*, pp. 87-88.

13. The 1976 OECD Decision provides that Member countries should, consistent with their need to maintain public order, protect their security interests, and fulfil their obligations regarding international peace and security, accord to foreign-controlled enterprises operating in their territory ... treatment under their laws, regulations and administrative practices no less favourable than that accorded to locally-owned enterprises.

14. Reproduced as Annex A to this study.

15. For a comment on this issue in the Canada-U.S. FTA, see Schott and Smith "Services and Investment", in Schott and Smith (ed.), *The Canada-United States Free Trade Agreement...* p. 139.

16. UNCTAD, *The Set of Multilaterally Agreed Equitable Principles and Rules for the Control of Restrictive Business Practices*, UN Sales No. E.81.II,D.5.

17. OECD: *Recommendation of the Council Concerning Co-operation between Member Countries on Restrictive Business Practices Affecting International Trade* (Paris, 1979), C(79) 154, Final.

18. UNCTAD: *Convention on a Code of Conduct for Liner Conferences*, April 6, 1974, UN, TD/Code/11/Rev. 1/1974, Final Act and Annexes. On insurance, see UNCTAD, Trade and Development Board, Study by the UNCTAD Secretariat, *Invisibles: Insurance/Methods Used for Increasing the Local Retention of Insurance Business/Regional and National Insurance Pools* TD/ B/C:3/160, 27 March 1980; UNCTAD

Third World Insurance at the End of the 1970s, TD/B/C.3/169 1981; José Ripolli, "Some Thoughts on Insurance and Development", *Best's Review*, (February 1975).

19. These UNCTAD studies are cited in the Bibliography.

20. For example, "U.S. Federal Standard for Interface ... ", 48 *Federal Register* No. 30 (July 6, 1983), pp. 311161-311167.

21. For a compact survey of investment protection agreements and double taxation agreements, see United Nations Centre on Transnational Corporations, Report of the Secretariat, *Bilateral, Regional and International Arrangements on Matters Relating to Transnational Corporations*, E/C.10/1984/8.

22. See note 18, Chapter IV.

23. See United Nations, International Tax Agreements, UN publication E.82.XVI.1; OECD, *Model Convention for the Avoidance of Double Taxation with Respect to Taxes on Income and on Capital* (Paris, 1977) and *United Nations Model Double Taxation Convention Between Developed and Developing Countries*, UN Publication E.80.XVI.3.

24. See *Canada Income Tax Conventions*, 1978, Schedule II, Article 8.

25. Cited in Note 13, Chapter IV.

26. *Financial Times* [London], April 3, 1986: "Business Law"; A.H, Herman: "Insurance Competition in the EEC", *Financial Times* [London], December 4, 1986.

27. *The Economist*, March 17, 1984.

28. Nick Garnett, "Government Moves to Restrict Cabotage", *Financial Times* [London], March 31, 1988.

29. This is essentially the view argued by Jackson in his recent paper, "Constructing a Constitution ... ", cited in note 40, Chapter II.

Chapter VI

Some Key Services Sectors

The purpose of this chapter is to examine in greater detail issues relating to a number of key services sectors, in the light of what has been said about the trade relations system and existing international regimes regarding services trade.

Information Services

We have argued that the development of an information economy is central to the emerging pattern of world trade and investments in services. Increasingly, other service industries—such as the various elements of the financial services complex, airlines, tourism, certain aspects of insurance—are dependent for efficiency on the use of modern techniques of storing, transmitting, and processing information. The same is true of manufacturing and resource exploitation, particularly at the exploration phase.

It seems reasonably obvious that a determined attempt to deal with restrictions in the information sector might well sweep up many of the more urgent issues in other services sectors. For example, one complaint often raised in discussions with U.S. airline representatives has been that in certain countries the national airlines control the airline seat reservation system—that is, they write the software for the reservations computer in ways that disadvantage foreign carriers. It is difficult to see why this sort of issue could not be attacked by negotiations either in the air transport sector or by negotiators in the information sector, without awaiting the outcome of the Uruguay Round. It also seems relatively obvious that it should be the many users of information whose interests are given priority, not the interests of producers of hardware (computers, terminals and telecommunications systems), operators of basic telecommunications services, software producers, or independent providers of information services. It is only in regard to the United States, with it vast market, that there may be a plausible case that restrictions on foreigners in these four components of the information industry would not impose very substantial costs on users. In smaller economies such as Canada's, the interests of users clearly outweigh those of other parties.[1] Clearly the special agreement on access for this sector in the Canada-U.S. FTA was drafted from this point of view.[2]

Despite the obvious importance of international flows of information, government policy has generally failed to keep pace with developments in the area of traded information or traded computer services over telecommunications links between countries. The basic rules of the international telecommunications system are, of course, developed under the International Telecommunications Convention administered by the ITU, as we have already noted. What we are addressing here are the services that can be called 'computer services' or 'enhanced services'. The several attempts to arrive at international rules for these services have resulted in either vague formulations or largely normative exhortations, such as the 1985 OECD Declaration on Transborder Data Flows on which we have already commented.[3] Concern with protecting information about individuals and corporations against inappropriate access has led to the enacting of legislation in various countries designed to protect such information and to ensure that individuals have access to and can verify information about themselves held in databanks. There is concern that governments may give way to pressure for restrictions to protect the position of domestically-oriented data service companies[4] and domestic suppliers of computer or telecommunications hardware. Such restrictions would, of course, be against the interests of data service companies that see their markets as international. More important, such restrictions would be against the interests of users of computerized data.

One effective way to solve these problems would be to formulate an international agreement that is more than mere exhortation. To provide the secure access that is essential to users of these services, a multilateral agreement controlling restrictions on flows of information services should not merely be normative; it should be drafted, not in terms of 'should' but in terms of 'shall'. One should try to avoid terms such as 'consider', 'develop', 'promote', 'seek'—the words used in the 1985 OECD TBDF Declaration. Only first-order rights—contractual rights—can provide the certainty on which private decisions to commit funds can be based. The Canada-U.S. FTA could, in this context, serve as a useful model, particularly for the EC.

If an international agreement is to be viable, no signatory country should feel that it has been required, possibly by pressures in some other sector, to assume a mass of burdensome obligations, that limit its freedom of action, without at least acquiring what are evidently equivalent rights with regard to the actions of other countries. This is a central issue with regard to information trade. It appears to many outside that country that the United States, an efficient and major supplier of information services, has much to gain from an international agreement limiting the rights of other countries to impose restrictions on the supply of such services originating in the United States. Many Americans also perceive this to be the case, and it is therefore not surprising that the United States has taken the lead in international discussions of information trade. Here, it seems, the United States has over-argued the case.

More specifically, the United States chose to use its trade law system to attack the Brazilian policy on informatics.[5] Whether it would make economic sense for the Brazilians to adopt a more outward looking policy was not really the issue. What was at issue is the right of a country, consistent with its obligations (e.g., the GATT), to protect a particular sector of activity, whether that sector produces goods or services, and to divert domestic resources to the building up of domestic capacity in that sector. Such a policy may be unwise and it may impose undue, unrecognized or incalculable costs on the economy of the country concerned, but as long as formal agreement obligations, such as the GATT obligations, are not breached there can be no legitimate ground for recourse to retaliation.

The United States should not assert that the Brazilians were in any sense behaving unacceptably—witness the broadly similar approach by the United States to its domestic sugar industry, in regard to which the United States prefers to encourage domestic producers and to limit imports by quantitative methods. What is acceptable conduct for the United States in regard to sugar is surely equally acceptable conduct for Brazil with regard to informatics. Whether, in each case, excessive costs are imposed on users or consumers is another matter. One need not be surprised that U.S. informatics firms argue the immorality, the wrong-headedness and anti-American character of Brazilian informatics policy, but it would be reasonable to expect trade policy officials to take a broader view and to see the parallel with other accepted but protectionist policies.

It would be possible to devise an agreement in the informatics sector that would address the emerging issues and provide some certainty about the degree of access of domestic producers to foreign markets and of foreigners to domestic markets. This writer has argued elsewhere that such a sectoral agreement, because it involves traded services, could follow the GATT fairly closely, although this is not necessarily the case for other services sectors.[6] An informatics sector agreement would have to address such issues as non-discrimination between foreign sources of traded information services (the MFN concept); national treatment for foreign information services (possibly after the payment of some sort of fee on imports or, perhaps more feasibly, an annual tax on such imports); the issue of what preference may be given domestic suppliers in regard to the procurement of information services by government; the issue of national treatment for foreign-controlled corporations (and the treatment of agencies or unincorporated branches of foreign corporations); the restrictive effect on user industries of regulations in this industry (e.g., the provisions regarding data storage in the Canadian Bank Act); and arrangements for adjudicating disputes.

For this latter and central issue, the GATT concept of "nullification and impairment" (in Article XXIII) may be a useful model. A dispute settlement provision of this sort would enable the signatories to an informatics sector agreement to deal with the nullification of the benefits of undertakings in regard to the flow of services if the nullification arose, for example, from restrictions imposed on the use of leased telecommunications facilities by a state-owned or state-regulated telecommunications body, from the imposition of hardware or interface standards, or from restrictions on international payments. It would not be necessary to address all these issues directly in an informatics sector agreement; it would be sufficient to provide that any measure undercutting the benefits that would reasonably be expected to flow from the agreement would be actionable. Indeed, there is much to be said for looking at the dispute settlement provisions first, then working back to the other substantive provisions of an agreement.

There is, of course, the key question of whether there is a basis for negotiating a multilateral agreement of such a contractual character. The lack of operational substance in the OECD Declaration on Transborder Data Flows suggests that, for the present, it will be difficult to secure any agreement that spells out meaningful rights and obligations in this sector. The key to working toward an agreement is for the United States, which is the *demandeur* and which is perceived to stand to gain most, to consider what concessions it can offer.

One issue that would have to be considered is the extent of the jurisdiction asserted by the United States over the offshore subsidiaries of U.S. parent firms and over the information concerning foreign firms—including subsidiaries incorporated abroad of U.S. parent firms—stored and/or processed in the United States. Issues of jurisdiction over information can arise in regard to securities and commodity trading, in regard to anti-trust actions (public or private), and in regard to the various export and re-export control regulations. Firms outside the United States may not be willing to have data processed and stored in that country if their computer links can be interrupted by U.S. authorities;[7] similarly they will not want to use U.S. information storage facilities if the information so stored is held to be within the jurisdiction of U.S. courts. Most governments assert some extra-territorial jurisdiction, and most governments object to other governments doing so. However, it is the case that the extent of the assertion of such jurisdiction by the United States goes beyond what seems acceptable to most other countries, including Canada.

Intellectual property rights are, of course, relevant to services trade in general and to information services in particular. The United States has taken the lead in identifying the functional inadequacies of the system of patents, copyright and trademarks as a general question affecting traded services and traded goods. In the information services sector, there is the particular difficulty of protecting effectively the rights of producers of software (that is, their copyright), of protecting the design rights (that is, as embodied in a patent) on a microprocessor, and of protecting the vested rights of compilers of databases. One approach suggested by the United States is to create a set of rules requiring governments to give more active protection to intellectual property rights created in other countries and to develop a complaint, conciliation and dispute settlement procedure for such rules. It is likely that what the United States seeks will, in the event, require new understandings, including concessions by the Untied States and by other countries, and not merely threats to deny protection on a reciprocal basis under U.S. domestic law, as envisaged in the 1984 U.S. legislation on the protection of computer chips.[8]

It is possible to approach the informatics sector by using some GATT concepts along the lines suggested above because, as we have noted, information is a product that is traded—that is, it can be sold by a provider in one country to a user in another or sent abroad for further processing; alternatively, it can be provided locally by a subsidiary of a foreign-controlled entity. Information transactions are not dissimilar to goods transactions, and accordingly the analytical approach and the trade agreement apparatus developed in regard to trade in goods are of some relevance as models. That is one reason why it is in this sector that Canada and the United States were able to work out a relatively detailed arrangement within the FTA. When we look at some other sectors, however, the parallels with goods trade are less evident.

Air Transport

We now look at a completely different sector—air transport. This sector is different in the sense that transactions do not relate to a product that crosses a border or is delivered by a subsidiary or affiliate (such as computer services) and different in the sense that there is already in place a significant—indeed, a very elaborate—body of internationally and bilaterally agreed rules.

But we should first note the key role of informatics in this sector. We have noted that the air transport system relies on computer services for its seat reservation systems. There exist various and competing systems on routing and pricing information and for data on seat availability. Travel agents are heavily dependent on the efficiency of such systems, and in metropolitan areas, where consumers have a range of choice among travel agencies and among airlines, biases in such programs—in terms of not providing adequate information on competing services—may be detected by experienced consumers. Most of these systems were devised and at first operated by individual airline companies; it is only recently that the European airlines have made serious efforts to establish a linked or 'umbrella' reservation system and to link such European computer reservation systems with U.S. systems.[9]

For the airlines' own use in routing, scheduling and other inter-airline purposes there is the worldwide SITA (Société Internationale de Télécommunications Aéronautiques) computer communications system.[10] The extent to which the major airlines have become dependent on computer systems for the economic use of their increasingly large transport units, as well as the extent to which actual aircraft flight operations are computer-controlled, are evidence of the validity of the assertion that the modern world economy is information-based or that it is an information economy.

Tariff-like charges on foreign carriers and user charges on carriers have been long established in the system of trade agreements regulating maritime and overland transport. Indeed, trade agreements prior to World War II typically included provisions in regard to transport charges and specified most-favoured-nation treatment or national treatment in regard to shipping. Gradually the notion of levying a tariff-like charge on foreign-owned ships was largely abandoned, although trade agreements, even since World War II, have frequently included provisions on port charges and other user fees. The usual format is to provide for an exchange of MFN treatment. In the air transport sector, the system based on bilateral negotiation has produced a structure of reciprocal and allegedly balanced rights and concessions. The right to serve a given point in one country from another country is determined by intergovernmental negotiation; indeed there are some 1,800 such air services arrangements, and they are regularly renegotiated as traffic patterns (i.e., demand) change and as the supply structure evolves (i.e., as new firms apply for rights).[11] Thus there is no requirement for a tariff-like charge on foreign aircraft; however, airport user charges and the obligations of countries with respect to the operation of the necessary air transport infrastructure are addressed in the Chicago Convention.

In the main, that Convention is drafted in terms of ensuring what would be called, in trade agreement terminology, national treatment. However, the Convention leaves the question of cabotage to national governments to decide, given that the Convention is based on the concept that the airspace over national territory is part of that national territory. As in maritime shipping, domestic services have been reserved by governments for domestically-controlled firms.[12] When it is suggested, in rather sweeping terms, that a multilateral or bilateral agreement on services should provide for national treatment, it is reasonable to ask whether it is seriously intended that cabotage no longer be reserved for domestic airlines. Even in the European Community, where there is much discussion about increasing competition in this service sector, it is not seriously argued that the concept of a common market for services would go as far as to allow a U.K. airline to fly domestic routes in France or for a Portuguese airline to compete for, say, London-Glasgow traffic. This illustrates the need in discussions about services negotiations to be specific about national treatment as a concept—i.e., national treatment with regard to what matters? In the air transport sector, these are specified in the Chicago Convention, but as we noted, it does not extend to cabotage. Article 7 of the Convention makes clear that cabotage rules are matters for individual states to determine. Moreover, there is the problem of airline ownership; it is a "common provision of bilateral air service agreements that the designated airline(s) of each party must be substantially owned and effectively controlled by that party or its nationals".[13]

Aside from the bilateral air route allocation agreements and the Chicago Convention, administered by ICAO, there are the activities of IATA. This association of carriers concerns itself with such matters as service standards and insurance issues and may be thought of as essentially an industry cartel. Certainly, some of its activities appear to be designed to limit competition between carriers.

There is also the International Air Service Transit Agreement (IASTA), which addresses transit rights, the rights to use a given national airspace and to land for refuelling or for emergencies. The IAST Agreement parallels the transit rights provisions in

Article V of the GATT, which were modelled on the transit rights provisions of early bilateral treaties.[14] Indeed, the GATT provisions are broadly drawn, reflecting the importance of transit traffic in Western Europe. Paragraph 7 of the GATT article explicitly exempts "the operation of aircraft in transit" from the provisions of the article; however it makes clear that the provisions do apply to the "air transit of *goods (including baggage)*". (Emphasis added.) This agreement is, of course, critical to the operation of the international air transport system, since many routes between two countries involve overflying a third country. Thus, much air traffic between Western Europe and the United States involves transit through Canadian airspace. Because of this Canada has a certain degree of leverage with European countries in bilateral air route negotiations.[15]

We have outlined these arrangements in the air transport sector to make clear that a complex web of arrangements already exists in this sector, covering, among other matters, market access. Despite the existence of these arrangements, U.S. officials have identified the following access issues:[16] (1) ground handling facilities that give preference to a national carrier and therefore discriminate against competing foreign carriers; (2) discriminatory use of airline reservation systems; (3) the setting of user fees at international airports to raise funds for domestic projects; (4) discriminatory tax practices (the taxation of airline companies is frequently addressed in agreements on the avoidance of double taxation); (5) discrimination by national carriers in freight forwarding, chartering, tour wholesaling and other aspects of the air transport sector; (6) preference in procurement (e.g., government travel) to national carriers; (7) the subsidization of nationally owned carriers; (8) differences in competition policy (e.g., the application of U.S. anti-trust law to carriers flying into the United States, as in the Laker case); and (9) the existence of 'illegal' (that is, contrary to IATA) fare discounts and charter fares.

The importance of these various restrictions on access to the air transport market (aside, of course, from the fact that cabotage is reserved to domestic carriers) has been changing, primarily because of deregulation in the United States and, more recently, because of the British government's emphasis on increased competition in this sector, particularly as regards air transport in Western Europe and, especially, in the European Communities. The structure of the industry is being affected by U.S. (and Canadian) deregulation, a willingness on the part of the regulatory authorities in the United States, Canada, the United Kingdom and France to permit more competition in domestic services, and privatization or potential privatization of nationally owned carriers in the U.K. and Canada. The economic effects of these changes seem to be much more important than the irritants noted by U.S. officials.

It is not entirely clear that the access problems identified in this sector could be dealt with more effectively under a GATT-like general services agreement or, indeed, under a new sectoral arrangement, rather than by amending or adding to the Chicago Convention or amending or adding to bilateral agreements.

The structure of arrangements in this sector draws our attention to one important issue. An obvious question to ask in regard to arrangements in the various services sectors is, what are the provisions for conciliation and dispute settlement? Clearly the notion of some sort of dispute settlement mechanism, applying to a number of service sectors and related in some way to the GATT dispute settlement arrangements, is central to the U.S. Services Proposal. It is therefore important to note that there are already in place a substantial number of dispute settlement arrangements in the air transport sector, to take this important sector as an example. Given that bilateral air route allocation agreements are routinely re-negotiated and revised at intervals, specific occasions are provided for bringing grievances or differing objectives or interpretations of rights and obligations to the bargaining table. Moreover, bilateral air route allocation agreements sometimes provide for conciliation, sometimes for binding arbitration.

In the 1960s the United States invoked the arbitration provisions in its air route allocation agreements with France and Italy in order to deal with differences of interpretation that had important economic consequences.[17] Moreover, the Chicago Convention provides for recourse to arbitration or to the International Court of Justice for disputes between its members.[18] ICAO itself has power to impose sanctions on airlines and on member countries that do not follow Convention rules.[19] Finally, the United States has legislative authority for its regulatory agencies (e.g., the Civil Aeronautics Board) to retaliate, within the scope of this sector, against foreign practices in the air transport sector that discriminate against U.S. carriers or treat them unreasonably.[20] That these powers have been rarely invoked tells us little about how effective their availability and the threat to invoke them may be.

It is important to understand that, as far as the air transport sector is concerned, there seems to be no obvious shortage of workable dispute resolution techniques nor any absence of bargaining or retaliatory power, and it is not clear whether or why the grievances said by U.S. officials to exist have not been addressed effectively enough under the existing arrangements. Certainly the much-ventilated grievances about discrimination in computerized reservation systems have been overtaken by major developments in the provision of this intermediate service, as noted above.

Maritime Transport

In the context of the Services Proposal, certain features of existing arrangements in the maritime transport sector should be noted. Like many service sectors, such as banking and air transport, the conduct of day-to-day operations is heavily dependent on telecommunications and computerized information handling. But the maritime transport sector has some special characteristics. First, there is the fact that most countries reserve domestic shipping services (i.e., cabotage, the carriage of domestic cargo from one national port to another) to national companies. Frequently there are requirements as to the ownership of such companies, as to the registration, even the construction, and certainly the crewing of vessels. U.S. cabotage is reserved by the Jones Act to U.S. flag vessels, built in the United States, and owned and crewed by U.S. citizens.[21] Given the wide differences in vessel operating costs (primarily, labour costs) between the United States or Canada on the one hand and, say, Taiwan or Korea on the other, such restrictions on cabotage lead to some unusual results.

For example, the transport of Alaskan oil from one U.S. port (in Alaska) to another U.S. port is cabotage, and if the Jones Act provisions are applied they are bound to impose costs higher than if tankers registered elsewhere and with foreign crews were employed. Similarly, the shipment of lumber by sea from the U.S. west coast to the U.S. east cost in U.S. bottoms is more expensive than the shipment of Canadian lumber from the Canadian west coast to the U.S. east coast, free from the restrictions of either U.S. or Canadian cabotage provisions. This has been, in fact, part of the problem of the trade in lumber between Canada and the United States. It is perhaps not surprising, but regrettable, that it was the objections of U.S. shipping firms to the proposed standstill in regard to possible new discriminatory measures that led to the transportation sector being excluded from the services provisions of the Canada-U.S. FTA.

We noted that cabotage restrictions are also receiving considerable attention in the European Communities. The U.K. authorities take the view that they are required, under the Treaty of Rome, to open U.K. coastal shipping to vessels of other EC member states, and they have done so. But other EC member states have continued to reserve cabotage to domestic shipping companies and ships. The U.K. authorities have recently threatened to reimpose restrictions on access to its domestic shipping market if the other member states do not move more quickly to open their cabotage to U.K. shipping companies and have taken steps to amend U.K. legislation accordingly.[22] We need not concern ourselves with the details of this controversy here, except to point out that, if in the European Communities it has not been possible, after 30 years, to achieve national treatment in shipping, then there is reason for scepticism as to whether national treatment, in any comprehensive sense, is a reasonable negotiating objective in the Uruguay Round for this sector.

There is also the significant use of cargo-preference or cargo-shipping arrangements, in a variety of forms and formats. For example, U.S. grain sold on concessional terms has usually been required to be shipped, to the extent of 50 per cent, in U.S. vessels. The United States has participated in bilateral cargo-sharing arrangements with certain developing countries, under which a portion of all goods moving directly between the United States and such a country must be transported in vessels of each country.[23] Such an arrangement is substantially in contradiction with the U.S. proposal to negotiate on services. However, it should be pointed out that such restrictive arrangements as Brazil apparently demanded could no doubt be justified, and perhaps for many years, under a balance of payments provision in a general services arrangement, analogous to GATT Article XII on restrictions on trade necessary to safeguard the balance of payments.

In the UNCTAD, the developing countries have devised, against the wishes of a number of developed nations, the Code of Conduct for Liner Conferences. The code contemplates the reservation of a portion of cargoes to and from a developing country to the vessels of that country.[24] This code, dating from 1974, has been much objected to by U.S. spokesmen; indeed one U.S. official suggested (in conversation with this writer) that it was the existence of the code that precluded the United States from considering UNCTAD as a forum for a possible negotiation on services. Yet the UNCTAD code is much more than the generalization of the cargo-preference and cargo-sharing concept—to which developing countries, not surprisingly, are attached and which the U.S. has accepted, not necessarily enthusiastically, in bilateral arrangements. However, such arrangements may, of course, guarantee U.S. shippers a much bigger piece of the action than they would get in conditions of open competition. It may be that, as a practical matter, a larger number of cargoes would be carried by ships of the non-market economy countries, which have been competing vigorously on a price basis, if arrangements were not in place to reserve cargoes for carriers of particular countries.[25]

A third feature of the maritime transport sector is the role of flags of convenience. Facilities are offered by certain countries, e.g., Liberia and Panama, for vessels to be registered under what are considered to be less onerous requirements than elsewhere.

This enables such vessels to compete more effectively than if they were registered in the countries where beneficial ownership and real control of such vessels may reside. (At least one developed nation—France—has countered this by providing facilities for the registration of domestically-controlled vessels in an offshore territory—the Kerguelen Islands—where the rules governing registration in the metropolitan territory need not apply.) What Liberia and Panama have to offer is, in effect, national treatment to foreign shipping companies and a virtual right of establishment, that is, a right for a foreign corporation to create a subsidiary in the jurisdiction.

Despite the broad formulation of the U.S. proposal that national treatment should be the rule for the services industries, national treatment is precisely what the international community has now agreed should *not* be available in this particular sector. In the UNCTAD resolution on open registries, it has been agreed that ships should not be registered in a given country unless there is a real and meaningful connection between the owners of the vessels and the country concerned.[26] This example should make clear, again, that national treatment is not necessarily the appropriate solution to perceived problems in all services sectors, and that national treatment is only an abstract formulation unless it is related to specific measures.

Another feature of the maritime transport sector is that there appears to be considerable scope for arrangements to restrict competition. It is a longstanding complaint by the United States against the European maritime countries that the influence of their shipping companies in the 'conferences'—that is, shipping companies' agreements in regard to particular shipping routes—has led to restrictive practices and discriminatory pricing. Other countries, including Canada, have also long held the view that European and Japanese shipping companies may be discriminating against them in the structure of their conference rules and in their detailed pricing. We do not intend to get into this very large and controversial issue (which is of reduced importance in a period when the supply of shipping exceeds demand) except to point out that, under the Havana Charter format, such restrictive practices would have been a legitimate subject for discussion, even for dispute, in the International Trade Organization. It remains to be seen whether a general services arrangement will contain any meaningful provisions on restrictive business practices. If that is the case, it is likely that the developing countries will defend their cargo-preference concept, as written into the Liner Conference Code, as a legitimate counter to long-established restrictive practices by the shipping interests of developed countries and to the domination of the shipping market by a limited number of maritime nations. In reality, of course, all cargo-preference arrangements are restrictions on competition, but in the present period of vigorous competition, they may seem justified as essentially protective mechanisms, possibly justifiable under a safeguards clause in a general agreement on services.

It is difficult to perceive just what could be added, as a practical matter, to the complex of arrangements in the maritime transport sector, except to institute a cross-sectoral dispute settlement mechanism and, less importantly, to register, as a set of reservations, the extensive exceptions to national treatment. An alternative approach might be to leave maritime transport (and possibly air transport) outside the scope of a multisectoral services agreement. Trying to include these two sectors may lead either to having to accept that there will be very little of substance in any general agreement, or that the formulation of such an agreement would become largely hortatory, rather than contractual, and not really trade liberalizing. The inability of the Canadian and U.S. negotiators to agree on even such a modest measures as a standstill on discrimination in this sector should make the problem evident.

Financial Services

The structure of this sector, together with the various international arrangements that have evolved or are evolving, present a quite different picture from the three sectors considered above. There are certain common features among these sectors—such as the influence of regulation on the structure of the industries involved and on the scope of operations of the major economic agents—and there is the important role of informatics. But to look at services at this level of generalization and abstraction may not be very relevant. The traditional distinctions made between the various types of financial services institutions (referred to in Canada as the 'four pillars') are breaking down because of market and technological innovation.

The objective of trade negotiations in this field would be to improve access, in some fashion, for firms wishing to help recycle, for a fee, the vast pools of available capital. The objective of deregulation is increased competition to reduce the fees and the interest rate margins paid to these firms and to stimulate further innovation in terms of the financial instruments available.

Within the *insurance sector*, there are distinct categories of activity (life insurance, health, liability, property, marine, reinsurance) and also insurance related to the use of particular assets or objects, such as automobile insurance (which packages liability, property, and even health insurance) or accident insurance (which packages various types of insurance against a variety of contingencies). Liability insurance appears in many insurance packages

—automobile insurance, householder's insurance, the insurance of directors of companies.

The regulatory regime for insurance varies from country to country. In Canada it is customary to speak of the insurance industry as one for the four pillars of the financial structure; more recently, at the federal level, insurance companies have become subject to the same regulators as the banks. However, the provinces retain separate regulatory authority as regards insurance firms. In the United States the life and health insurance industry is essentially a state-regulated industry.[27] In the United Kingdom the decision has been made, for the present, not to bring Lloyd's, the central underwriting market for domestic as well as international insurance and reinsurance contracts, under the new Financial Services Act, but rather to assign the regulatory role to a separate authority.[28]

In the insurance sector, an important issue within the European Communities is better access by insurance firms of one member state to the markets of other member states. We need not review this issue in detail, except to observe that if the EC has not been able to resolve these access issues after 30 years, then one should not assume that it will be easy to negotiate in a broader forum.[29] The internal EC problem regarding insurance would appear to be more important than the discriminatory rules applying to foreign insurers in South Korea, or discrimination against foreign firms by Argentina in regard to marine insurance, to list two examples of restrictions on access for U.S. insurers. Both have been the subject of action under Section 301 of the Trade Act of 1974, which addresses alleged unfair trading practices of foreign governments.[30] Certain insurance circles in the U.K. hold the view that a general and multilateral negotiation on services trade restrictions will put pressure on those EC member states, such as West Germany, that restrict access by British insurers to their markets. Countries outside the EC may not find this rationale convincing. In any event, the major issue in the insurance sector appears to be an issue primarily within the EC, and that is not an issue that can easily be negotiated in the Geneva discussions.

In the *banking sector* there are various distinct types of activity, each creating different problems for regulators in domestic markets and for the emerging structure of rules and norms at the international level. Banks that want to expand in other countries are impatient with restrictions on access to those countries. The easing of restrictions on the operations of U.S.-controlled banks in Japan over the past four or five years has made this particular issue somewhat less acute. As for Canada and the United States, the FTA includes a set of arrangements, clearly not intended to be the last word, but that deals in detail with the more important of the current grievances of U.S. banks about access to the Canadian market.[31]

International banking as an industry reflects the existence of very large balances available for short-term speculation; with the easing of exchange controls, these balances may be moved from one market to the other in search of a higher interest return or an exchange rate gain. International banking now depends on the technical improvement in financial market mechanisms resulting from the availability of informatics, a consequent reduction in transaction costs and, in turn, the wave of innovation in the creation of financial instruments. This development has been authoritatively described in the Cross Report, a study prepared by a group convened by the Bank for International Settlements.[32] That study drew particular attention to the shift from international lending by banks to the issuing of securities on the international market by companies seeking fresh capital ('securitization') and lower interest expenditures.

Beyond these changes and beyond the increased competition, there are two major issues of greater importance than the narrow access issues of the Services Proposal. One is the emerging problem of how to—and who is to—regulate activity in the international markets, that is, the Euro-currencies markets and offshore markets, such as the Cayman Islands and those being created in New York, Japan and perhaps even in Montreal and Vancouver. Second, there is the problem for banking authorities in countries where major money-centre banks have made extensive loans to certain developing countries and may face major difficulties if some of these loans are not serviced or if there are defaults. This problem for domestic banking regulators is compounded in regard to banks that have also made what now appear to be imprudent loans in the energy and agricultural sectors.

In a climate characterized by rapid change and intense competition for business, one finds that while some banks are eager to expand into new markets, there are others whose range of activities is shrinking.[33] In this environment, the fact that, at the federal level, the United States follows a policy of national treatment must have a major influence on how other countries view access to their local banking industry for foreign-controlled banks. But the access issue, important as it is to particular banks, now seems less important than the attempt to formulate a set of detailed rules, or at least to agree on modalities of regulation, and how to deal with the overhang of excessive debt. Perhaps for this reason, other issues—and not necessarily issues to be dealt with in a services negotiation—have become more apparent.

In addressing these issues, regulators and representatives of the major banks are, one might well argue, beginning to evolve a

structure of international rules.   One component is the Bâle
Concordat which sets out, *inter alia*, the agreement of regulators as
to how responsibility for regulating a foreign-controlled bank
should be shared between the regulators in the host country and
the regulators in the country of the parent bank.[34]   Another
component is the agreement between regulators as to how banks
should manage 'off-balance-sheet' risks.   This too has been a
product of discussion in Bâle under the aegis of the Bank for
International Settlements and resulted in the issuance of
consultative documents by the authorities in certain major
financial centres.[35]   This was followed, in January 1987, by an
agreement between the Bank of England and the various U.S.
federal banking authorities on how to define bank capital and how
various types of assets should be weighed according to risk,
including both on-balance-sheet and off-balance-sheet assets.[36]
These agreed rules, having been examined in Bâle, are now being
put in place by other countries, including Japan and Canada.
These emerging international arrangements, this set of rules for
this services sector, are highly developed, detailed responses to
changes in banking as an industry.

If we take *securities dealing* as a sector, it is obvious that the
issue of the ownership of securities firms—be they in Tokyo or
Toronto—is a major issue to those firms that are excluded and wish
to enter particular markets.   It is also an issue for the political
authorities, who have to balance a number of conflicting
considerations.   There was pressure on them to keep the domestic
market for existing participants, there are the benefits of
additional competition and an enhanced role for the local
securities market, and there are the obvious reciprocity considerations. If the authorities choose to exclude particular foreign firms
from operating in their domestic securities markets, then their
domestic firms may be excluded from the foreign market
concerned.   Thus Canadian (i.e., Ontario) securities firms have not
been allowed to manage an issue of securities in London because
British-controlled subsidiaries in Canada have not been allowed to
lead an underwriting in Toronto.

These reciprocity considerations in an industry where some
physical presence or facility in the market may be necessary to
carry on business are obviously difficult to apply in regard to
activities, such as membership in an exchange, where it has been
necessary or appropriate to limit the number of participating
firms.   Thus the Japanese authorities have not been willing to
permit all comers from abroad to do business in the Tokyo stock
exchange (or in the markets for other types of securities).   Clearly,
limitations in entry have had the effect—perhaps the intended
effect—of restricting competition. It is of interest that as a result
of the substantial changes in the regulation of London's

International Stock Exchange (e.g., the abolition of the distinction between brokers and jobbers and the abolition of fixed commissions) and the merger of the membership of the exchange with the membership of the International Securities Regulatory Organization, the number of member firms allowed to do business in London has increased significantly, including the number of foreign-controlled firms.

Access is essentially an issue of importance to the firms concerned. It is because of pressure by potential entrants, and the reality of reciprocity considerations, that the authorities in Britain, Quebec, Ontario and Japan have, in one fashion or another, allowed foreign firms increased rights to participate in their markets. The issue of access by foreign firms looks rather less important now than, say, five years ago, when the proposal to negotiate rules on services trade and investment was beginning to get attention. It follows that there is less, in substance, to negotiate about, although it remains the view in London and Washington that foreign firms in Japan do not have rights equal to the rights enjoyed by Japanese firms in London and New York.

However, to the public at large the major issue in regard to the securities sector is a different issue: Can the securities market be regulated effectively? Can we agree on what practices should be forbidden and then police the market with any hope of success? This is a technical question, in a sense. For example, if we agree that trading on inside information can be defined and should be prohibited, can we assume that such trading will in fact be detected? A related and separate question is whether regulation should be essentially self-regulation, perhaps under the authority or subject to the rule making of some institution with statutory power (the pattern adopted, for the present, in the United Kingdom, under the Financial Services Act); or should regulation and policing be carried out by separate, outside entities (the pattern followed in the United States and in Ontario, for example). These issues are being debated in the light of the current inquiries into insider trading activities in London and New York and the alleged breaches of U.K. companies legislation with regard to purchases of a company's own stock. These issues, like other regulatory issues, are being approached by working out new international arrangements, such as the memorandum of understanding reached in September 1986 between the U.S. and U.K. securities authorities providing for the exchange of detailed information on securities transactions. It is expected that other countries will enter into such arrangements, essentially on a bilateral basis.[37] In any event, the issues involved in making regulation effective are likely to seem to the public to be more important than whether an additional British or American securities firm can be allowed to operate in Toronto.

A final comment on financial services as a group of sectors: the buying and selling of securities and the making of a market in a security are activities quite different from commercial banking or investment banking. In certain jurisdictions, banks may be permitted to buy and sell securities on behalf of clients or, in others, to own controlling interest in a securities firm. Consumer credit subsidiaries of automobile manufacturers are competing with banks in the U.S. in offering consumer loans and may expand their activities into other aspects of retail banking. But these developments should not obscure the fact that, to the extent that such activities are deemed to require regulation, the regulation must relate to particular functions, not to particular corporate structures. In one jurisdiction or another, it may be judged appropriate to limit or narrowly define the role of a commercial bank, to define what securities firms may or may not do, or to limit ownership links between firms carrying out different functions. These are separate issues, which, of course, do have implications not only for the regulatory process, but also for the structure of the various industries and their ability to compete.

Professional Services

Finally, it may be helpful to look at a quite different sector— different in terms of the structure of the economic agents involved and the structure of regulation. In professional services the service is delivered to the consumer of the services by an individual (or group of individuals), usually, but not always, as employees or partners of a specialized firm. In many cases the rendering of the professional service requires the mobility of people—i.e., either the service provider goes to the client or the client goes to the service provider. In some cases, professional services may be provided without direct physical contact (e.g, architectural drawings transmitted over telephone lines to the client's computer.) However, the issues in the field of professional services arise not in relation to such computer flows but in relation to the provision of services by individuals. There are two main issues: (1) the recognition by the authorities in one country of professional qualifications recognized in another country; and (2) the question of whether a particular individual may be allowed to enter another country for the purpose of providing that service.

Within the European Communities some progress has been made in establishing that qualifications obtained in one member state are recognized in another member state, e.g., for law, accounting and medicine. Given the ease with which persons may move for short periods within the EC, many professional services are no doubt provided for periods of time by professionals of one member state to customers in another member state without formal permission from the immigration authorities. But movement from one member state to another on a permanent basis, in order to carry on a profession, is a matter for the professional body in the member state concerned, and residence requirements are usually related to recognition of professional qualifications.

Another example: both the European Communities and the United States have been pressing Japan to allow foreign lawyers to practise in Japan. Presumably foreign lawyers in Japan advise foreign-controlled firms in Japan about foreign (non-Japanese) issues; they may advise Japanese firms about foreign law, and only rarely could they advise regarding Japanese legal issues. But of course there are matters, such as the avoidance of double taxation and choice of law, in which knowledge of the law in Japan as well as the other countries is relevant. These issues are still being negotiated, essentially bilaterally, but there is much complaint that the Japanese professional group lays down requirements that no foreign lawyer could easily meet.[38]

Professional services, of course, have been addressed in bilateral treaties on commerce and navigation (FCN treaties). They are addressed, for example, in the 1962 treaty between the U.K. and Japan and in the U.S./Japan FCN treaty. However, when the U.S. treaty came before the Senate for approval, the Senate added a proviso that the rights for individuals of one country to carry on business in the other country, as specified in the treaty, could not be extended to those professions that, in the United States, are regulated by the states or by professional bodies or associations to which state power is delegated.[39] In general, the more recent FCN treaties negotiated by the United States have created few rights for professional services; these are being negotiated bilaterally between the professional groups involved.[40] This approach is reflected in the Canada-U.S. FTA, in regard to the profession of architecture;[41] and we should note that the agreement does attempt to improve the procedures at the border for certain professionals travelling between the two countries or carrying out their profession in the other country.[42]

The issue of professional services concerns the movement of a limited number of individuals possessing valuable and expensive skills, the availability of which, to the importing country, is assumed to produce gains. However, it is not apparent that these are gains of the same order as the gains that would be realized if less-skilled labour, for which differences in pay are substantial between countries, were allowed to move. But it is not at all apparent that, for example, the use of Korean or Thai construction crews on major projects in Canada, the United States or Western Europe will be a matter of urgent business in the Uruguay Round.

Conclusions

The main conclusion emerging from the foregoing is that there are important structural and organizational differences between services sectors and between the systems of international rules that apply in the various sectors. Because of this reality, the basis for a general agreement on services is not very extensive. That is not to say that agreement to make all measures transparent, to make all restrictions, in principle, negotiable, and to set up a dispute settlement mechanism are minor matters. Rather it is to say that an agreement along these lines leaves a great deal of detail to be addressed at the level of particular sectors, and that this is necessarily so. A related conclusion is that the problems facing particular services sectors—facing entrepreneurs, managers, regulators and legislators—include a number of issues other than the issue of access to foreign markets. Indeed, some of those issues may be much more important than negotiating about restrictions on access. It is tempting, when we look at the current state of the financial services industry or at shipping or air transport, to argue that restrictions on access to foreign markets are only intermittently, and only for some entities, a first-order issue.

Another conclusion is that while the Services Proposal was being articulated, while the investigative and consultative machinery was being cranked up in the United States, the United Kingdom, Europe, Japan and Canada, and while trade policy personnel were finding their way into new territory, a number of access problems facing particular services corporations were resolved or partially resolved. It is perhaps partly for this reason that some of the earlier pressure from U.S. private interests seems to have abated; a lot more concern and effort are being deployed now about trade in agriculture and the trade policy aspects of intellectual property rights systems. What remains is a suspicion that U.S. policy spokesman and some U.S. private sector representatives want a general arrangement for services that will allow retaliation in the goods sector if other countries restrict U.S. services operations in their markets. The U.S. approach is understood by certain developing countries in these terms—hence their opposition to dealing with services issues in the same tent as goods issues. It is discouraging to see a U.S. GATT expert describing this understandable caution on the part of developing countries as being a preference for keeping trade in services "out of the liberal trade rules".[43]

Notes

1. This writer has addressed these issues in two previous publications: *Traded Computer Services/An Analysis of a Proposal for Canada/U.S. Agreement* (Montreal: Royal Bank of Canada, 1983); "The Elements of a General Agreement in Information Trade", paper prepared in 1985 for the Atwater Institute of Montreal and published in *Inter Media* (London: 1987). The section that follows is based on this second paper.

2. Canada-U.S. FTA, Sectoral Annex C to Annex 1404.

3. OECD, *Declaration on Transborder Data Flows*.

4. The requirement in Canada's Act that certain data required by the regulatory authorities (that is, the Superintendent of Financial Institutions) be held in Canada and not solely in foreign data banks was long viewed in the United States as a measure designed only to protect Canadian computer services companies.

5. United Nations Centre on Transnational Corporations, *Transborder Data Flows and Brazil* (New York: United Nations, 1983), E.83 II.A.3.

6. See note 1 above.

7. For discussion of this issue, see Rodney de C. Grey, "Notes for a statement on 'The Canadian View on Extraterritoriality and Export Controls' " Trilateral Conference [Los Angeles], 1983, photocopied; for the U.S. controls referred to see 47 *Federal Register* No. 122 (June 24, 1982), p. 27250.

8. See Karen A. Amner, "The Semiconductor Chip Protection Act of 1984", 17 *Law and Policy in International Business* No. 2 (1985), pp. 395-420.

9. See Roderick Oram, "Airlines buy into Apollo ticket system", *Financial Times* [London], May 3, 1988; Michael Donne, "Airlines club together in war of the computers", *Financial Times* [London], May 5, 1988; David Churchill, "American Airlines, BA resolve computer reservation dispute", *Financial Times* [London], June 27, 1988.

10. See Barbro Beer, "Informatics in International Trade", 19 *Journal of World Trade Law* (November/December 1985), pp. 570-578.

11. There is, of course, a complex of bilateral agreements in the air transport sector going beyond the primary issue of route

allocation. As of April 1986 there were 17 air transport sector agreements between Canada and the United States.

12. In the United States, for example, cabotage is reserved to domestic carriers under section 1108 of the Federal Aviation Act.

13. From ICAO's reply to the MTN/GNS enquiry, MTN.GNS/W/36, 16 May 1988.

14. For an early and detailed transit rights provision, see Article XXIX of the Treaty of Washington (1871) between Great Britain and the U.S., in *Treaties and Agreements Affecting Canada/in force between/His Majesty and the United States of America*, (Ottawa: King's Printer), 1927, p. 46.

15. According to the *Financial Times* [London], November 14, 1986 ("Canada Threatens to Pull Out of Air Agreement") and *The Globe and Mail*, November 18, 1986 ("Canada Raises Stakes in Air Dispute with U.K."), the Canadian government gave the required one year notice of withdrawal to the agreement (IASTA) following the U.K.'s notice of withdrawal from the 1981 Canada/U.K. air services agreement: "Exchanges of Notes Between Canada and the United Kingdom of Great Britain and Northern Ireland Amending the Agreement for Air Services Signed at Ottawa August 19, 1949, as Amended on August 18, 1958 and September 6, 1960", London, April 14, 1981; in force January, 1981." (Not published in Canada Treaty Series.)

16. Unpublished U.S.T.R. air transport sector paper, made available to this writer.

17. For the U.S./France arbitration see Paul B. Larsen, "Arbitration of the United States-France Air Traffic Rights Dispute" 30 *Journal of Air Law and Commerce* No. 3 (1964), pp. 231-247; for the U.S./Italy arbitration, see Paul B. Larsen, "The United States-Italy Air Transport Arbitration: Problems of Treaty Interpretation and Enforcement", 61 *American Journal of International Law* No. 2 (1967), pp. 496-520.

18. Articles 84 and 85 of the Chicago Convention.

19. Articles 87 and 88 of the Chicago Convention.

20. See Part 213 of the U.S. CAB regulations (14 C.F.R.).

21. Section 20 of the Merchant Marine Act of 1920—the Jones Act. For a recent list of restrictions on maritime transport,

see International Chamber of Commerce/Commission on Sea Transport, *List of Obstacles to Trade in International Maritime Services* (Paris: 1986), Doc. 321/315 bis.

22. Paul Cheeseright, "Britain Ready to Close Coastal Waters to EEC", *Financial Times* [London], March 15, 1986; Nick Garnett, "Government moves to restrict cabotage", *Financial Times* [London], March 31, 1988.

23. Walter Conte, "U.S. and Brazil Set Maritime Pact Despite Implication for Free Trade", *Wall Street Journal*, December 20, 1985.

24. UNCTAD: *Code of Conduct for Liner Conferences*, Vol II, Final Ad. (New York: United Nations, 1975). For U.S. comments, see Stephen C. Neff, "The UN Code of Conduct for Liner Conferences", 14 *Journal of World Trade Law* No. 5 (September/ October 1980), 398-423; Paul B. Larsen and Valerie Vetterick, "The UNCTAD Code of Conduct for Liner Conferences: Reservations, Reactions and U.S. Alternatives" 13 *Law and Policy in International Business* No. 1 (1981), pp. 223-280.

25. "Red Bottoms on Blue Water", Editorial in *The Times* [London], 26 July 1984.

26. For a commentary on and text of the 1981 resolution of the UNCTAD committee on shipping, see "UNCTAD Flags of Convenience," in 15 *Journal of World Trade Law* No. 5 (September/October 1981), pp. 466-468; see also UNCTAD, Trade and Development Board, "Action on the question of open registries", TC/B/C.4/220, 3 March 1981.

27. See *Statement of Principles Respecting Trade in Services by Life and Health Insurance Companies between the United States and Canada*, Health Insurance Association of America et al., November 28, 1986.

28. U.K. Financial Services Act giving effect to the proposals in the White Paper, "Financial Services in the United Kingdom . . .", Cmnd. 9432, 1985; Lloyd's Act, 1982.

29. A useful short and authoritative discussion is A. H. Herman, "Insurance: A Time to do Business", *Financial Times* [London], March 26, 1987.

30. For 301 complaints against South Korea insurance practices, see 45 *Federal Register* No. 203 (November 26, 1980), 78850; for a discussion of how this matter was resolved, see Che

Yoon-Je, "How the United States Broke into Korea's Insurance Market", 10 *The World Economy* No. 4 (December 1987), pp. 483-496; for 301 complaint regarding Argentine marine insurance, see 45 *Federal Registry* No. 145 (July 25, 1980).

31. Canada-U.S. FTA, Chapter Seventeen, "Financial Services"; for comments see evidence by N. LePan and Raymond Labrosse (of the Department of Finance) before the Standing Committee of the Senate of Canada (July 25, 1988); and Carl J. Lohmann and William C. Murden, "Policies for the Treatment of Foreign Participation in Financial Markets and their Application in the U.S.-Canada Free Trade Agreement", Paper prepared for a conference at the University of Ottawa, January 22, 1988.

32. Bank for International Settlements, *Recent Innovations in International Banking*, The Cross Report (Basel: 1986). See also David Smith, "Competition will spur financial innovation", *The Times* [London] March 1986.

33. An example is Midland Bank (of the U.K.) selling off its affiliate, acquired only recently in California (Crocker) and abandoning some types of activity in the domestic (U.K.) market.

34. Bank for International Settlements, Committee on Banking Regulations and Supervisory Practices, "Principles for the supervision of banks' foreign establishments", Bâle, 1983.

35. In March 1986 the Bank of England issued a consultative document on off-balance-sheet risks: *Off-Balance-Sheet Business of Banks/A Consultative Paper by the Bank of England*. See also Peter Truell, "Bank of England Plans Rules on Off-Balance-Sheet Risks", *Wall Street Journal* [Europe], March 21, 1986.

36. For text of Bank of England/Federal Reserve Board, Comptroller of the Currency and Federal Deposit Insurance Corporation agreement, see *Financial Times* [London], January 9, 1987; for developments in other countries see, for example, Stefan Wagstyl, "BIS forcing Japan's banks to toughen up", *Financial Times* [London], May 20, 1988; George Graham, "French win country risk argument", *Financial Times* [London], March 30, 1988; Haig Simorian, "Bundesbank Chafes at Cooke report", *Financial Times* [London], March 15, 1988; [no author], "BIS maps out sounder basis for banking", *Financial Times* [London], December 11, 1987; John Kohut, "Canadian Banks a target

for new capital standards", *The Globe and Mail*, August 30, 1988.

37. For details of the U.K./U.S. "Memorandum of Understanding", see "U.K. and U.S. sign agreement on fraud", *Financial Times* [London], September 24, 1986.

38. Christopher Sheehey, "Japan's New Foreign Lawyer Law", 19 *Law and Policy in International Business* No. 2 (1987), pp. 361-383.

39. *Treaty of Friendship, Commerce and Navigation Between the United States of America and Japan*, TIAS 2863, April 2, 1953; the Senate Provision, p. 2132.

40. *U.S. National Study*, pp. 230-239.

41. Canada-U.S. FTA, *Annex 1404*, A. Architecture.

42. Canada-U.S. FTA, Chapter Fifteen, and Annex 1502.1, C. Professionals.

43. John H. Jackson, "Constructing a Constitution...", note 12 at page 202.

Chapter VII

The Issues in the Geneva Services Negotiations

In terms of traditional trade theory, the key questions raised by the Services Proposal are whether the theory of comparative advantage applies to traded services and therefore whether there are gains from trade in services. The assumption seems to be that if it can be established that there are indeed gains from trade in services, it follows that all countries would gain from the reduction or elimination of barriers to trade in services. If all countries accepted this assumption, it would be easier to conduct the negotiations, as each country would be agreeing to actions that benefit itself. The problem is that, although this assumption may be valid, it is not very persuasive in practical, political terms. It is certainly far from convincing when the logic is extended uncritically to services delivered by establishments.

This argument is not persuasive for politicians and their advisers because the issue is not whether there are gains from trade, but rather how large these gains are in relation to other gains, such as the gain or public good that is thought to accrue through the building up of domestic capacity in a particular industry,[1] or by securing what may appear in some countries to be an important psychological benefit—i.e., the benefit of having only a few foreign-controlled corporations active in the economy. The gains from reducing barriers to trade, which are distributed unequally among the players, have been discussed at great length with regard to trade in goods, but the magnitude of those gains depends on such questions as whether there are increasing returns to scale in a given industry and whether an industry is labour-intensive, given that there are great differences in wage costs between countries. In a number of modern industries, such as automotive parts manufacturing, the increasing returns to scale are substantial. In some service industries, such as tourism or dry cleaning, they may be relatively less important. Not all industries, and certainly not all service industries, enjoy the same returns to scale. The issue that most proponents of the Services Proposal seem to want to ignore is that there are other non-economic goals that governments legitimately pursue and that the potential gains from removing restrictions on trade and establishment in the services sector have to be measured, in the political process, against these other goals.

There are, of course, goods-producing industries in which governments pursue non-economic goals and forego manifest economic gains—agriculture, textiles, automobiles are obvious examples. Through the political process, non-economic goals have been given priority in these sectors; to put the issue more pejoratively, protectionist sentiment has prevailed. There is certainly some protectionist sentiment in services industries—in air transport and insurance, for example. This protectionism will have to be taken into account as negotiations proceed.

In regard to activities in the data processing or banking sectors, for example, there is likely to be consideration given in many smaller countries to the potential and largely unquantifiable benefits of developing domestically-controlled capability and capacity and of maintaining sovereignty, whatever that is thought to be, over the operation of foreign corporations. From the point of view of the large service entities in the large economies, these arguments are likely to seem bogus. The problem is how to measure these essentially psychological gains against the economic gains from trade. The fact that sovereignty—one of the alleged benefits of having domestically-controlled corporations provide these services—can be a cover for protectionism should not prevent us from realizing that there is a difficult issue in determining how to measure one category of gains against another.

However, if we accept, for purposes of discussion and debate, that it might be useful to try to think out some general rules about services, we could classify the issues that will have to be addressed under various headings, not all of which are of equal importance.[2] Much of what we have to say here follows fairly directly from the analysis in Chapter IV of how the GATT works.

Dispute Settlement

The GATT, and the Tokyo Round Codes, have developed dispute settlement practice around the careful formulations of Article XXIII. It might be argued that this could well be an analogue for consultation, conciliation and dispute settlement provisions in a broad agreement on services—both those that are traded and those that are delivered by establishments. To the advocates of a more legalistic, adjudicatory system, the GATT system may seem to be far from satisfactory in practice; in terms of adjudication, it certainly falls considerably short of providing for recourse to the International Court of Justice, as contemplated in the Havana Charter. The shortcomings in the dispute settlement system relate, however, more to the unwillingness of contracting parties to abide by the GATT structure of rights and obligations—for example, to use Article XIX and not evade its conditions and criteria. For dispute settlement, this would mean having to abide by the advice of GATT panels. This in turn means that GATT panels must invariably come up with the correct answers and formulate them in acceptable terms. For issues as politicized as trade policy issues are, this is no more than a council of perfection.

The negotiating issue implicit in the Geneva services talks is whether there should be one single trade relations system of dispute settlement or two. The related issue—whether compensatory, countervailing or retaliatory action would be taken before or after or without regard to scrutiny by some international authority—is equally critical. Big countries can have recourse to retaliation[3] (or to insisting on adequate compensation) with relative equanimity, particularly in dealing with smaller countries. Smaller countries, particularly the developing countries, are not in the retaliation business; it is not a profitable way for them to conduct their trade policy.

Given this element of practical asymmetry, what we could call a unified dispute settlement/retaliation system would increase the leverage of the larger entities vis-à-vis the smaller ones. It would represent an important increase in the scope for retaliation as a commercial policy instrument for the European Communities and the United States with respect to the practices of other countries. With a single unified system for the settlement of trade disputes, it might be possible to retaliate in the goods sector against alleged restrictions in the services sector, or vice versa. For example, if your insurance firms want action against the allegedly discriminatory practices of country X, you may be able to oblige your domestic garment industry by restricting imports of garments from country X. Retaliation can be, in such a short-term and mercantilist calculus, an attractive option. A question for negotiators representing smaller countries will therefore be: Is it prudent to buttress the retaliatory power of the European

Communities and the United States, the major services exporters, by agreeing to a unified dispute settlement system?

One can describe in fairly simple terms what would be a retrograde, unsatisfactory outcome of discussions of the dispute settlement component of the services negotiation in Geneva, and contrast it with a less damaging outcome. An unsatisfactory outcome would be a dispute settlement mechanism which allows countries to suspend GATT concessions on goods in response to alleged derogations from the agreement on services, and allowed this to take place essentially under domestic legal procedures and without adequate prior international scrutiny. Clearly, such a system would favor large countries.

A better, less damaging outcome would be to confine dispute settlement in a services agreement to the Services Sector, to preclude retaliation by the withdrawal of concessions on goods, and to provide for effective international surveillance and evaluation of any proposed retaliation before such action is taken.

Non-discrimination

The term non-discrimination is sometimes used in a very far-reaching sense, that is, to indicate that the same treatment should be received by imported products (or foreign-controlled entities) as by domestic products or domestically-controlled entities. In the OECD and the GATT, that is called national treatment. In other context, non-discrimination stands for most-favoured-nation treatment, perhaps conditional, perhaps unconditional. As noted above, one of the two objectives of the GATT was to establish the principle and practice of non-discrimination in trade relations; this was embodied in the provisions of Article I, an unconditional most-favoured-nation clause, and by the provisions of Article III, requiring national treatment of imported goods once the tariff levied at the frontier has been paid or the requirements of a quota met.

Although Article I, the MFN clause, is drafted in the unconditional form, the GATT system has important elements of conditionality. For example, new signatories had to accept, in adhering to the GATT, a complex parcel of obligations worked out at Geneva and Havana; these imposed meaningful limitations on rights to use quotas and to discriminate and included a system of compensatory sanctions (Articles VI, XIX and XXVIII, for example). Countries that could not accept all the GATT obligations, such as Switzerland and Poland, had to enter into special negotiations to develop special regimes between them and the rest of the GATT signatories, each to be embodied in a 'protocol of accession'. The bargaining power of existing signatories as against a potential new signatory was enhanced by the provisions of

Article XXXV, which allows an existing signatory to deny GATT rights to any potential new signatory (as many European countries, e.g., France and the U.K., did at the time of Japan's accession in 1955). Moreover, new signatories had to enter into tariff negotiations, with the result that they reduced and bound their tariffs against increase in order to pay for the GATT-bound rates of existing signatories to which, by adhering to the GATT, they in turn acquired rights.

This price of admission to the club and the assumption that all major trading countries would take part in each successive round of negotiations, were intended to deal with the problem of free-riders. Thus, in a very real sense, the GATT MFN provisions were developed in a context of conditionality; as long as the conditions set out above were met, the MFN clause would be applied between GATT signatories without precise item-by-item conditionality or reciprocity being required.

However, in the Tokyo Round it became evident that with regard to certain codes relating to non-tariff barriers, i.e., the codes on subsidies/countervail and on procurement, there would be real difficulties—in the United States at least—in extending the benefits of the particular codes to countries that did not accept the obligations of the codes. The U.S. Administration took the view, from the beginning of the negotiation, that it could not extend the benefit of the injury test for countervail to GATT countries that did not adhere to the subsidies/countervail agreement. Similarly, the benefits of the procurement rules—that is, access to that portion of the U.S. procurement market specified in the Procurement Code after payment of the requisite tariffs—could not be extended to countries that did not sign that Code, i.e., those countries that refused to accord to U.S. firms the right to compete for some negotiated portion of their procurement markets. Thus, in the working out of these two codes during the Tokyo Round, the essential conditionality of MFN under the GATT became more evident.

Some confusion arose as to the meaning of GATT Article I from a decision by the United States that several countries (not necessarily GATT signatories) that had bilateral trade treaties with the United States containing *unconditional* MFN clauses were in fact entitled to the benefits (e.g., the injury test) in the Subsidies/Countervail Code. This development implied that the GATT MFN provision had less meaning to the United States than its bilateral treaty articles. Then there was a dispute with India (a non-signatory of the GATT Code) as to whether the United States could deny India the benefits of the injury test in the Code, given the MFN provisions of Article I. The dispute was referred to a GATT panel but was settled 'out of court'.

On balance, one should accept that, as a practical matter, an element of conditionality is inherent in the GATT concept of non-discrimination.[4]

The Uruguay Round of multilateral trade negotiations will likely involve, as Schott and Hufbauer have indicated,[5] much more use of explicitly conditional (or reciprocal) agreements, particularly those seeking to resolve problems of trade in those products now dealt with outside the GATT system, i.e., steel, textiles, automobiles and dairy products, among others. It is likely that, as the United States has proposed, important concessions with regard to traded services (including those delivered by establishments) will not be extended to countries that do not reciprocate with equivalent concessions.

For example, the United States, at the federal level, adheres to a policy of giving national treatment to foreign-controlled banks to be established in the United States, whether or not the countries where the parent firms are located give national treatment to U.S.-controlled banks. The U.S. government may or may not wish to continue to do so, but it is most unlikely that the United States could accept an obligation to do so without some agreed reciprocity.

In the services area generally there may be many examples of situations where countries may be willing to accept imported services (or foreign-controlled services establishments) on a national treatment basis or on an MFN basis but where they will be unwilling to accept an obligation to do so, except on a reciprocal or conditional basis. Some developing countries will assert, as a matter of principle or as an aspect of 'special and differential treatment', that they are entitled to all the benefits of such agreements on services as may be negotiated; however, the fact is that major trading countries cannot expect the United States or the EC to tolerate free-riders.

To sum up: any comprehensive (general or sector) negotiation on services will go forward under the banner of conditionality and reciprocity.

Right of Commercial Presence

The concept of a 'right of commercial presence' is one aspect of the services debate in which it is evident that discussion in the OECD has advanced understanding; more recently, the formulation developed in the Canada-U.S. FTA has provided some precise drafting that may serve as a model for drafting in Geneva.[6] Earlier discussion, as we have noted, turned on the more conventional concept of right of establishment and the related issue of the right to invest in such establishment as may be necessary to deliver a service.

In conventional trade policy—i.e., policy concerned with trade in goods—the notion of establishment has not been an issue. For example, in the early 1930s, Canada enacted a set of high tariff rates and helped put in place a system of preferential tariff margins between Commonwealth countries. Some of the high tariffs were designed to protect Canadian producers against U.S. or other foreign competition. Others were designed to encourage foreign firms to establish subsidiaries in Canada to serve the Canadian market and the preferential market in the United Kingdom, Australia and other Commonwealth countries. Clearly such a policy of encouraging the construction of branch plants implied that there be no limitation on the right of establishment in the goods-producing sectors. In Canada, as in the United States, limitations on the right of establishment have been related to particular sectors, such as banking and telecommunications; otherwise foreign enterprises have been able to establish (that is, until the Foreign Investment Review Act).

However, post-war negotiations to reduce tariffs clearly created many new possibilities for serving a given market (such as Canada) through exports, thus reducing the incentive to establishment (i.e., investment in branch plants). Only in developing countries, such as Mexico, has there continued to be very high protection for domestic producers (by high tariffs and restrictive quotas) and restrictions on and detailed conditions attached to establishment by potential foreign investors.

The GATT, which was addressed to reducing barriers to trade, did not deal with the issue of establishment, which lay outside the narrow trade agreement nexus of what was, after all, only Chapter IV of the Havana Charter. In a limited sense, establishment as a concept was subsumed, in the Havana Charter, in the broader subject of international investment. This was addressed particularly in Article 12, "International Investment for Economic Development and Reconstruction", in Chapter III of the Charter, entitled "Economic Development and Reconstruction". Article 12 contains an interesting, if cautious provision: "Members therefore undertake . . . (ii) to give due regard to the desirability of avoiding discrimination as between foreign investments . . .".

One might ask, however, why the GATT did not address the issue of the right to do business, or what we can now call a 'right of commercial presence'. The short answer is probably that, with respect to trade in goods, such a provision would have been unnecessary between the original GATT signatories. In both domestic law and bilateral treaties there was sufficient protection for nationals of one country wishing to buy or sell goods in another country. Such issues have been addressed, in some detail, in such relatively modern bilateral instruments as the U.K./Japan Agreement of 1962 and the U.S./Japan FCN treaty of 1953.[7]

Indeed, there is a network of FCN-type treaties conveying MFN rights to national treatment, including aspects of "commercial presence" very much like the pre-World War II system of trade agreements.

It is important, for an understanding of the Canada-U.S. FTA, and of Canada's prospects in the Uruguay Round to keep in mind that Canada, unlike many other countries, does not have comprehensive FCN-type treaties with the United States, with the EC (or its member states), or with Japan.[8]

Provisions very much like a right of commercial presence have, in fact, been developed in many bilateral FCN-type treaties; there are, of course, particular sectoral exceptions for each country. One might ask, why not rely on these treaties rather than seek to develop some multilateral provision? One may assume that the answer is, first, that such a right does not exist in regard to a number of trading countries and, second, that there is no generally accepted specialized forum for conciliation and dispute settlement, other than the International Court, and certainly no mechanism of sanctions (compensation or retaliation) to ensure adherence to the treaty provisions. Certainly there is no provision in FCN-type treaties under which retaliatory action could be contemplated under the procedures of domestic law (such as Section 301 of the U.S. Trade Act of 1974).

National Treatment

The notion of national treatment figures importantly in the U.S./Japan FCN treaty, and the concept is important in a wide variety of trade agreement contexts. To review its main uses, first, there is the use in the OECD, where it is the standard adopted for the treatment of foreign-controlled enterprises with regard to such matters as taxation. Second, the term is used in the GATT (in Article III) in the context of ensuring that the only measure that can legitimately be applied in relation to imports but not to like domestic products is the tariff at the frontier (and a quantitative restriction, in defined circumstances). Any differential in the application of such measures as, for example, the levying of a commodity tax, is recognized as being merely as disguised tariff. The one important exception to national treatment is in regard to procurement. Third, there is the concept that the treatment accorded under domestic law to nationals (individuals or companies) is a standard to which access can be accorded, by agreement, to individuals and companies of another country. Through MFN clauses, such a standard of treatment agreed with one country may be extended to the persons and companies of another.

It is important to note that national treatment, as a concept, can be disaggregated: that is, we can specify to what types of action by the state the obligation shall apply. This notion of disaggregation is important in regard to certain services. For example, it may be agreed that national treatment in air transport is to be accorded to such matters as landing charges, but not accorded in regard to access to domestic routes.

One may predict that in some fashion any general agreement on services will invoke the concept of national treatment, and that there will be either detailed lists of national exceptions or reservations, detailed exceptions by sector, or both. Moreover, many countries may be willing in practice to accord defined and specified national treatment in particular sectors, but not willing to bind themselves by treaty to do so.

Roles of States and Provinces

The issues of what obligations will be assumed, in a meaningful and binding sense, by governments of states, provinces and other sub-national authorities will be more acute in the services sector than in the goods area. The regulation of commerce with foreign nations is, in the U.S. and Canadian constitutional systems, assigned to the central government. Thus it is only in regard to a narrow range of issues that the competence of other levels of government has arisen: for example, whether subsidies paid by such governments were actionable under the obligations of the central government as contained in the GATT and the Subsidies/Countervail Code;[9] whether a provincial commodity tax was in conflict with the national treatment provisions of Article III of the GATT; and whether buy-provincial or buy-state procurement provisions constituted a breach of Article III.

In the Tokyo Round, aside from provincial practices in the marketing of wines and spirits, the one subject that Canadian federal authorities deemed expedient to pursue with provincial authorities was the scope for possible provincial undertakings regarding procurement; in the event, the procurement negotiation did not go that far. These quasi-legal issues were conditioned by the vague wording of the one GATT provision that specifically addresses the issue of to what extent GATT obligations bear on the actions of state/provincial authorities. That is Article XXIV (paragraph 12), which reads: "Each contracting party shall take such reasonable measures as may be available to it to ensure observance of the provisions of this Agreement by the regional and local governments and authorities within its territory." In the Canada-U.S. FTA the role of sub-national governments is referred to in a number of provisions; in regard to services covered by Chapter Fourteen, the sub-national governments are to accord national treatment to "persons of the other party"; with regard to financial services (excluding insurance), Article 1701 makes clear the provisions "shall not apply to any measure of a political subdivision of either party."

For the services negotiations in Geneva the issue will be substantive. In the United States the separate states have regulatory authority in regard to certain major services activities, including banking and insurance. Many professions are regulated by autonomous bodies acting under state legislation. Much the same is true in Canada; the provinces do not have authority in regard to banking but they do in regard to credit unions, which are a form of near-bank. It has been observed by a number of senior U.S. trade policy experts that, despite the Services Proposal, it seems unlikely that the present U.S. Administration will wish to usurp the authority of the states in regard to any important service sector. The FTA drafting, which is very sector-specific for financial services, may be found useful in Geneva.

'Unfair' Trade

As we noted earlier, there have been suggestions from the private sector in the United States that the unfair trade provisions (anti-dumping, countervail, Section 337 of the Tariff Act and Section 301 of the Trade Act) should be extended to the services area before any negotiation of general rules regarding traded services begins.

The elaboration of a system of sanctions in domestic law against unfair trade practices, under the aegis of GATT Article VI and the two Article VI Codes (on Anti-dumping Duties and on Subsidies/ Countervail) has been, on balance, a retrograde and protectionist development. That is not to say that there are not instances of unfair trade, of predatory dumping and of export subsidization, that must seem intolerable to domestic competitors in the markets at issue; it is only to say that the Article VI system, which has become the virtual centrepiece of trade policy in practice, is essentially protectionist and discriminatory.[10] There are now some members of the U.S. trade bar—where 'unfair trade' is a growth industry—who share this view.[11] From this point of view, it would be thoroughly retrograde to extend the Article VI concepts to services; there is simply no case for doing so. There is a case, however, for addressing examples of unfair trading practices, such as subsidization or dumping of airline fares, under some sort of nullification and impairment provision analogous to GATT Article XXIII.

In my view, this should be considered a make-or-break issue by Canada, by developing countries and indeed by all smaller trading countries. If it were seriously suggested that there should be anti-dumping provisions with regard to dumped insurance, or countervail with regard to allegedly subsidized airfares, then the negotiations should be judged as being aimed at increasing protection, not at liberalization. In that event, the smaller participants (in which category we must include Canada) should be prepared to walk away from the negotiating table. Surely the unwillingness of the United States to work out arrangements on anti-dumping and countervail in the FTA should put smaller countries on the alert. Article VI-type measures—as now developed in domestic legislation in the United States, the European Communities, Australia and, of course, in Canada—are essentially protectionist. One aim of the negotiation should be to reduce these systems to their proper role—that of dealing with predatory price discrimination and genuinely damaging export subsidization—rather than to extend these systems to new areas of trade. If there are, in fact, cases of really damaging unfair trade practices in the services area, they could and should be dealt with under an Article XXIII-type system. This will, of course, make the conciliation and the dispute settlement mechanism all the more central to any general agreement on services.

'Exceptions'

It is evident from our discussion of the GATT system as it actually functions that the various exceptions to the general rules are, in fact, central to the GATT system. In a sense, GATT trade policy is about exceptions. Moreover, there is the overriding problem that major trading countries have chosen not to confine their exceptional action to the terms of the GATT provisions that authorize exceptions. For example, many preferential systems would not withstand the rigorous application of the criteria set out in Article XXIV; few, in fact, have been legally sanitized by the use of a waiver from Article I obligations under the provisions of Article XXV.[12] Another example is the widespread recourse to 'surrogate' measures in lieu of action under Article XIX; measures taken under the Multi-Fibre Arrangement are an obvious example.

In a comprehensive agreement on services, what sort of exceptions would be necessary? First, and most obviously, there is the question of how to handle the special provisions or measures that it is accepted may apply in particular sectors, though not necessarily in every jurisdiction. This is particularly evident where the service is a public monopoly or is extensively regulated; examples include radio and television broadcasting. Another important example is air transport. It is perhaps only a matter of drafting to provide that domestic air transport may be reserved to domestic carriers—an exception to the notion of national treatment and to the principle or concept of the right of commercial presence. This could be achieved, at one extreme, by excluding this sector entirely (as in the Canada-U.S. FTA and in the United

Kingdom/Japan treaty), thus leaving the definition of what measures are to be applied on a national treatment basis (e.g., airport fees and landing charges) to ICAO. An alternative would be to subsume all this in the general agreement on services and provide for the allocation of domestic routes as an exception to national treatment. The former approach seems more practical.

For publicly-owned services entities or monopolies, some provision regarding the obligations to be assumed by governments in regard to such entities, perhaps along the lines of GATT Article XVII, covering state trading enterprises, may well be appropriate. However, it may be that this GATT provision itself requires updating; the services negotiations may provide an opportunity for working toward its revision.

No doubt (as discussion in the OECD makes clear)[13] there will have to be a provision analogous to the GATT "General Exceptions" provision (Article XX) and the "security exception" (Article XXI); we say analogous because some of the GATT provisions in Article XX may not be relevant (e.g., (h), relating to obligations under any intergovernmental commodity agreement and (j), relating to products in short supply). But presumably there will be pressure to except measures alleged to be justified on national security grounds or "necessary to protect public morals" and measures "necessary to secure compliance with laws or regulations [for] the protection of patents, trade marks and copyrights, and the prevention of deceptive practices".

Given the importance the United States attaches to the issue of intellectual property on the MTN agenda, it may be that an exception along the lines noted above would require very detailed discussion, and the GATT provision itself will be addressed in intellectual property negotiations.[14]

Another major category of exceptions is the notion of free trade areas or customs unions, as allowed for in GATT Article XXIV. Should we accept that the European Communities, for example, may have a more liberal regime between its members states, in conformity with the Treaty of Rome, in regard to, say, insurance or air transport, than is agreed between the EC and other countries? Certainly the current view in Brussels is that access to the EC market for foreign services firms will be strictly on a basis of reciprocity. This is already an issue being debated between the EC Commission and the member states.[15] To the extent that what is contemplated in the U.S. proposals, for some sectors at least, is national treatment, with narrowly drawn national exceptions (like the OECD Codes), the question of preferences may not arise; for other sectors, it may be a substantive issue. For example, if in a customs union, an economic union or a free trade area foreign air carriers were permitted to serve domestic traffic, this would clearly open scope for maintaining a preferential barrier against the enterprises of third countries.

A separate question arises with regard to the nature of international scrutiny of preferential arrangements. GATT Article XXIV provides for scrutiny if the measures being applied are of a transitional character, though designed to lead to the creation of a regime in conformity with the Article. This provision has broken down in practice. Countries proposing Article XXIV measures may take the position that the arrangement entered into does meet the test of Article XXIV, thus putting the onus on third countries to demonstrate that it does not. Clearly, this is far from satisfactory, yet the creation of preferential areas that may not necessarily meet the Article XXIV criterion has been one of the main activities of post-war trade policy.

Another somewhat related issue is the question of a special dispensation of some sort for developing countries, such as the Tokyo Round concept of "special and differential" treatment. A number of observers have felt that one way to deal with a demand for special treatment for developing countries is to provide for a delay before developing countries are required to apply the stated obligations. Another technique, analogous to the GATT technique of tariff negotiation, would be negotiated lists of national exceptions by specific sectors; this could take account of development considerations. Possibly developed countries might follow a reservations or exceptions procedure while developing countries might be allowed to table only positive detailed obligations.

Another GATT-type exception, which, it is understood, has been discussed in the OECD, is a provision allowing restrictions to be imposed on imports in order to protect the balance of payments position of a signatory. It is inevitable that this issue will arise in discussion of any proposed general rules, if only with respect to the position of developing countries. Such an exception might very well enable some developing countries to maintain restrictions, possibly of a discriminatory character, on imported services for decades (given the balance of payments implications of the burden of servicing existing debt).

Finally, under the heading of exceptions, is the issue of what action should be sanctioned if imports of a particular service (or the activities of foreign-controlled services companies) cause or threaten "serious" injury to domestic producers, or "retard" the establishment of a domestic industry—that is, the analogue of the emergency provision of GATT Article XIX, the safeguard provision. No doubt the argument will be made that the existence of such a provision will enable governments to proceed further with liberalization than they would otherwise; this was the logic of Article XIX. At this stage, however, when it is not clear that such a provision is necessary, one should not proceed simply to copy

these GATT provisions, which had their origin in the particu-
larities of tariff negotiations. Carefully negotiated exceptions to
general rules, coupled with an agreement to review such
exceptions periodically, as well as provision for some sort of waiver
or temporary release from obligations (along the lines of the GATT
Article XXV), may be all that is necessary.

If a sector-specific safeguard provision along the lines of
Article XIX were to be agreed, however, a separate question would
be just how willing countries would be to abide by the rules. After
all, the central fact about GATT Article XIX is the unwillingness
of major trading countries to abide by the discipline of that article.

Conclusion

From this exposition, it is clear that the two key issues—the make-
or-break issues in a services negotiation—are how to address so-
called unfair trade practices and the question of dispute settlement. On the second issue, the smaller countries will be much
involved, particularly those developing countries with few services
exports that are striving to improve their exports of manufactured
or semi-manufactured goods. Their interests are likely to be at
risk. On the first, it seems clear that the interests of no country
will be served by extending the concepts of GATT Article VI, and
the other legal concepts of unfair trade, to the services sector. That
is not to say that the issue of unfair trade does not have to be
addressed, but rather that the Article VI system is now a
retrograde approach to this problem.

There remains the question of what is the Canadian interest.
Canadian representatives joined early with those from the United
States in urging that there be negotiations to bring restrictions on
traded services within some sort of framework of rules. One
overriding consideration has virtually determined Canadian
support for the U.S. initiative and required that Canada would be
one of the first countries to give some support to the U.S. proposal:
namely, that if the United States concludes that its interests would
be served by launching such a negotiation, Canada cannot oppose
the proposal without paying a very high price. In economic terms
we are so closely integrated with the United States, regardless of
the FTA arrangements now in place, that, as a practical matter,
our interests are not likely to be much different from those of the
United States over a range of subjects.

Moreover, it can be argued that if a major trading country
takes the view that a particular issue should be examined in the
GATT, the very minimum that is required of other signatories is
that they allow that country to have its day in the international
forum. In this particular situation, it would appear that the U.S.
Administration, or some elements or senior personalities in it,

have come to believe that the only way domestic protectionist pressures can be contained is to put together a new domestic political coalition of freer trading interests, composed of those major multinational corporations that favor trade liberalization and those major services entities that wish to remove restrictions on U.S. services exports and on U.S. investment in services facilities abroad. If the Canadian interest is trying to maintain a relatively open trading system, we must accept the result of the U.S. Administration's political calculations.

The Canadian national study on services for the GATT did not suggest that Canadian interests would be threatened by a GATT-like negotiation on services. Of course, there would be many hypothetical outcomes of such a negotiation that would be unacceptable to this or that Canadian service industry and therefore likely to be unacceptable to Canadian negotiators, just as there are possible outcomes that would be negative. The Canadian inquiry did suggest that, because of the great variations between services sectors, the most appropriate negotiating approach would be a bottom-up approach, that is, to concentrate on dealing with restrictions sector by sector, rather than trying to formulate general rules in a vacuum. Despite the effort that has gone into trying to formulate a conceptual approach, most notably at the OECD, it is hard to disagree with this early Canadian appreciation. The real issues in services are at the sectoral level, not at the level of over-drafted but vague generalities.

To say that, as a practical matter, we cannot effectively oppose the U.S. proposal for negotiations on services does not mean that, in the detail of the negotiations, as they develop, there may not be many matters where Canada will dissent from the U.S. position; it is in the detail of the negotiations that particular Canadian interests will be advanced. We are likely to find, as the negotiation proceeds, that the real risk to Canadian interests arises from premature agreement being reached in bilateral discussions between the European Communities and the United States—agreement in which Canadian interests are simply overlooked because of ignorance or misunderstanding, or agreement in which one of the big entities seeks to advance its interests, in a particular sector or across the board, by securing the consent of the other large trading entity in advance of general negotiations. The real risk to Canadian interests—in any GATT negotiation—arises in the main from the first case and from the fact that Canada has no sympathy or support in Europe, where Canada is perceived as no more than a snow-bound satellite of the United States.

Canada's support for the U.S. proposal does not mean that we are necessarily of the view that services are the most important issue to be addressed in the GATT. The importance of the Services Proposal arises from the logic of the U.S. Administration's decision to try to cobble together a new domestic alliance in support of what is presented as a liberal trade policy. There are obviously other issues that may seem, from other perspectives, to have greater priority on the MTN agenda.

As I have observed elsewhere,

> ... None of the literature on services makes an effective case for giving overwhelming priority to the "services proposal"; the priority being accorded in Washington is simply a reflection of the lobbying skills of particular interests. The priorities for governments are surely improving international monetary management, achieving more stable growth; bringing some sort of order to those sectors of traded goods where there is now autarchy and anarchy—e.g., to the trade in steel, textiles, agriculture, autos, and doing something about the access to industrial markets of the manufactured exports of developing countries. The Canadian interest, in broad economic and narrower trade terms, and in terms of foreign policy, particularly in regard to the major developing countries in the Americas, remains very much involved in these issues.[16]

Those words were written more than three years ago, but there seems to me to be no reason to alter them. I would, however, add to the agenda an item that ought to have priority, in terms of time and resources, before services—the issue of reform of the contingency protection system, particularly those elements based on Article VI of the GATT and said to be addressed to unfair trading practices. In a country like Canada, which exports so much of its production of goods, that should be a priority item on our agenda for negotiations, both in Washington and Geneva.

What we have been discussing are Canada's priorities for the Uruguay Round agenda. As the negotiations advance, new interests or concerns are becoming manifest. One is that, for a small trading country, it is vital, once a major multilateral trade negotiation is actually launched, that it not be allowed to fail. The consequences for the United States or the European Communities of a collapse or, more likely, of a failure to reach a positive conclusion may be serious; but for a country like Canada, heavily dependent on trade, a failure could be much more serious, though less serious with the FTA in place. (The same could be said for Japan and Korea; moreover, if the trade negotiations failed to conclude successfully, these two countries would be the victims of bilateral discrimination for the foreseeable future.)

It would be encouraging to think that a shared will exists to make the negotiations succeed. That applies to services as well as other items on the agenda. It is profoundly disturbing that the United States had to expend so much effort securing a reluctant and unenthusiastic consensus that services be on the agenda. That result having been achieved, U.S. enthusiasm seems to be less than maximum. This may merely reflect the fact that some of the (few) substantive and nagging problems of restrictions on services have been successfully tackled bilaterally, such as restrictions on U.S. insurance sales in Korea. However the MTN develops, and however the services issue actually gets addressed, an overriding Canadian interest is that somehow the negotiation must be concluded successfully. A successful conclusion may, of course, involve the sacrifice of some particular Canadian interest or concern; that is what it means not to be one of the major negotiating entities.

Another concern, one that many observers and, indeed, many participants fail to recognize, is the risk of securing a perverse result. The practical results of what is agreed may be not at all what the negotiators intended, or rather not what all of them intended, and certainly not what outside observers may think they see in the results. For example, it was an article of faith that the Kennedy Round negotiation of the Anti-dumping Code resulted in a moderation in and an agreed regulation of the use of anti-dumping duties, particularly by the United States and Canada. But that was true only with regard to certain aspects of the system. With regard to other aspects, the post-Kennedy Round systems of anti-dumping duties—particularly but not only in the European Communities—were more onerous (i.e., more restrictive of legitimate trade) than what existed before. This was attributable in part to one of the inevitable features of trying to negotiate rules about the application of complex administration systems. Each negotiating country insists on putting in the agreement some cover for its favorite administrative device, and at the end of the day all signatories have acquired the right to use all of them. The total of these administrative devices is likely to be more restrictive than the previous separate national systems.

The same sort of process was at work in the Tokyo Round negotiations on countervail. It has been argued that securing the application by the United States of an injury test for countervail was a clear gain in terms of liberalization, but is this evident from the record of countervail cases in the United States since the Tokyo Round? For Canada, particularly, there was the loss of the regional offset provision, which has made U.S. countervail, in that respect, more restrictive since the Tokyo Round than before it.[17] This latter result was in part the outcome—some would think inevitable—of the compromises forced on the U.S. Administration by protectionist elements in Congress. Given that not all aspects of the administrative procedures associated with a particular non-tariff measure can be specified in an international agreement, there will likely always be some scope for adding a margin of administrative protectionism when the necessary domestic legislation is being prepared.[18] One could analyze Canada's post-Kennedy Round Anti-dumping Act and the post-Tokyo Round Special Import Measures Act from this point of view, and indeed certain commentators have identified several restrictive (i.e., protectionist) features in the administration of these two acts.[19]

There is certainly some prospect that the results of a negotiation on services could yield perverse or negative results. For example, in a given sector, one country or another may agree to a less open regime than it applies; sectoral services issues that are now addressed in sectoral industry bodies (public or private) may be elevated to formal disputes involving retaliation.

My only purpose in emphasizing this negative aspect of negotiation—this propensity to produce perverse results by one route or another—is that often the negative results bear most heavily on the smaller entities. The larger entities have more bargaining power and more resources to apply to the detailed scrutiny of draft agreements and to the subsequent domestic legislative processes in other countries.[20] This element alone should incline Canadians to a relatively cautious preference for dealing with services issues sector by sector.

At this particular juncture the Canadian interest in services negotiations in Geneva is obviously closely related to the Canada-U.S. FTA. A key consideration in regard to services in the bilateral arrangement is whether it will be proposed to maintain some sort of preferential barrier against third countries. In regard to trade in goods, it may well be that for some producers there is much attraction in getting tariff-free access to the U.S. market but in maintaining, perhaps reinforcing, the barriers against imports from third countries. This would be a rational and understandable policy for both U.S. and Canadian textile producers, for example. But with regard to services, the perspective may vary from industry to industry, and a given service industry in one country or the other may conclude that its interests would not be served by a permanently preferential arrangement.

If we consider the key informatics sector, it is fairly clear from the text of the FTA that the United States contemplates a significant arrangement with Canada, but it may not wish to tie its hands in regard to other countries. I explored this issue in a short study for the Royal Bank of Canada in 1983; on the question of whether an arrangement for free trade in informatics or data processing should be preferential, I said:

> ... the United States would not be served by a preferential arrangement with Canada. A 'preferential arrangement'

is an exchange of privileges accorded by one signatory to the products of the other which it is not prepared to accord to products of a third country. It does not seem that Canada would have any particular interest in securing an advantage in the United States in this sector over other countries; moreover, the United States would have no interest in negotiating such an arrangement. The U.S. could contemplate only an open-ended arrangement, that is, an arrangement open to a third country which was prepared to offer approximately equally favorable terms of access to both Canadian and U.S. computer services.[21]

There is no reason to change this assessment. The U.S. interest in informatics is to secure the least restricted access to Europe and Japan, and it could not contemplate limiting its ability to enter into an arrangement with the European Communities (or with individual member states, such as Britain and France) or with Japan merely to create a preferential position for Canadian data-processing firms.

It is not yet clear how the transport sectors can be addressed in the MTN services discussion, although the United Kingdom long ago served notice that U.S. shipping restrictions had to be on the table.[22] The FTA outcome makes clear how difficult this will be. Canada, as an exporting country, may therefore wish to use the services discussion in Geneva to press for the removal of restrictions that raise the costs of shipping services or that discriminate against Canadian exports.

Sector by sector, Canadian interests in a services negotiation will be very much affected, if not determined, by what may be finally put in place as a result of the FTA. The issue of preferences will vary by sector. It remains that there is very little in the arguments presented by U.S. official representatives or by private advocates of a general services negotiation that responds to any perceived Canadian interest. Canada's Task Force on Trade in Services did report a number of restrictions on Canadian services exports, but it is not clear from the Task Force study that these restrictions could be removed through the technique of a general negotiation and at an acceptable price. Indeed, putting aside the Canadian interest in working with our trading partners and helping them to address the issues they perceive to be important, it is the case that the general services negotiation, as now seems the prospect, could create some real risks for Canada and for other small countries.

These risks fall under three headings. First, there is a risk that all that will be agreed are some wordy formulations that do not create real rights and obligations of the kind on which business decisions can be based. Such an exercise would be essentially futile, and not without cost. The main cost is the loss of confidence in the international order—confidence in the ability of governments to devise functionally effective rules between sovereign nations. A moment's reflection on the fact that most of what is being proposed is already covered, after a fashion, by the OECD Invisibles Code, or the fact that the Treaty of Rome long ago envisaged a common market for services, ought to make clear that it is entirely possible for governments, including the governments of the United States and Canada, to devise ineffective agreements about services. It is not desirable to proceed yet again in this fashion, but one is not persuaded, by what has been advanced by various governments or by various international secretariats, that the elements of an exchange of meaningful rights and obligations of a general, across-the-board character has as yet been devised. Surely, the reality of negotiation about services is at the sectoral level. The FTA outcome makes that, at least, fairly clear.

Second, there is a risk that the system of contingency protection (anti-dumping duties, countervailing duties, safeguards, and surrogates for safeguards) will, in time, be extended to services. If one purpose of the proposed negotiation is to protect the U.S. market against alleged unfair competition, it may well be argued that there is some sort of case for extending GATT Articles VI and XIX to services. But if unfair methods of competition are a serious concern in regard to services, then surely there is enough scope for dealing with such issues within the existing legal and regulatory framework. For example, U.S. legislation in regard to air transport and maritime transport provides domestic legal authority for retaliation against discriminatory practices by other countries. It is unlikely that most countries are not already armed in some way to deal with unfair trade in services. Radical reform of the GATT-endorsed system of contingency protection, as it applies to goods, should, ideally, be on the MTN agenda; it is more likely that the MTN will be an opportunity to secure international cover for new protectionist applications of the contingency system. It is inconceivable that Canada's interests will be served by that, or by the extension of the system to services. Nor will Canada's interest be served by adopting normative language that will provide moral justification for the United States invoking Section 301 of the Trade Act—despite the hypothetical shelter of the FTA arrangements.

Third, there is the issue of dispute settlement, so central to the U.S. position on services. I do not sense that, once away from the services industries' lobbyists in Washington, there is any great need for a *comprehensive* international dispute settlement mechanism for services, as distinct from sector-specific mechanisms. The existing sectoral arrangements surely provide well enough with such issues. For a sector, such as insurance, where there is no sectoral intergovernmental body, why not create one? The logic of the U.S. proposal on dispute settlement is that the United States wishes to get into a position where concessions on goods can be withdrawn as retaliation for restrictions on services. Clearly, this is aimed at developing countries that may not have much in the way of services exports or services companies operating in the United States; it is not particularly aimed at Canada, although if such a system had been in place, the United States might have considered restricting some Canadian export of goods, say rail cars, as retaliation for Canadian restrictions on border broadcasting.

It is not obvious that Canada has any interest in increasing the retaliatory leverage of the larger trading entities or in increasing the inherent bias of the GATT rules (or any multilateral GATT-like rules) in favor of the larger entities. Nor do I see that Canada has any interest in being seen to line up with the United States and the European Communities on this issue and against the developing countries, which should now perceive that their interests are at risk.

Many Canadian readers of this paper may have concluded that the FTA with the United States means we have much less interest in the services negotiation in Geneva. That does not appear to be the case, for various reasons. One is that, in regard to discrimination in services, the FTA provides a standstill, not a removal of discriminatory provisions—it applies only to new legislation. We have already Jeffrey Schott's comment: "The [FTA] is long on rules and short on liberalization"; this somewhat under estimates what is, in effect, the binding of existing levels of protection for a wide range of services activities. Another reason for Canada attaching importance to the multilateral negotiation is that the FTA does not cover certain key services sectors—trucking, air transport, shipping; for these sectors there is no standstill on discrimination. Schott observes that there will have to be some real liberalization emerging from Geneva (or, presumably, U.S. services industries lobbyists will not be pleased) but he notes, too, that as a practical matter, a standstill may be one of the results of the Geneva negotiation.[23] It is hard to avoid the conclusion, in looking at the FTA in regard to services, that positive liberalization will be difficult to achieve in Geneva, and that it is likely to be set out in sector-specific arrangements. Indeed, the negotiators are now turning to discuss two key services sectors: telecommunications and construction.

Epilogue – Montreal: Possibly a Beginning

The text of this study was written before trade ministers met in Montreal for the Uruguay Round mid-term assessment. Now that that meeting has taken place, this paper can be read as a discussion of how negotiators arrived at the text on services (reproduced as Annex F) agreed at Montreal, and put "on hold" until agreement was reached (in April 1989) on agriculture, intellectual property issue, textiles and safeguards.[24]

There is little point in trying to analyze what is clearly heavily negotiated and deliberately vague text, but one can offer some comments to help evaluate it.

First, one should say that, given the inherent difficulty of devising comprehensive agreements in the services area, particularly when the trade policy framework for goods is less than fully effective, the Montreal text is perhaps better, more coherent than might have been feared would be agreed.

Second, we should take the Montreal text as expressing agreement on what is essentially an agenda for negotiations on services, not as a substantive agreement in itself. The anonymous editorial writer of the London *Financial Times*, writing shortly after Ministers (and their staffs) packed their bags and left Montreal, observed that "the task before ministers at Montreal was a modest one, not so much to agree on trade policy as to agree on how to reach agreement, on trade policy." But later he continued: "The services agreement . . . describes the essential principles and objectives of progressive liberalization of trade in services, policy transparency, national treatment and non-discrimination in weasel words, as concepts, principles and rules [that] are considered relevant [to the negotiations]".[25] But to expect more than a vaguely worded agreement on an agenda for negotiating on services is, at this stage, probably unrealistic.

Third, one should note that, despite the vagueness of the Montreal text, it appears that U.S. services industries spokesmen are not dissatisfied, or at least have chosen publicly to express a degree of enthusiasm for the result. Thus James D. Robinson III, chairman and chief executive officer of American Express, chairman of the U.S. Advisory Committee on Trade Negotiations, a member of the U.S. delegation in Montreal, and a leading spokesman for the services industries, has stated that ". . . the truth is that real progress was made [at Montreal] toward international commercial disarmament." And later: ". . . the breakthrough on services lays out a timetable for continued negotiation in 1989, as well as procedures for determining how different services will be covered in the final agreement."[26] Just why the Montreal text is described as a "breakthrough" is not really clear; indeed, this expression of view is like much of the positions and postures of the U.S. services industry in the run-up to the Uruguay Round—that is, the rationale is not entirely clear to an outside observer. That is merely to say that in the Uruguay Round, U.S. services industries have their own agendas, which they may choose to keep hidden.

A fourth comment one should make on the Montreal services paper is that it reflects a substantial difference of view between the United States and the EC on services issues. Before Montreal, EC representatives pressed for a definition of 'reciprocity' in regard to services activities that would reflect both the increasing concern in Brussels that the EC must insist on some form of substantial reciprocity in such areas as financial services in regard to the United States and Japan (and Canada), but also an understanding that such an approach could not be imposed on developing countries. The United States found this difficult to accept; the U.S. view has been, and remains, that national treatment should be the standard for financial services, and that an adequate measures of reciprocity will be achieved by the adoption of a national treatment rule. Of course, national treatment is not contemplated for such sectors as air transport.[27] The debate on "reciprocity", what it is, how to find it, will continue.

A fifth comment is that the Montreal text reflects the fact the United States has more recently taken less of a leading position on services in the Uruguay Round, primarily, it appears, because U.S. officials have begun to give more weight to the implications, for their relations with countries with which they have FCN treaties, of accepting new obligations in regard to services activities. (We examined the roles of FCN treaties in Chapter IV.) This may explain why the Montreal text has only the briefest reference to "most-favoured-nation/non-discrimination". At the same time the Commission of the European Communities has become somewhat more committed to the services negotiations; this reflects the view that broad international negotiation on a subject for which the Commission is trying to devise new rules to impose on the member states serves a useful purpose. In the Tokyo Round the Commission was active in urging onward the negotiation of a code on procurement; this reflected merely the Commission's concern with prying open national procurement markets within the EC for EC suppliers; the negotiation in Geneva was thought to be a useful lever in the internal negotiation. The concern of the Commission with services in the Uruguay Round may be explained in similar terms.

These comments may help in interpreting the Montreal text; we have asserted that it is merely an agenda for negotiations, and that it is possibly a beginning. But there are other, more sombre views. The prevailing view in official Washington is that the United States must have recourse to unilateral retaliation to enforce its trade agreement rights; the growing enthusiasm for this approach to trade relations is bound to make it more difficult to reach substantive agreement in the Uruguay Round, on services and on other issues. To an extent the existence of a multilateral trade negotiation can serve as a brake on unilateralism in

Washington (and elsewhere), but there is a limit to what the traffic will bear. The outlook for 1989-1990 is, to say the least, not very promising; Professor Lester Thurow of MIT is reported to have stated (at Davos) that 1989 will be a year of "incredibly sharp trade disputes".28 Thurow is reported to have argued that the Uruguay Round should be abandoned and that GATT should be replaced by a new agreement between the emerging trading blocs: East Asia, the EC, and United States-Canada.

Given that sort of perspective, the negotiators on services (and on other issues) in Geneva will have to make a great deal of progress, to put a lot of substance against the headings of their agenda, if the Uruguay Round is to be successful.

Notes

1. See the study of Brazilian informatics policy: United Nations Centre on Transnational Corporations, *Transborder Data Flows and Brazil/A Case Study.* The public debate which developed in Britain in early 1986 as to whether it was appropriate for British Leyland, a British-controlled automobile manufacturer, to be sold to U.S. firms shows that the same sort of problem or perception sometimes and in some places exists in relation to goods.

2. The comments in this chapter relating to conventional trade agreement concepts are treated at much greater length in a study by this writer to be published shortly by the Trade Policy Research Centre in London.

3. For a detailed comment on the relationship between international rules and domestic law and procedures, see Robert G. Hudec, "Retaliation Against 'Unreasonable' Foreign Trade Practices: The New Section 301 and GATT Nullification and Impairment" 59 *Minnesota Law Review*, 1975, pp. 461-500. This discusses the case of U.S. retaliation against Canadian restrictions, which retaliation, in U.S. law, was held to be authorized by virtue of a provision (Section 252a of the Trade Expansion Act of 1962) allowing the President to retaliate against another country's alleged breach of its trade agreements obligations, as determined under U.S. domestic procedures, but which was subsequently presented to the GATT Contracting Parties as merely being the exercise of the U.S. rights to take retaliatory action under GATT Article XIX. The Canadian record in regard to the restrictions at issue was not attractive, and this may have inhibited Canadian representatives from scrutinizing carefully the U.S. action in legal terms; however, Hudec's careful analysis

of this case should be considered by Canadians who support the notion of extending the GATT to services.

4. These issues are examined in detail in Gary Clyde Hufbauer, J. Shelton Erb and H.P. Star, "The GATT Codes and the Unconditional Most-Favored-Nation Principle" 12 *Law and Policy in International Business*, No. 1, 1980, pp. 59-94; and Gary Clyde Hufbauer, "Should Unconditional MFN be Revived, Retired or Recast?" in R.H. Snape (ed.), *Issues in World Trade Policy*. For the report of the GATT Panel on the complaint of India, see *BISD* 28S, p. 113.

5. Gary Clyde Hufbauer and Jeffrey J. Schott, *Trading For Growth: The Next Round of Negotiations*, Institute for International Economics [Washington], 1985, pp. 73-74.

6. Canada-U.S. FTA, Article 1401.

7. For U.K./Japan treaty, see *Treaty of Commerce, Establishment and Navigation etc.*, November 14, 1962; for U.S./Japan treaty, see TIAS 2863, pp. 2063-2133.

8. See Jeffrey J. Schott and Murray G. Smith, "Services and Investment" in Schott and Smith (ed.), *The Canada-United States Free Trade Agreement, etc.*, p. 137. Schott and Smith are among the few commentators who have taken account of the relevance for the FTA of Canada not having an FCN Treaty with the United States.

9. See 26S *BISD*: Footnote 1 of Article 7 of the Subsidies/ Countervail Code, at p. 67.

10. See Rodney de C. Grey, *U.S. Trade Policy Legislation/A Canadian View*, Montreal, IRPP, 1983; Rodney de C. Grey: *Trade Policy and the System of Contingency Protection in the Perspective of Competition Policy*, a report prepared for the OECD Committee of Experts on Restrictive Business Practices, OECD, Paris, DAFFE/RBP/WPI/86.3; not published.

11. See, as an important example, Noel Hemmendinger, "Shifting Sands: An Examination of the Philosophical Bases of U.S. Trade Laws" in Jackson, Cunningham and Fontheim (eds.): *International Trade Policy: A Lawyer's Perspective* (New York: Matthew Bender for the American Bar Association, 1985).

12. One preference scheme for which there is a waiver is the U.S. tariff preference for Canadian automotive products. 14S

BISD, U.S. imports of automotive products; *Decision of 20 December 1965*, p. 37 and p. 181.

13. OECD, *Elements of a Conceptual Framework for Trade in Services*, p. 13.

14. It was reported in the *Financial Times* [London] (April 24, 1986) that it was the view of the U.K. authorities that trying to add intellectual property to the MTN agenda would be "overloading" and would discourage developing countries from participating. Nonetheless, the inclusion of this item was endorsed by the OECD Council of Ministers meeting in Paris, April 18, 1986 and then accepted at Punta del Este.

15. Mr. Willy de Clercq, the EC Commission for External Trade, is reported to have said: "Where international obligations do not exist, as for example, in the field of services, we see no reason why the benefits of our internal liberalization should be extended unilaterally to their country." William Dawkins, "de Clercq renews warning on EC trade after 1992" *Financial Times* [London] August 31, 1988. See also the detailed and important analysis by Bernard Cassen, "Dans la jungle du grande marché" *Le Monde Diplomatique* (Paris), September 1988.

16. Rodney de C. Grey, "The Services Industries: A Note of Caution about the Proposal to Negotiate General Rules About Traded Services" in *Canada and the Multilateral Trading System* p. 38.

17. See Rodney de C. Grey, *U.S. Trade Policy Legislation*, p. 41, for a discussion of the offset issue.

18. For an account of the political processing of the Tokyo Round results in Washington, see Gilbert R. Winham: "Robert Strauss, the MTN and the Control of Faction", 14 *Journal of World Trade Law*, No. 5, September-October 1980. Winham underestimates the protectionist features that Strauss accepted as part of the price for getting the Trade Agreements Act through Congress; the offset issue mentioned above is only one example, although an important one for Canada.

19. Notably, Klauss Stegemann. A recent paper on this subject is "Anti-dumping Policy and the Consumer", 19 *Journal of World Trade Law*, No. 5, September-October 1985, pp. 466-484. See Rodney de C. Grey, *Trade Policy and the System of Contingent Protection in the Perspective of Competition Policy*, for a more detailed discussion and for more detailed biblio-

graphical references, particularly to American writing on this issue.

20. A case in point: During the congressional consideration of the Trade Agreements Act, the EC Commission retained leading U.S. trade policy insiders, who filed a daily report as the draft legislation was examined, section by section, in *in-camera* hearings. Canada, by contrast, relied on Embassy officials for reporting on this rapidly moving process, to which, because it was taking place in closed meetings, they had little access.

21. Rodney de C. Grey, *Traded Computer Services*, p. 2.

22. See Cecil Parkinson, "Liberalization of International Trade in Services", Notes for a Speech by the Minister of Trade, Lloyd's of London, 17 September 1980. "The Americans are perhaps instinctively a little more liberal about other people's markets than about their own—witness the difficulties U.K. interests have run into trying to get into U.S. banking [*sic*] and insurance. It might be undiplomatic but it is hardly an exaggeration to say their restrictiveness in shipping matters is notorious."

23. Jeffrey J. Schott, "Implications for the Uruguay Round" in Schott and Smith (eds.), *The Canada-United States Free Trade Agreement*, p. 165. One should note the contrary views of Jules Katz, an experienced U.S. negotiator, at p. 179.

24. The decision to put the decision on services and other issues on hold until April 1989 is set out in MTN.TNC/7(MIN) 9 December 1988, p.1.

25. "Teetering on the brink" Editorial in *Financial Times* [London], December 13, 1988.

26. James D. Robinson III, "Progress Has Been Made Toward Trade Disarmament", *International Herald Tribune*, January 7-8, 1989.

27. William Dullforce and Peter Montagnon, "U.S. and EC at odds over trade in services" *Financial Times* [London], December 7, 1988; Anthony Harris, "Fed warns EC against reciprocity in banking", *Financial Times* [London], November 3, 1988; Tim Dickson, "EC 'favors' banking reciprocity changes", *Financial Times* [London], April 18, 1989; Stefan Wagstyl, EC warned [by Japanese] about reciprocity", *Financial Times* [London], April 19, 1989.

28. William Dullforce, "Year of bitter trade disputes predicted", *Financial Times* [London], January 28, 1989; Paul Magnusson, "On Trade, the U.S. Sounds the Charge—And Comes Out Firing Blanks", *Business Week*, February 6, 1989.

Selected Bibliography

There is now a very substantial literature addressed to general issues arising in regard to international services transactions and direct foreign investment in services facilities, as well as many specialized works addressed to issues in regard to particular services sectors. This bibliography lists some of the most important in the first category and a number of recent publications in the second category. The bibliography does not list more than a few economic analyses of services industries or of employment patterns as affected by the growth of services; it is intended to serve as a short guide to the literature relevant to the proposal to negotiate new multilateral general and sector-specific rules governing restrictions on services trade and investment.

Atinc, T. et al. "International Transactions in Services and Economic Development" 5 *Trade and Development* (1984), 141-214.

Balasubramanyam, U.N. "Interests of Developing Countries in the Liberalization of Trade in Services". Paper prepared for Commonwealth Seminar, London, 1988.

Beheney, Jr., Thomas Amos. "Case Comment: Federal and State Regulation of Foreign Bank Entry: *Conference of State Banking Supervisors v. Conover*" 15 *Law and Policy in International Business* No. 4 (1983), pp. 1223-1258.

Bellis, Jean-Francois, Edwin Vermulst and Phillip Miesquar. "The New EEC Regulation on Unfair Pricing Practices in Maritime Transport: A Forerunner of the Extension of Unfair Trade Concepts to Services?" 22 *Journal of World Trade* No. 1 (1988), pp. 47- 65.

Benz, Stephen F. "Trade Liberalization and the Global Service Economy" 19 *Journal of World Trade Law* No. 2 (March-April 1985), pp. 95-120.

Bernier, Ivan. "Trade in Services and the Experience of the European Economic Community". Victoria, B.C.: Institute for Research on Public Policy, 1987.

Bhagwati, Jagdish N. and Douglas A. Irwin. "The Return of the Reciprocitarians: U.S. Trade Policy Today" 10 *The World Economy* No. 2 (June 1987), pp. 109-130.

Bhagwati, Jagdish. "Splintering and Disembodiment of Services and Developing Nations" 7 *The World Economy* No. 2 (June 1984), pp. 133-144.

Bhagwati, Jagdish N. "Trade In Services and the Multilateral Trade Negotiations" 1 *World Bank Economic Review* No. 4 (September 1987), pp. 549-569.

Bhagwati, Jagdish. "Services". In J. Michael Finger and Andrzej Mechowski (ed.). *The Uruguay Round.* World Bank, 1987.

Blades, Derek. "Goods and Services in OECD Countries" 8 *OECD Economic Studies* (Spring 1987), pp. 159-184.

Böhme, Hans. *Restraints on Competition in World Shipping.* Thames Essay No. 15, London: Trade Policy Research Centre, 1978.

Brender, Anton and Joaquiem Oliveira-Martins. "Les échanges mondiaux d'invisibles: une mise en perspective statistique". *Monnaies et Finances Internationales* (n.d.).

Bressand, Albert. "Services, Corporate Strategies and GATT Negotiations. A New Challenge for Europe". Paper prepared for Ditchley Park Conference, February 1986.

Brock, William E. "A simple plan for negotiating on trade in services" 5 *The World Economy* No. 3 (November 1982), pp. 229-240.

Bylensky, Gene. "Invasion of the Service Robots" 116 *Fortune* No. 6 (September 14, 1987).

Camps, Miriam and William Diebold. *The New Multilateralism: Can the World Trading System be Saved?* New York: Council on Foreign Relations, 1983.

Carter, R.L. and G.M. Dickinson. *Barriers to Trade in Insurance* Thames Essay No. 19. London: Trade Policy Research Centre, 1979.

Chand, U.K. Ranga. "The Growth of the Service Sector in the Canadian Economy" *Social Indicators Research* No. 13 (1983) D. Reidel Publishing Company.

Chant, John F. "The Canadian Treatment of Foreign Banks: A Case Study in the Workings of the National Treatment Approach". In Stern (ed.). *Trade and Investment in Services.*

Clairmonte, F. and J. Cavanagh. "Transnational Corporations and Services: The Final Frontier", *Trade and Development, an UNCTAD Review* No. 5. UN Publication Sales No. 3.84.II.D.8.

Clendenning, E. Wayne. *The Euro-Currency Markets and the International Activities of Canadian Banks.* Ottawa: Economic Council of Canada, 1976.

Cline, William R. *"Reciprocity": A New Approach to World Trade Policy.* Policy Analyses in International Economic, No. 2. Washington: Institute for International Economics, September 1982.

Cobhan, Murray. "Small States and the Uruguay Round Negotiations on Trade in Services". Paper prepared for Commonwealth Seminar, Canada, 1988.

Cohen, Michael and Thomas Morante. "Elimination of Non-tariff Barriers to Trade in Services: Recommendations for Future Negotiations" 13 *Law and Policy in International Business* No. 2 (1981), pp. 495-519.

Colegate, Raymond. "Airline De-regulation in the United States Eight Years On" 9 *The World Economy* No. 4 (December 1986).

Collado III, Emilio. "Reciprocity Legislation". In G.C. Hufbauer (ed). *U.S. International Economic Policy, 1981/A Draft Report.* Washington: ILI, Georgetown University Law Centre, 1982.

Curzon, Gerard and Victoria Curzon-Price. "The Undermining of the World Trade Order" *30 Jahrbuch fur die Ordnung von Wirtschaft und Gesellschaft* (1979), pp. 383-407.

Curzon, Gerard and Victoria Curzon. "The Multi-Tier GATT System". In *The New Economic Nationalism.* A Battelle Conference, ed. Otto Hieronymi. London: Macmillan, 1980.

Deardorff, Alan V. "Comparative Advantage and International Trade and Investment in Services". In Stern (ed.). *Trade and Investment in Services.*

Diebold, Jr., William and Helena Stalson. "Negotiating Issues in International Service Transactions". In William R. Cline (ed.). *Trade Policy for the 1980s.* Washington, D.C.: Institute for International Economics, 1983.

Duck-woo, Nam. "A General Agreement on Trade and Services?" Paper prepared for Commonwealth Seminar. London, 1988.

Ernst, Martin L. "The Mechanization of Commerce" 247 *Scientific American* No. 3 (September 1982), pp. 111-122.

Everard, James A. "The OECD Declaration and Trade in Services". Discussion Paper. Victoria, B.C.: Institute for Research on Public Policy, 1987.

Ewing, A.F. "Why Freer Trade in Services is in the Interest of Developing Countries" 19 *Journal of World Trade Law* No. 2 (March-April 1985), pp. 147-167.

Faulhaber, Gerald R. "Financial Services: Markets in Transition". Discussion Paper No. 27, Fishman-Davidson Center for the Study of the Service Sector, Wharton School, University of Pennsylvania, 1987.

Feinman, Michael V. "National Treatment of Foreign Banks Operating in the United States: The International Banking Act of 1978" 11 *Law and Policy in International Business* No. 3 (1979), pp. 1109-1147.

Feketekuty, Geza and Kathryn Hauser. "Information Technology and Trade in Services" 52 *Economic Impact* (1985).

Feketekuty, Geza. "Negotiating Strategies in Liberalizing Trade and Investment in Services". In Stern (ed.), *Trade and Investment in Services.*

Feketekuty, Geza. *"Trade in Professional Services: An Overview,* Barriers to International Trade in Professional Services", Chicago, Legal Forum, No. 1, 1986.

Feketekuty, Geza and Jonathan Aronson. "Meeting the Challenges of the World Information Economy" 7 *The World Economy* No. 1 (March 1984), pp. 63-86.

Feketekuty, Geza. "Negotiations on Trade in Services in the Uruguay Round of Multilateral Trade Negotiations". Paper prepared for NBER conference, August 1987.

Feketekuty, Geza. *International Trade in Services/An Overview and Blueprint for Negotiations* Cambridge, Mass.: AEI/ Ballinger, 1988.

Findlay, Christopher. *A Framework for Services Trade Policy Questions.* Pacific Economic Papers, No. 126. Canberra: ANU, 1985.

Fisher, Bart S. and Ralph G. Stienhardt III. "Section 301 of the Trade Act of 1974: Protection for U.S. Exporters of Goods, Services and Capital" 14 *Law and Policy in International Business* No. 3 (1982), pp. 569-690.

Fortune International, No. 12, June 10, 1985. "The Fortune Service 500/The Largest U.S. Non-Industrial Corporation."

Frazee, Rowland C. *Trade and Technology: It's Canada's Move,* Montreal: Royal Bank of Canada, 1983.

Friedman, Kenneth J. "The 1980 Canadian Banks and Banking Law Revision Act: Competitive Stimulus or Protectionist Barrier?" 13 *Law and Policy in International Business* No. 3 (1981), pp. 483-810.

Gadbaw, R. Michael. "Reciprocity and Its Implications for U.S. Trade Policy" 14 *Law and Policy in International Business* No. 3 (1982), pp. 691-746

Ganley, Oswald H. *The United States–Canadian Communications and Information Resources Relationship and Its Possible Significance for Worldwide Diplomacy* Harvard University (n.d.).

Gavin, Brigit. "A GATT for International Banking?" 19 *Journal of World Trade Law* No. 2 (March/April 1985), pp. 121-135.

Geehan, Randall. *A Survey and Analysis of the Availability of Data on Canada's Exports and Imports of Services. Report to Task Force on Trade in Services.* Ottawa: April 1982.

Gershuny, Jonathan and Ian Miles. *The New Service Economy/ The Transformation of Employment in Industrial Societies.* London: Frances Pinter, 1983.

Giarini, Orio (ed.). *The Emerging Service Economy.* Oxford: Pergamon for the Services World Forum, 1987.

Gibbs, Murray. "Continuing the International Debate on Services" 19 *Journal of World Trade Law* No. 3 (May-June 1985), pp. 199-218.

Ginzberg, Eli and George J. Vojta. "The Services Sector of the U.S. Economy" 244 *Scientific American* Number 3 (March 1981), pp. 32-39.

Giuliano, Vincent E. "The Mechanization of Office Work" 247 *Scientific American* No. 3 (September 1982), pp. 124-135.

Goldberg, Paul M. and Charles P. Kindleberger. "Towards a GATT for Investment: A Proposal for Supervision of the International Corporation" 2 *Law and Policy in International Business* (1970), pp. 225-325.

Gotlieb, Alan, C. Dalfen, and K. Katz. "The Transborder Transfer of Information by Communications and Computer Systems: Issues and Approaches to Guiding Principles" 68 *American Journal of International Law*, (1974).

Gray, Peter H. "A Negotiating Strategy for Trade on Services" 17 *Journal of World Trade Law* No. 5 (September/October 1983), pp. 377-388.

Grey, Rodney de C. "The Services Industries: A Note of Caution about the Proposal to Negotiate General Rules about Traded Services". Paper for the Royal Commission on the Economic Union and Economic Development Prospects for Canada. Ottawa: 1984. In John Whalley (ed.) *Canada and the Multilateral Trading System,* Toronto: University of Toronto Press, 1985.

Grey, Rodney de C. *U.S. Trade Policy Legislation/A Canadian View.* Montreal: Institute for Research on Public Policy, 1982.

Grey, Rodney de C. "The General Agreement After the Tokyo Round". In John Quinn and Philip Kayton (ed.). *Non-Tariff Barriers After the Tokyo Round.* Montreal: Institute for Research on Public Policy, 1982.

Grey, Rodney de C. *Traded Computer Services: An Analysis of a Proposal for Canada/U.S.A. Agreement.* Montreal: Royal Bank of Canada, 1983.

Grey, Rodney de C. "Contingent Protection, Managed Trade, and the Decay of the Trade Relations System". In R.H. Snape (ed). *Issues in World Trade Policy.* London: Macmillan, 1986.

Grey, Rodney de C. "Negotiations About Trade and Investment in Services". In Stern (ed.). *Trade and Investment in Services.*

Grey, Rodney de C. "Elements of a General Agreement in Information Trade" 15 *Inter Media* (March 1987).

Grey, Rodney de C. "The Conflict Between Trade Policy and Competition Policy". In E-V Petersmann and Meinhard Hilf, *The New GATT Round of Multilateral Trade Negotiations/ Legal and Economic Problems.* Deventer/Boston: Kluwer, 1988.

Griffiths, Brian. *Invisible Barriers to Invisible Trade.* London: Macmillan for the Trade Policy Research Centre, 1975.

Grubel, Herbert G. "Does the World Need a GATT for Services" Discussion Paper. Vancouver: The Fraser Institute.

Grubel, Herbert G. "Traded Services Are Embodied in Materials or People" 10 *The World Economy* No. 3 (Spring 1987), pp. 319-330.

Hansen, David P. "Regulation of the Shipping Industry: An Economic Analysis of the Need for Reform" 12 *Law and Policy in International Business* No. 4 (1980), pp. 973-999.

Hindley, Brian and Alasdair Smith. "Comparative Advantage and Trade in Services" 7 *The World Economy* No. 4 (December 1984), pp. 369-89.

Hindley, Brian. "Introducing Services into GATT". Paper prepared for conference organized by the Spanish Ministry of Finance and the Economy and the Trade Policy Research Centre, 1986.

Hudec, R. "GATT Dispute Settlement After the Tokyo Round: An Unfinished Business" 31 *Cornell International Law Journal* (1981), pp. 391-432.

Hufbauer, G.C. "Should Unconditional MFN be Revived, Retired or Recast?". In R.H. Snape (ed.). *Issues in World Trade Policy*. London: Macmillan, 1986.

Hufbauer, G.C., J.S. Erb, and H.P. Starr. "The GATT Codes and the Unconditional Most-Favored-Nation Principle" 12 *Law and Policy in International Business* No. 1 (1980), pp. 59-93.

Haltman, Charles W. "International Banking and U.S. Commercial Policy" 19 *Journal of World Trade Law* No. 3 (May-June 1985), pp. 219-228.

Inman, Robert P. (ed.). *Managing the Service Economy/Prospects and Problems*. Cambridge University Press for Wharton School, 1985.

Jackson, John H. "Constructing a Constitution for Trade in Services" 11 *The World Economy* No. 2 (June 1988), pp. 187-202.

Jackson, John H. "The Crumbling Institutions of the Liberal Trade System" 12 *Journal of World Trade Law* 2 (March-April 1978).

Jackson, John H. (ed.). *Legal Problems of International Economic Relations*. St. Paul, Minnesota: West Publishing Co., 1977.

Jackson, John H. *World Trade and the Law of the GATT*. Indianapolis: Bobbs-Merrill, 1969.

Jones, Ronald W. "A Comment on Comparative Advantage and International Trade in Services". In Stern (ed.): *Trade and Investment in Services*.

Kakabadse, Mario A. *International Trade in Services/Prospects for Liberalization in the 1990s*. The Atlantic Institute for International Affairs, 1987.

Kasper, Daniel M. "Trade Liberalization in Air Services: How to Get There from Here" 11 *The World Economy* No. 1 (March 1988), pp. 91-107.

Keiner, Bruce R. Jr. "The 1966 Carrier Agreements: The United States Retains the Warsaw Convention" 7 *Virginia Journal of International Law* No. 1 (December 1966), 140-256.

(T.S.T. Key). "Services in the U.K. Economy" 25 *Bank of England Quarterly Bulletin* No. 3 (September 1986), 404-414.

Kierzkowski, Henryk. *Services in the Development Process and Theory on International Trade.* Geneva: UNCTAD, June 1984.

Kirkland, Jr., Richard I. "Are Service Jobs Good Jobs?" *Fortune International* No. 12 (June 10, 1985).

Koekkock, K.A. "Trade in Services, the Developing Countries and the Uruguay Round" 11 *The World Economy* No. 1 (March 1988), pp. 151-155.

Kommenacker, Raymond J. *World Traded Services: The Challenges for the Eighties.* Dedham, MA: Artech House, Inc., 1984.

Kommenacker, Raymond J. "Trade Related Services in GATT" 13 *Journal of World Trade Law* No. 6 (1979), pp. 510-522.

Kommenacker, Raymond J. "Services Negotiations: From Interest-Lateralization to Multilateralism in the Context of the Servicization of the Economy". Conference paper, 1987 (forthcoming).

Larsen, Paul B. and Valerie Vetterick. "The UNCTAD Code of Conduct for Liner Conferences: Reservations, Reactions and U.S. Alternatives" 13 *Law and Policy in International Business* No. 1 (1981), pp. 223-280.

Lissilzyn, Oliver J. "Bilateral Agreements on Air Transportation" 30 *Journal of Air Law and Commerce* No. 3 (1964), pp. 248-263.

Lohmann, Carl J. and William C. Murden. "Policies for the Treatment of Foreign Participation in Financial Markets and Their Application in the U.S.-Canada Free Trade Agreement". Conference paper, (January, 1988).

Malmgren, Harald B. "Negotiating International Rules for Services" 8 *The World Economy* No. 1 (March 1985), pp. 11-26.

Malmgren, Harald B. "Threats to the Multilateral System". In William R. Cline (ed.). *Trade Policy In the 1980s.*

Marston, Geoffrey. "The U.N. Convention on Registration of Ships" 20 *Journal of World Trade Laws* No. 5 (September/ October 1986), pp. 573-580.

McKellar, Neil L. *A Classification of Services for International Trade/Report to Task Force on Trade in Services.* Ottawa: March 1982.

Moroz, Andrew R. "Legal, Institutional and Negotiating Issues in Trade in Services". Conference paper. The Fraser Institute, 1986.

Noyelle, Thierry. "International Trade and FDI in Services: A Review Essay" *CTC Reporter* No. 23 (Spring 1987).

Nusbaumer, Jacques. *Les Services/Nouvelle Donné de l'Économie.* Paris: Economica, 1984.

Nusbaumer, Jacques. *The GATT and Services—Issues and Prospects.* Paper prepared for CSI/LOTIS Services Industries Conference, February 1986.

Pecchioli, R.M. *The Internationalization of Banking: The Policy Issues.* Paris: OECD, 1983.

Pryke, Richard. *Competition Among International Airlines* London: Trade Policy Centre, 1987.

Quinn, James Brian, Jordan J. Baruch and Penny Cushman Paquette. "Technology in Services" 257 *Scientific American* (December 1987), pp. 24-32.

Quinn, James Brian and Christopher E. Gagnon. "Will Services Follow Manufacturing into Decline?" *Harvard Business Review* (November/December 1986), pp. 95-103.

Rada, J. *International Division of Labour and New Information Technology with Special Reference to Services.* Geneva: ILO, 1984.

Randhawa, P.S. "Punta del Este and After: Negotiations on Trade in Services and the Uruguay Round" 21 *Journal of World Trade Law* (August 1987), pp. 163-171.

Revell, J.R.S. *Banking and Electronic Fund Transfers.* Paris: OECD, 1983.

Riddle, Dorothy I. "Critical Issues in Services Research/A Literature Review". November 1985 (photocopy).

Riddle, Dorothy I. *Service-Led Growth/The Role of the Service Sector in World Development.* Westport, Conn.: Greenwood Press, 1986.

Roseman, Daniel. "Trade in Services: Lessons of the Canada/ United States Free Trade Agreement". Notes for a presentation to the Annual Conference of the Services World Forum, Geneva, 1988.

Rothschild, Emma. "The Real Reagan Economy" *New York Review of Books* (June 30, 1988).

Sampson, Gary P. and Richard H. Snape. "Identifying the Issues in Trade in Services" 8 *The World Economy* No. 2 (June 1985), pp. 141-181.

Sapir, André. "Determinants of Trade in Services". CEME Discussion Paper No. 8104, Université Libre de Bruxelles, 1981.

Sapir, André. "Trade in Services: Policy Issues for the Eighties" *Columbia Journal of World Business* (Fall 1982), pp. 77-83.

Sapir, André. "The Role of Services in the International Division of Labour between the Industrialized and the Developing Countries". Presented at Conference on Restrictions on Transactions in the International Market for Services, May 13-June 2, 1984.

Sapir, André and Ernst Lutz. *Trade in Non-Factor Services: Past Trends and Current Issues.* World Bank Staff Working Paper No. 410, 1980.

Sapir, André and Ernst Lutz. *Trade in Services: Economic Determinants and Development-Related Issues.* World Bank Staff Working Paper No. 480, 1981.

Sapir, André. "North-South Issues in Trade in Services" 8 *The World Economy* No. 1 (March 1985), pp. 27-42.

Sauvant, Karl P. *Trade and Foreign Direct Investment in Data Services.* Boulder and London: Westview/Praeger, 1984.

Sauvant, Karl P. *International Transactions in Services/The Politics of Transborder Data Flows* Boulder and London: Westview, 1986.

Sauvant, Karl P. "Services in the Japanese Economy". In Robert P. Inman (ed.) *Managing the Services Economy.*

Saxonhouse, Gary R. "Services in the Japanese Economy". In Robert P. Inman (ed.) *Managing the Services Economy.*

Schott, Jeffrey J. "Protectionist Threat to Trade and Investment in Services" 6 *The World Economy* No. 2 (June 1983), pp. 195-214.

Schott, Jeffrey J. "Services and the World Trading System". Statement before the Subcommittee on Economic Stabilization, Committee on Banking, Finance, and Urban Affairs, House of Representatives, June 4, 1984.

Schott, Jeffrey J. and Jacqueline Mazza. "Trade in Services and Developing Countries" 20 *Journal of World Trade Law* No. 3 (May/June 1986), pp. 253-273.

Schott, Jeffrey J. and Murray G. Smith. "Services and Investment". In Schott and Smith (ed.). *The Canada-United States Free Trade Agreement: The Global Impact.* Washington: Institute for International Economics; Ottawa: Institute for Research on Public Policy, 1988.

Schott, Jeffrey J. "Implications for the Uruguay Round". In Schott and Smith (ed.). *The Canada-United States Free Trade Agreement.*

Semkow, Brian W. "Japanese Banking Law: Current Deregulation and Liberalization of Domestic and External Financial Transactions" 17 *Law and Policy in International Business* No. 1 (1985), pp. 81-156.

Sheehey, Christopher. "Japan's New Foreign Lawyer Law" 19 *Law and Policy in International Business* No. 2 (1987), pp. 361-383.

Shelp, Ronald Kent et al. *Service Industries and Economic Development.* New York: Praeger, 1984.

Shelp, Ronald K. *Beyond Industrialization: Ascendancy of the Global Service Economy.* New York: Praeger, 1981.

Shelp, Ronald K. "The Proliferation of Foreign Insurance Laws: Reform or Regression" 8 *Law and Policy in International Business* (1976), pp. 701-735.

Siegel, Brenda. "The Internationalization of Service Transactions: The Role of Foreign Direct Investment in International Trade In Services". *Discussion Paper.* Victoria, B.C.: Institute for Research on Public Policy, 1987.

Sion, L. Gilles. "Multilateral Air Transport Agreement Reconsidered: The Possibility of a Regional Agreement Between North Atlantic States" 22 *Virginia Journal of International Law* No. 1 (Fall 1981), pp. 155-218.

Spero, Joan Edelman. "Information: The Policy Void" 48 *Foreign Policy* (Fall 1982).

Spero, Joan Edelman. "Barriers to U.S. Services Trade". Statement before the Subcommittee on International Finance and Monetary Policy, Senate Committee on Banking, Housing and Urban Affairs, November 9, 1981.

Stalson, Helena. "International Service Transactions". In Robert P. Inman (ed.). *Managing the Services Economy.*

Stern, Robert (ed.). *Trade and Investment in Services: Canada/ U.S. Perspectives.* Toronto: Ontario Economic Council, 1985.

Summers, Robert. "Services in the International Economy". In Robert P. Inman (ed.). *Managing the Services Economy.*

Summers, Robert and Alan Heston. "The International Demand for Services". Discussion Paper #32, Fishman-Davidson Centre for the Study of the Service Sector, Wharton School, University of Pennsylvania.

Tumlir, Jan. "Need for an Open Multilateral Trading System" 6 *The World Economy* No. 4 (December 1983), pp. 393-408.

Tumlir, Jan. "International Economic Order: Can the Trend be Reversed?" 5 *The World Economy* No. 1 (March 1982), pp. 29-41.

Tumlir, Jan. "The Protectionist Threat to International Order" 34 *International Journal* (1978- 79), pp. 53-63.

VanGrasstech, Craig. "Trade in Services: Obstacles and Opportunities" 59 *Economic Impact* No. 3 (1987).

Walter, Ingo. *Barriers to Trade in Banking and Financial Services.* London: Trade Policy Research Centre, 1985.

Ward, G. et al. *The Marine Insurance Industry in Canada.* Ottawa: Canadian Transport Commission, (April 1978).

Yachelsar, John N. and Gordon Cloney (ed.) *Services and U.S. Trade Policy.* Washington: Georgetown University, (1982).

Bank for International Settlements. *Recent Innovations in International Banking.* Bâle: (April 1986) (The Cross Report).

Government of Canada, Department of Industry, Trade and Commerce. *Task Force on Trade in Services, Background Report.* Ottawa: October, 1982.

Organization for Economic Cooperation and Development (OECD) *International Trade in Services: Banking.* Paris: 1984.

OECD Secretariat. *Deregulation and Airline Competition.* Paris: 1988.

OECD. *International Trade in Services: Insurance; Identification and Analysis of Obstacles.* Paris: 1983.

OECD. *Code of Liberalization of Current Invisible Operations.* Paris: December 1976 (Update of March 1973 Edition).

OECD. *Elements of a Conceptual Framework for Trade in Services.* OECD Secretariat (Trade Committee) TC/WP/85/9. Paris: 1985.

U.K. *Regulatory Arrangements at Lloyd's, Report of the Committee of Inquiry.* (Neil Report). CM 59. London: HMSO, 1987.

UNCTAD. *Action on the Question of Open Registries.* Report by the UNCTAD Secretariat. TD/B/C.4/220, March 3, 1981.

UNCTAD. *Production and Trade in Services: Policies and their Underlying Factors Bearing upon International Services Transactions.* TD/B/941/Rev 1.

UNCTAD. *Services and the Development Process.* TD/B/1000/Rev. 1.

UNCTAD. *Services.* Report by the UNCTAD Secretariat. TD/B/1162, February 1988.

UNCTAD. *Trade and Development Report 1988.* UN Sales No. E.88.11.D.8. "Part Two: Services in the World Economy", pp. 135-219.

UN Centre for Transnational Corporations. *Transnational Banks: Operations, Strategies and Their Effects on Developing Countries.* New York: 1981.

United Nations, *Work by the United Nations Centre on Transitional Corporations on Transitional Corporation in Services and Transborder data flows.* February 1987. (A bibliography of UNCTC material).

U.S. Office of the Comptroller of the Currency, *Acquisitions of U.S. Banks.* 1982.

U.S. Department of the Treasury, *Report to Congress on Foreign Government Treatment of U.S. Commercial Banking Organizations.* 1979, up-dated 1984.

U.S. Department of Commerce, International Trade Administration. *Current Developments in U.S. International Service Industries.* March 1980.

U.S. Office of the United States Trade Representative. *U.S. National Study on Trade in Services.* Washington; 1983.

U.S. Congress, Office of Technology Assessment. *Trade in Services: Exports and Foreign Revenues.* Special Report. OTA-ITE-316. Washington: September 1986.

U.S. Congress, House of Representatives. Sub-Committee on Economic Stabilization, Committee on Banking, Finance and Urban Affairs. *Service Industries: The Changing Shape of the American Economy,* 98th Congress, Second Session. November 1984.

U.S. Congress, Office of Technology Assessment. *International Competition in Services/Banking, Building, Software, Know-How.* Washington: July 1987.

Walker, R.J. and Dermot Tremble. "Japanese Banks in London" 27 *Bank of England Quarterly Bulletin* (November 1987), pp. 518-524.

Walter, Ingo. "Global Competition in Financial Services". Conference paper. November 1987 (photocopy).

Yoon-Je, Cho. "How the United States Broke into Korean's Insurance Market" 10 *The World Economy* No. 4 (December 1987), pp. 483-496.

Ypsilanti, Dimitri and Robin Marsell. "Reforming Telecommunications Policy in OECD Countries" *OECD Observer* No. 148 (October/November 1987), pp. 18-23.

Annex A

Text of the notification in 1976 by the
Canadian Delegation to the OECD of

"Canadian Exceptions to National Treatment"

This text identifies the extent to which, for Canada, 'national treatment' has not been extended in certain services sectors.

Quote: Attached is a list of laws and regulations of the Canadian Federal Government and certain provinces which provide for treatment of foreign controlled enterprises different to that accorded domestic enterprises.

Canada, as is the case with other OECD countries, has legislation which identifies particular sectors considered to be of strategic economic or cultural importance. These sectors include banking and other financial institutions, insurance, certain aspects of resource development, and publishing. The right of establishment by a foreign investor in these sectors is regulated in some manner. The instrument of national treatment does not cover the right of establishment and as such these items have not been listed.

Finally, in the field of tax obligations, the Canadian tax system does not generally provide for differential treatment when it comes to the operations of foreign interests as opposed to Canadian owned and/or controlled operations, because liability for tax is based on the notion of residence rather than nationally. There is a very limited number of exceptions to this principle such as some special roll-over provisions only applicable to Canadian partnerships and Canadian corporations and some special tax provisions for Canadian corporations that are Investment Corporations, Mortgage Investment Corporations or Mutual Fund Corporations. These are included in the attached list.

BY NATURE OF OPERATIONS

1. *Tax obligations*

(i) FEDERAL

Income Tax Act

Corporations formed in accordance with the laws of a foreign state and not resident in Canada on and after 18th June, 1971 (non-Canadian corporations) are not entitled to tax-free roll-over provisions and cannot qualify under certain special status corporations rules such as Investment Corporations or Mortgage Investment Corporations. Non-Canadian partnership (e.g. where one or more members are not resident in Canada) are also not entitled to tax-free roll-overs of assets.

(ii) PROVINCIAL

(a) Ontario

The Land Transfer Tax Act

Under this Act, effective 10th April, 1974, the Land Transfer Tax on acquisitions of land by non-residents was increased to 20 per cent of the value of the consideration for sale. The rate for residents remained at 3/10 of 1 per cent on the first $35,000 and 6/10 of 1 per cent on the balance. A "non-resident" is an individual who is not ordinarily resident in Canada or if resident in Canada is neither a Canadian citizen nor lawfully admitted to Canada for permanent residence. A non-resident corporation is defined in the context of ownership of its shareholdings or occupancy of directors' positions by non-resident individuals.

A deferral or remission may be made where it can be shown that the acquisition was or is to be used for the purpose of development and subsequent resale of residential, commercial or industrial projects, or for the purpose of establishing, expanding, or relocating an active business.

The Land Speculation Tax Act

Under the Act, a tax of 20 per cent is imposed on the taxable value of designated land (all real property in Ontario except Canadian resource property). Where the transfer of controlling interests in a corporation, more than 50 per cent of whose assets are comprised of designated land, is considered to be a takeover by a non-resident corporation, as defined in the Land Transfer Tax Act, then an additional tax is imposed at the rate of 20 per cent of the proceeds of dispositions on designated land.

(b) Québec
Land Transfer Duties Act

Under this Act a duty is levied on the transfer of land to "non-resident persons". In addition, when in control of and existing corporation owning principally land is acquired by "non-resident persons", either from a resident or another non-resident, such corporation becomes liable for land transfer duties. A non-resident is an individual who is not ordinarily resident in Canada or if resident in Canada is neither a Canadian citizen nor lawfully admitted to Canada for permanent residence. A corporation is non-resident when more than 50 per cent of its voting capital stock or more than 50 per cent of its directors are non-resident individuals. The Act provides for exemptions from duties in several defined circumstances.

2. *Right to official aid and subsidies*

(i) FEDERAL
Northern Mineral Exploration Assistance Regulations

These regulations provide for grants to persons who intend to do exploratory work in Northern Canada. Such persons must in general be either Canadian citizens or a Canadian corporation whose shares are either owned at least 50 per cent by Canadians . . . .

Western Grains Stabilization Act

The Act provides for stabilization payments to grain producers. To be eligible for such payments the producer must be (a) a Canadian citizen or a landed immigrant or (b) a corporation with more than 50 per cent of its shares owned by Canadian citizens or landed immigrants.

(ii) PROVINCIAL

(a) Alberta

Agricultural Development Act

Under the Agricultural Development Act, to be eligible for a loan or loan guarantee by the Alberta Agricultural Development Corporation, an applicant must be a Canadian resident. A corporation is eligible for a loan provided that it is a resident of Alberta; that it is incorporated in Canada; and that non-resident ownership and control does not exceed 20 per cent of the issued and outstanding shares. A non-resident includes an individual who is not a Canadian citizen or a landed immigrant.

A partnership having non-resident partners is not eligible for a loan if the beneficial interest of non-resident partners exceeds 20 per cent of the fair market value of the partnership property or 20 per cent of the actual purchase price of the partnership property at the time the application for a loan is made, whichever is greater, and if the profits to which the non-resident partners are entitled exceed 20 per cent of the total profits.

Alberta Opportunity Fund Act

Under this Act the Alberta Opportunity Company, in providing loans or other assistance to commercial enterprises in Alberta, is required to give priority to those enterprises owned and operated by Canadian citizens residing in Alberta.

(b) Québec

Booksellers Accreditation Act

Regulations made under this Act stipulate that the Québec government may grant subsidies for the publication and distribution of books only to companies or corporations provided that:

- they are incorporated under Québec laws;

- they have their main place of business in Québec;

- the majority of the directors are Canadian citizens domiciled in Québec;

- the president, the general manager, the assistant manager and the secretary treasurer are Canadian citizens domiciled in Québec;

- 50 per cent of the shares issued, representing at least 50 per cent of the votes which may be cast at a meeting of the shareholders and 50 per cent of the combined paid-up capital and acquired surplus belong to one or more corporations satisfying the conditions specified above.

An Act respecting the guarantee of certain loans to Publishers and Booksellers and to amend the Québec Industrial Development Assistance Act

Under this Act the Minister of Cultural Affairs, after approval, where required, of the Lieutenant-Governor in Council, will authorize the guarantee of loans to eligible publishers or booksellers. To be considered eligible an individual must be a Canadian citizen or landed immigrant domiciled in Québec. In the case of a corporation the majority of its directors must be Canadian citizens and more than 50 per cent of the shares must be owned by Canadian citizens domiciled in Québec.

(b) Saskatchewan

Agricultural Incentives Act

Under the Agricultural Incentives Act, to be considered eligible for financial assistance, a farmer must be a *Canadian citizen* or a landed immigrant residing in Saskatchewan. The same conditions hold for each member in respect of a farming partnership or co-operative farming association, and for each shareholder of a farming association.

3.   *Access to bank credit and capital market*

4. *Government purchasing and public contracts*

(i) PROVINCIAL

(a) Ontario

Under administrative guidelines Ontario government advertising contracts are only to be awarded to 100 per cent Canadian controlled corporations based in Ontario.

5. *Other*

(i) Foreign Investment Review Act

The Act gives the Government authority to review investment proposals by non-eligible persons in the context of "significant benefit to Canada" criteria. Generally speaking a non-eligible person is an individual who is not a Canadian citizen or a Canadian citizen who is not ordinarily resident in Canada (with some exceptions); a foreign government or an agency of a foreign government; or a corporation that is controlled by one or more non-eligible persons.

The Act applies to a foreign controlled corporation already in Canada if that corporation acquires control of another business enterprise in Canada. There is an exception if the business enterprise being acquired has gross assets not exceeding $250,000 and gross revenues not exceeding $3,000,000 and if the business in Canada of the enterprise being acquired is related to the business in Canada of the foreign controlled corporation making the acquisition. The Act also applies to a foreign controlled corporation with an existing business in Canada if that corporation establishes a new business in Canada and the new business is unrelated to the existing business.

BY SECTORS

6. *Sectors where investment at second remove requires authorization*

See the Foreign Investment Review Act above.

7. *Sectors subject to internal regulation*

(i) FEDERAL

Broadcasting Act

Directives issued under the Broadcasting Act stipulate that a licence to operate a broadcasting station, or permission to operate a network of broadcasting stations, can only be granted to a Canadian citizen; or to a Canadian corporation of which the Chairman and each of the directors are Canadian citizens and of which four-fifths of the shares are owned either by Canadian citizens or by Canadian-controlled corporations. An exception may be allowed in the case of an application for the removal of a broadcasting licence that was outstanding on 1st April, 1968, providing the Commission is satisfied that granting a renewal would not run contrary to public interest and providing the Governor in Council, by order, approves such a renewal.

Canadian Mining Regulations

Mining leases in the Northwest Territories can only be granted to a Canadian citizen, or to a corporation incorporated in Canada the shares of which are either 50 per cent beneficially-owed by Canadian citizens or listed on a recognized Canadian stock exchange, and Canadians will have an opportunity of participating in the financing and ownership of the corporation.

Canada Oil and Gas Land Regulations

An oil and gas lease in the Yukon or Northwest Territories shall not be granted to a person who is not a Canadian citizen, to a corporation incorporated outside of Canada or to a corporation unless at least 50 per cent of the issued shares are beneficially-owned by persons who are Canadian citizens or the shares of the corporation are listed on a recognized Canadian stock exchange and Canadians have an opportunity of participating in the financing and ownership of the corporation.

(ii) PROVINCIAL

(a) Alberta

Public Lands Act

Under this Act an applicant for homestead sale must be a Canadian citizen or a British subject or must declare in his application his intention to become a Canadian citizen.

Regulations under this Act provide for the issue of grazing leases only to corporations the majority of whose shares are owned by Canadian citizens resident in Alberta for their own exclusive use and benefit.

Under the Farm Development Regulations only a Canadian citizen may apply to exchange, lease or purchase public land.

(b) British Columbia

Land Act

Under this Act non-Canadian citizens are not entitled to a Crown grant. There is an exception in the case of non-Canadian citizens whose application for a disposition of Crown land was allowed prior to 3rd April, 1970.

(c) Ontario

Securities Act

Regulations promulgated pursuant to the Securities Act constitute a complex network of restrictions with respect to the renewal of registrations for non-residents dealing in securities. The manner in which non-resident registrants may conduct their operations are also governed by regulations. Unquote.

Annex B

OECD Declaration on Transborder Data Flows

This text makes clear how difficult it will be to agree on precise, meaningful, contractual obligations in some services sectors.

Quote: This Declaration represents the first international effort to address economic issues raised by the information revolution. It addresses the policy issues arising from transborder data flows such as flows of data and information related to trading activities, intracorporate flows, computerised information services and scientific and technological exchanges. These flows are playing an increasingly important role in the economies of Member countries and in international trade and services.

In adopting this Declaration, the governments of OECD Member countries expressed their intention to promote access to data and information, and to develop common approaches for dealing with transborder data flows issues. They agreed to undertake further work on the main issues emerging from transborder data flows.

Declaration

Rapid technological developments in the field of information, computers and communications are leading to significant structural changes in the economies of Member countries. Flows of computerised data and information are an important consequence of technological advances and are playing an increasing role in national economies. With the growing economic interdependence of Member countries, these flows acquire an international dimension, known as Transborder Data Flows. It is therefore appropriate for the OECD to pay attention to policy issues connected with these transborder data flows.

This declaration is intended to make clear the general spirit in which Member countries will address these issues. In view of the above, the Governments of OECD member countries:

Acknowledged that computerised data and information now circulate, by and large, freely on an international scale;

Considering the OECD Guidelines on the Protection of Privacy and Transborder Flows of Personal Data and the significant progress that has been achieved in the area of privacy protection at national and international levels;

Recognising the diversity of participants in transborder data flows, such as commercial and non-commercial organisations, individuals and governments, and recognising the wide variety of computerised data and information, traded or exchanged across national borders, such as data and information related to trading activities, intracorporate flows, computerised information services and scientific and technological exchanges;

Recognising the growing importance of transborder data flows and the benefits that can be derived from transborder data flows; and recognising that the ability of Member countries to reap such benefits may vary;

Recognising that investment and trade in this field cannot but benefit from transparency and stability of policies, regulations and practices;

Recognising that national policies which affect transborder data flows reflect a range of social and economic goals, and that governments may adopt different means to achieve their policy goals;

Aware of the social and economic benefits resulting from access to a variety of sources of information and of efficient and effective information services;

Recognising that Member countries have a common interest in facilitating transborder data flows, and in reconciling different policy objectives in this field.

Having due regard to their national laws, do hereby declare their intention to:

- Promote access to data and information and related services, and avoid the creation of unjustified barriers to the international exchange of data and information;

- Seek transparency in regulations and policies relating to information, computer and communications services affecting transborder data flows;

- Develop common approaches for dealing with issues related to transborder data flows and, when appropriate, develop harmonized solutions;

- Consider possible implications for other countries when dealing with issues related to transborder data flows.

Bearing in mind the intention expressed above, and taking into account the work being carried out in other international fora, the Governments of OECD member countries,

Agree that further work should be undertaken and that such work should concentrate at the outset on issues emerging from the following types of transborder data flows:

- Flows of data accompanying international trade;

- Marketed computer services and computerised information services; and

- Intra-corporate data flows.

The Governments of OECD member countries agreed to co-operate and consult with each other in carrying out this important work, and in furthering the objectives of this Declaration. Unquote.

Annex C

GATT Decisions on Services

These texts make clear how cautiously the Contracting Parties to the GATT have approached the Services Proposal.

Quote: **Ministerial Declaration of 29 November, 1982**

Services

The Contracting Parties decide:

1.   To recommend to each contracting party with an interest in services of different types to undertake, as far as it is able, national examination of the issues in this sector.

2.   To invite contracting parties to exchange information on such matters among themselves, *inter alia* through international organizations such as GATT. The compilation and distribution of such information should be based on as uniform a format as possible.

3.   To review the results of these examinations, along with the information and comments provided by relevant international organizations, at their 1984 Session and to consider whether any multilateral action in these matters is appropriate and desirable. Unquote.

Fortieth Session of the Contracting Parties: Action taken on 30 November 1984

Quote: The CONTRACTING PARTIES adopted the following agreed conclusions:[1]

The CONTRACTING PARTIES,

Noting:

that a number of contracting parties with an interest in services have undertaken and circulated national examinations of the issues in this sector, and that other such examinations are recommended,

and that the process of carrying out the Ministerial Decision highlights the complexity of the issues involved.

In pursuance of the 1982 Ministerial Decision on services,

Agree to the following arrangements within GATT:

1.   That the Chairman of the CONTRACTING PARTIES will organize the exchange of information provided for in the Ministerial Decision on issues in the services sector, essentially on the basis of national examinations, which could refer to any considerations in the area of services which appear relevant to the contracting party concerned, and the compilation and distribution of such information based on as uniform a format as possible;

2.   The GATT secretariat will provide the support necessary for this process;

3.   The Chairman of the CONTRACTING PARTIES will keep the Council informed of the progress made and report to the CONTRACTING PARTIES;

---

1   After adoption of the agreed conclusions, the CONTRACTING PARTIES took note of the following statement by the Chairman:

"With reference to the arrangements just agreed by the CONTRACTING PARTIES which provide for the organization of the exchange of information on issues in the sector of services, it is understood that:

In addition to servicing and keeping records of meetings, the secretariat would prepare an analytical summary of national examinations together with information made available by relevant international organizations and a summary of issues raised in the exchange of information. Concurrently the secretariat would propose a format, for the compilation and distribution by it of the information exchanged among contracting parties, to be progressively elaborated in order to make it as uniform as possible.

It is also understood that the secretariat could, on an agreed basis, undertake additional tasks as required."

4. The CONTRACTING PARTIES decide to review the results of these examinations, along with the information and comments provided by relevant international organizations, at their next regular session and to consider whether any multilateral action in these matters is appropriate and desirable. Unquote.

CONTRACTING PARTIES
Forty-First Session
November 1985

Decision by the CONTRACTING PARTIES

The CONTRACTING PARTIES,

In pursuance of the 1982 Ministerial Decision on Services, and

In accordance with the Agreed conclusions adopted by the CONTRACTING PARTIES on 30 November 1984,

Decide to invite contracting parties to continue the exchange of information undertaken in pursuance of the Agreed conclusions of 30 November 1984, and to prepare recommendations for consideration by the CONTRACTING PARTIES at their next session.

Extract from Declaration of Ministers at Punta del Este, September, 1986

Negotiations on Trade in Services

Ministers, also decided, as part of the Multilateral Trade Negotiations, to launch negotiations on trade in services.

Negotiations in this area shall aim to establish a multilateral framework of principles and rules for trade in services, including elaboration of possible disciplines for individual sectors, with a view to expansion of such trade under conditions of transparency and progressive liberalization and as a means of promoting economic growth of all trading partners and the development of developing countries. Such framework shall respect the policy objectives of national laws and regulations applying to services and shall take into account the work of relevant international organizations.

GATT procedures and practices shall apply to these negotiations. A Group on Negotiations on Services is established to deal with these matters. Participation in the negotiations under this Part of the Declaration will be open to the same countries as Under Part 1. GATT secretariat support will be provided, with technical support from other organizations as decided by the Group on Negotiations on Services.

The Group on Negotiations on Services shall report to the Trade Negotiations Committee.

Annex D

Concepts for a Framework Agreement on Services

(paper submitted by the United States, October 1987)

Introduction

The Ministerial Declaration calls for negotiations to establish a multilateral framework of principles and rules for trade in services. The United States believes that the GNS [Group on Negotiations on Services] should concentrate its efforts on the elaboration of such a framework and work towards agreement on this framework as soon as possible. Early agreement on a framework and its coverage will allow the GNS maximum scope for subsequent negotiation on individual sector agreements.

In order to assist the GNS in its efforts to elaborate a framework of principles and rules for trade in services, the United States sets forth in this paper a number of considerations and concepts to facilitate this process. To date, there have been useful discussions in the GNS on several concepts of great relevance to a framework agreement, including those of transparency, non-discrimination and national treatment. The United States has taken into account these discussions in formulating its views on these concepts. In addition, the United States believes that there are additional concepts which should be reflected in a framework agreement.

This paper begins with a discussion of general considerations that should be taken into account in elaborating the framework and then proceeds to a discussion of a number of specific concepts.

General Considerations

The United States believes that the following general considerations should be given great weight as work proceeds on the elaboration of a framework for trade in services:

1. The framework should be designed to achieve a progressive liberalization of a wide range of services sectors in as many countries as possible.

2. The framework should recognize the sovereign right of every country to regulate its services industries. At the same time, it should be agreed that the framework is intended to deal only with those measures whose purpose or effect is to restrict the access and operations of foreign service providers. The framework must ensure against the adoption or application of measures whose purpose or effect is restrictive or distortive of trade.

3. Under the framework there should be agreement by countries to avoid adopting new restrictive measures on foreign service providers and to apply the framework to the greatest extent possible to existing measures.

4. The framework should be of benefit to every country, regardless of its stage of economic development. It should therefore result in a progressive and time-phased liberalization of the world services markets which contribute to development in a positive way, without compromising any individual country's development objectives. This will provide a more competitive environment within all services markets, enabling local consumers to utilize services bearing the most advanced technology with the lowest possible prices.

5. The framework should apply to the cross border movement of services as well as to the establishment of foreign branches and subsidiaries for purposes of producing or delivering the service within the host country.

6. The coverage of the framework should be broad but flexible. In this regard, once the content of the framework has been agreed, the GNS initially should attempt to extend its coverage to a wide range of services sectors. Using the framework as a point of reference, the GNS should then attempt to negotiate individual sector agreements as needed. These would provide additional, more detailed rules and should allow for greater precision and flexibility in attaining appropriate degrees of liberalization, depending on the sector in question.

Specific Concepts

Transparency

The general objective of including obligations on transparency in a services framework agreement is to ensure that government measures affecting service industries are developed and maintained in a clear and predictable manner and that information on such measures is readily accessible and is made known to all interested parties on an equal basis. Since measures used by governments to control services industries are often promulgated for reasons unrelated to trade, it is necessary to provide a structure that allows for the examination of such measures, existing and future, directed at services and service providers and affecting the coverage of a services framework agreement. Such a structure would allow for the identification of both intended and unintended effects of government measures on the access and treatment of foreign services and service providers to a particular market.

Obligations on transparency should be twofold: (1) The obligation to publish proposed and final rules and regulations affecting services and subject to certain exceptions to provide interested parties the opportunity to comment on proposed rules and regulations. The advance publication requirement would not be required in the case of emergency measures to protect fiduciary, health, safety and national security. The same is true for measures undertaken by courts and legislatures, where the timing and substance of a measure cannot always be determined in advance. The opportunity for comments by interested parties in advance of the regulation would not extend to a review of the proposal by an international body. It would be available to private parties and interested governments within a reasonable review period set by the regulator. Once they are legally effective, laws and regulations whose content are considered to be inconsistent with the framework could be subject to review under the traditional notification/consultation procedure referred to below; and (2) The obligation to notify other countries through an agreed procedure a certain category of government measures affecting services. Measures subject to this notification procedure would include those that the notifying country itself recognized as potentially having an adverse impact on the trade of others, either through its own internal assessment or by virtue of the measure having been called to its attention by other signatories. Measures having been so notified would be subject to consultations.

Non-discrimination

In general, signatories to the framework agreement should extend the benefits of agreement unconditionally to all signatories. Although the widest possible adherence of countries to the framework agreement is the most desirable, it is inevitable that some countries may elect not to become signatories. The United States believes that the benefits of the framework agreement need not be extended to non-signatories. It should be recognized that some countries will not be capable of applying the obligations of the framework agreement to some service sectors. In this regard, the United States offers the following preliminary observations. There could be flexibility allowed for signatories to take exceptions to the coverage of the agreement. However, the number and extent of these exceptions to the agreement should be limited. One possible approach would be that signatories, upon entry into force of the framework, could invoke non-application to those countries that have taken exceptions excessively. This would avoid upsetting the balance of rights and obligations of the framework agreement.

National Treatment

The concept of national treatment should be a fundamental element of a framework agreement. National treatment should generally require that foreign service providers receive treatment no less favorable in like circumstances than that accorded to domestic service providers with respect to government measures affecting the service sector in question. The primary objective of national treatment is to prevent discrimination against foreign service providers as compared with their domestic counterparts. At the same time, the concept allows governments to take measures affecting services on a non-discriminatory basis in order to fulfil domestic policy goals.

In most cases, national treatment for foreign service providers would be treatment identical to that provided to domestic service providers in the service sector in question. Occasionally, differences in institutional structures and regulatory systems may require a modified approach to national treatment, which should be allowed under the framework such as in the case of national security considerations and fiduciary responsibilities. However, such treatment would have to be at least equivalent in effect. Parties would be obligated to substantiate such equivalency both in terms of establishing the necessity for non-identical treatment and ensuring that there is no disguised violation of the national treatment principle.

- Access to Local Distribution Networks. Many service industries rely on access to local distribution networks to effectively deliver their product to customers. Equal and non-discriminatory access to the means of distribution and delivery, such as transportation and telecommunications networks, are essential to all service providers.

- Access to Local Firms and Personnel. The ability to deal with local firms and personnel on a contractual basis or otherwise is critical to the production, marketing and delivery of some services. Foreign service providers should have the option, but not be forced, to form partnerships locally when it facilitates participation in a market.

- Access to Customers. Direct access of foreign service providers to domestic customers and of domestic customers to foreign providers can provide critical communication and information needed to effectively participate in a services market.

- Right to Use Brand Names. The right to sell under a brand name is important to effectively market some services. Foreign service providers should be allowed this right on the same basis as their domestic counterparts.

National treatment alone will not assure a liberal international trading regime in services. For example, regulators will sometimes impose market needs tests that limit or prohibit new entrants, whether foreign or domestic, into a given market. In some cases in the past, regulators have effectively cartelized a given services market by denying the issuance of new licenses for decades. National treatment obviously has no value in these instances from the standpoint of trade liberalization. While in a few instances regulators have established a legitimate need to limit the number of participants, a framework agreement should provide for a degree of foreign participation if such restricted circumstances recur. Another related issue exists with respect to establishment or investment requirements imposed on foreign service providers where such requirements bear no relationship to legitimate regulatory needs. Where there is no reasonable basis to require local establishment or investments, service providers should be able to sell their service across the border.

Discipline on State Sanctioned Monopolies

Governments sometimes choose to provide services through a single monopoly entity which can be either a state enterprise or a private party. The framework agreement should provide disciplines governing the behavior of such a monopoly entity in its capacity as a sole service provider as well as in its activities when engaged in a competitive service. It should also assure that appropriate compensation to affected signatories or their affected entities is provided when a government decides to transform the provision of a service from a competitive to a monopoly environment.

The framework should not interfere with a government's sovereignty to provide a service by way of a monopoly. It should, however, oblige the monopoly entity to provide its service to foreign-based users on a non-discriminatory basis with respect to price, quality and quantity.

Special disciplines should be established to guard against abusive and anti-competitive practices of monopoly entities that also engage in competitive services. The framework should prohibit the monopoly entity from cross-subsidizing its competitive services with monopoly revenues. There should also be safeguards to prevent the monopoly entity from denying its monopoly service to potential customers that are also offering a service in competition with the monopoly entity.

Subsidies

The provision of subsidies by governments to their service providers can distort international trade in services. The services framework should therefore contain rules governing the use of such subsidies, whether they be domestic or export subsidies.

The rules should take account of the fact that such subsidies can have adverse effects on foreign competitors in the foreign competitor's own market; in third country markets; and the market of the country providing the subsidy. The rules might be analogous to some of the approaches existing for trade in goods in various GATT instruments. For instance, the framework could prohibit the use of export subsidies to service providers altogether and set out in an illustrative list specific examples of such export subsidies. As for domestic subsidies, there might be an obligation to seek to avoid those domestic subsidies that could have an injurious effect on service providers of other signatories.

The signatories should provide a mechanism for the resolution of disputes over the interpretation of the subsidy provisions. Authority to take offsetting measures equivalent to the impact of the injurious subsidy would be allowed. However, countervailing duties, in the traditional sense are not viewed as a practical way of dealing with subsidy practices, given the different means of trading services across borders.

Non-discriminatory Accreditation Procedures

Services frequently require the presence of a provider to effectively produce and convey the service. Governments, and in some cases, self-regulating professional bodies, often impose extensive requirements for minimum standards of competence and ability in order to perform the service. Such measures arise from a legitimate concern for consumer protection and the desire to maintain the highest professional standards. However, these measures can sometimes extend beyond the legitimate standards of assuring competence and ability to perform a service and constitute an unjustifiable barrier to accreditation by foreign applicants.

A services framework should therefore discourage licensing measures that are unrelated to competence and ability to perform. It should also prohibit those measures whose purpose or effect is to discriminate against foreign providers of licensed services.

More specific rules for individual professions would be reserved for the sectoral agreements dealing with any such professions.

Consultation/Dispute Settlement

The services framework should contain appropriate consultation and dispute settlement provisions. Such provisions might be similar in concept to Article XXII and XXIII of the General Agreement or on similar provisions of the various Non-tariff Measure Agreements. Improvements in the traditional GATT dispute settlement mechanisms negotiated in the Uruguay Round should be taken into consideration by the GNS.

Conclusion

The considerations and concepts set forth in this paper represent, in the view of the United States, a solid basis for the elaboration of a framework agreement to govern the conduct of international trade in services. In the U.S. view, such a framework should be negotiated and, if possible, implemented at an early stage of the Uruguay Round. The framework could then be the point of departure for the negotiation of sectoral agreements during the later stages of the Round.

While participants in the GNS should continue to deepen their analysis of all the elements of the 1987 work plan of the GNS, the focus of these various elements should now be directed toward the elaboration of the framework, as called for in the Ministerial Declaration.

Annex E

Notes for an Opening Statement Delegation of Canada

MTN-Group Negotiating Services Meeting
23-25 February, 1987
Geneva

Canada is pleased that the first meeting of Group of Negotiations on Services has now assembled to address the negotiating objectives agreed to by our respective Ministers at Punta del Este. Canada is aware of the difficult task in front of us and the pioneering spirit which will be necessary to ensure progress in this new area of international trade relations.

Canada has made extensive preparations for these important discussions by assessing our domestic service sectors, and the role which they play as crucial elements in our economy, not only indirectly in support of manufacturing but also natural resources and agriculture, as well as directly over a wide range of business, transportation, financial, information and consumer services. Our efforts to date have improved our understanding of services and the comparative strengths and weaknesses in our own service sectors. Yet we remain well aware of the difficulties ahead, in particular the continuing lack of consistent data on trade in services and the difficult conceptual problems to be overcome. Despite these problems, we are keenly aware of the clear trend towards the increasing importance of services as a generator of economic growth and employment. Globalization of services trade, and the increasing linkages between producers and consumers of services across borders, are now a fact of life.

The efforts of the Canadian Government to improve its understanding of the role of services in the domestic economy have allowed us to develop a better appreciation of the trends in services trade across borders—by commercial presence, by trade through networks, or by the personal delivery of services through the temporary movement of people. Here we have an interest in ensuring that the dynamics of existing trade flows, both imports and exports, are secured and that increased trade and economic development are fostered. In order to address this challenge in a practical and meaningful way in the course of the work of the GNS, we shall need to examine the question of the coverage of an agreement dealing with trade in services, to ensure that we focus on the commercially traded services which are the life blood of so many sectors. We must focus our analysis on the transborder transactions in services which are bought and sold in a commercial market. We must explore how this issue touches upon the temporary access to markets for skilled service workers and also upon the separate question of investment. In addition we must take account of rapidly developing sectors such as information and telecommunications services which together could come eventually to be traded on a competitive basis.

In terms of immediate objectives for the GNS, Canada would like to see the development of a framework or "rules of the road" based on trade principles for services which will eventually require participants to bind themselves to a discipline on services trade. This framework must build upon familiar trade policy concepts such as non-discrimination, national treatment, transparency, nullification and impairment, dispute settlement. We, of course, recognize that we must gain a better understanding of the consequences of applying such a framework in the real world of international commerce and also refine, as necessary, its principles and rules. This process will require a determination of which sectors should be covered, and how the rules will apply in the chosen sectors.

After rules have been developed covering a range of services sectors, we foresee countries agreeing progressively to bring regulations and practices affecting their respective service industries under multilateral discipline; identifying barriers to trade in services and proposing concessions which could be exchanged to produce liberalization. One step on the road of "progressive liberalization" could involve freezing or standstill. The goal, of course, remains enhanced economic development for all members of an agreement, while respecting the policy objectives of national laws and regulations.

Canada is a major trading nation with almost 32 per cent of its GNP dependent on foreign trade, and with 75 per cent of GNP in services. As a net importer of technology and capital, Canada has had a services trade deficit consistently since the 1950s. In particular, our trade in some services, in particular those we class as "business related services" for statistical purposes is in an increasingly deficit position. However, these facts have not made us any less in favour of rules for trade in services. We realize that our long term interest requires access to world class service inputs from both domestic and foreign sources. These inputs not only enhance the competitiveness of our own services industry but also increase the productivity of our agricultural, natural resources and manufacturing industries. We also have confidence in our ability to export our services to other parts of the world.

The GNS has a difficult task ahead and Canada is committed to making progress in this vitally important new area of international trade. We will have ideas and suggestions to contribute to the discussion of specific elements arising over the course of our coming meetings.

Annex F

Trade Negotiations Committee Meeting at Ministerial Level

Montreal, December 1988

Negotiations on Trade in Services

1.   Ministers reaffirm the objectives for negotiations on trade in services agreed at Punta del Este.   Ministers agree that substantial progress has been achieved in pursuit of these objectives.

2.   Ministers take note of the report of the GNS to the TNC contained in MTN.GNS/21 which they consider an important basis for further work directed towards the achievement of these negotiating objectives.   This work should proceed in a parallel and interrelated fashion.

3.   Ministers note the understanding reached on statistics and on existing international arrangements and disciplines as set out in paragraphs 7 and 8 of the GNS report.

4.   Work on definition should proceed on the basis that the multilateral framework may include trade in services involving cross-border movement of services, cross-border movement of consumers, and cross-border movement of factors of production where such movement is essential to suppliers.   However, this should be examined further in the light of, *inter alia*, the following:

    (a) Cross-border movement of service and payment.

    (b) Specificity of purpose.

    (c) Discreteness of transactions.

    (d) Limited duration.

5.   Ministers agree that work should proceed, without excluding any sector of trade in services on an *a priori* basis, with a view to reaching agreement on the sectoral coverage under the multilateral framework in accordance, *inter alia*, with the considerations that coverage should permit a balance of interests for all participants, that sectors of export interest to developing countries should be included, that certain sectors could be excluded in whole or in part for certain overriding considerations, and that the framework should provide for the broadest possible coverage of sectors of interest to participants.

6.   Ministers agree that, before the concepts, principles and rules which comprise a multilateral framework for trade in services are finally agreed, these concepts, principles and rules will have to be examined with regard to their applicability and the implications of their application to individual sectors and the types of transactions to be covered by the multilateral framework.

7.   Ministers agree that negotiations on the elaboration of a multilateral framework of principles and rules for trade in services should proceed expeditiously. To this end, the following concepts, principles and rules are considered relevant:

(a)   *Transparency*

Provisions should ensure information with respect to all laws, regulations and administrative guidelines as well as international agreements relating to services trade to which the signatories are parties through adequate provisions regarding their availability. Agreement should be reached with respect to any outstanding issues in this regard.

(b)   *Progressive Liberalization*

The negotiations should establish rules, modalities and procedures in the multilateral framework agreement that provide for progressive liberalization of trade in services with due respect for national policy objectives including provisions that allow for the application of principles to sectors and measures. Provisions should also be established for further negotiations after the Uruguay Round. Specific procedures may be required for the liberalization of particular sectors.

The aim of these rules, modalities and procedures should be to achieve, in this round and future negotiations, a progressively higher level of liberalization taking due account of the level of development of individual signatories. To this end the adverse effects of all laws, regulations and administrative guidelines should be reduced as part of the process to provide effective market access, including national treatment.

The rules, modalities and procedures for progressive liberalization should provide appropriate flexibility for individual developing countries for opening fewer sectors or liberalizing fewer types of transactions or in progressively extending market access in line with their development situation.

(c) *National Treatment*

When accorded in conformity with other provisions of the multilateral framework, it is understood that national treatment means that the services exports and/or exporters of any signatory are accorded in the market of any other signatory, in respect of all laws, regulations and administrative practices, treatment "no less favourable" than that accorded domestic services or services providers in the same market.

(d) *Most-Favoured-Nation/Non-Discrimination*

The multilateral framework shall contain a provision on m.f.n./non-discrimination.

(e) *Market Access*

When market access is made available to signatories it should be on the basis that consistent with the other provisions of the multilateral framework and in accordance with the definition of trade in services, foreign services may be supplied according to the preferred mode of delivery.

(f) *Increasing Participation of Developing Countries*

The framework should provide for the increasing participation of developing countries in world trade and for the expansion of their service exports, including *inter alia* through the strengthening of their domestic services capacity and its efficiency and competitiveness.

Provisions should facilitate effective market access for services exports of developing countries through, *inter alia*, improved access to distribution channels and information networks. These provisions should facilitate liberalization of market access in sectors of export interest to developing countries.

Autonomous liberalization of market access in favour of services exports of developing countries should be allowed.

Particular account shall be taken of the serious difficulty of the least-developed countries in accepting negotiated commitments in view of their special economic situation and their development, trade and financial needs.

(g) *Safeguards and Exceptions*

Further negotiations will be necessary on provisions for safeguards, e.g., for balance-of-payments reasons, and exceptions, e.g., based on security and cultural policy objectives.

(h) *Regulatory Situation*

It is recognized that governments regulate services sectors, e.g., by granting exclusive rights in certain sectors, by attaching conditions to the operations of enterprises within their markets for consumer protection purposes and in pursuance of macro-economic policies. Asymmetries exist with respect to the degree of development of services regulations in different countries. Consequently, the right of countries, in particular of developing countries, to introduce new regulations is recognized. This should be consistent with commitments under the framework.

8.   Other elements mentioned in MTN.GNS/21, as well as new ideas and concepts participants may wish to put forward, will also be considered.

9.   It is understood that the acceptability of the multilateral framework will be dependent on the initial level of negotiated commitments of signatories.

Future Work

10.   Future work should provide for:

(a) The compilation by the secretariat of a reference list of sectors by February 1989. This process could be assisted by submissions by participants.

(b) Invitation to participants to submit indicative lists of sectors of interest to them with a target date of May 1989.

(c) The process of examining the implications and applicability of concepts, principles and rules for particular sectors and specific transactions should begin as lists become available.

(d) Further work as necessary on the role of international disciplines and arrangements and on the question of definition and statistics.

11. The GNS should endeavour, by the end of 1989, to assemble the necessary elements for a draft which would permit negotiations to take place for the completion of all parts of the multilateral framework and its entry into force by the end of the Uruguay Round.

Related Publications

Order Address

The Institute for Research on Public Policy
P.O. Box 3670 South
Halifax, Nova Scotia
B3J 3K6

1-800-565-0659 (toll free)

James J. McRae and
Martine M. Desbois, eds.

Traded and Non-traded Services: Theory, Measurement and Policy.
1988 $22.00
ISBN 0-88645-066-7

Donald M. McRae and
Debra P. Steger, eds.

Understanding the Free Trade Agreement. 1988 $19.95
ISBN 0-88645-079-9

Jeffrey J. Schott and
Murray G. Smith, eds.

The Canada-United States Free Trade Agreement: The Global Impact.
1988 $15.95
ISBN 0-88132-073-0

199

Roger Verreault et Mario Polèse	*L'exportation de services par les firmes canadiennes de génie-conseil : évolution récente et avantages concurrentiels.* 1989 19,95 $ ISBN 0-88645-078-0
Mario Polèse, Julie Archambault, Marcel Gaudreau et Roger Verreault	*Les exportations de services de gestion et de promotion immobilières : sur quoi repose l'avantage concurrentiel des firmes canadiennes?* 1989 19,95 $ ISBN 0-88645-093-4
William J. Coffey and James J. McRae	*Service Industries in Regional Development.* 1989 $24.95 ISBN 0-88645-103-5
James R. Melvin	*Trade in Services: A Theoretical Analysis.* 1989 $24.95 ISBN 0-88645-090-X
Murray G. Smith, ed.	*Canada, the Pacific and Global Trade.* 1989 $20.00 ISBN 0-88645-100-0
H.E. English, ed.	*Pacific Initiatives in Global Trade.* 1990 $25.00 ISBN 0-88645-105-1
Frank Stone	*Canada, the GATT and the International Trade System.* (2nd edition) forthcoming
Richard G. Dearden, Michael M. Hart and Debra P. Steger, eds.	*Living with Free Trade: Canada, the Free Trade Agreement and the GATT.* (forthcoming)

PLUS: Some 40 overview and discussion papers are also available. Discussion papers cost $7.50 each, or $200.00 for the set. Overviews cost $15.00 each. A complete set of papers and overviews is available for $250.00. For the complete list, please write to the address shown above.